Digby Collins

The Horse Trainer's and Sportsman's Guide

Digby Collins

The Horse Trainer's and Sportsman's Guide

ISBN/EAN: 9783744678773

Printed in Europe, USA, Canada, Australia, Japan

Cover: Foto ©Andreas Hilbeck / pixelio.de

More available books at **www.hansebooks.com**

THE

HORSE-TRAINER'S AND SPORTSMAN'S GUIDE;

WITH ADDITIONAL CONSIDERATIONS
ON THE DUTIES OF GROOMS, ON PURCHASING BLOOD STOCK,
AND ON VETERINARY EXAMINATION.

BY DIGBY COLLINS.

LONDON:
LONGMANS, GREEN, AND CO.
1865.

PREFACE.

A BRIEF TREATISE on the formation of the horse, so far as it is of importance with regard to his action— of training the racehorse, steeplechaser, and hunter—together with his management in health and disease—has long since appeared to me as wanting in the sportsman's and groom's library.

I was induced to believe that a work on this subject, published at as small a cost as possible, so as to bring it within the reach of every stableman in the land, might be beneficial in rooting out old and carefully-cherished prejudices, which have thriven with greater luxuriance in stable management than in any branch of industry with which I am acquainted.

I am unwilling to lay myself open to the suspicion of wishing to claim for this work any importance as a literary or scientific production. I have endeavoured, in each portion of it, sedulously to avoid all technicalities, and never to use two sentences where one would sufficiently explain the matter in hand.

It is a practical subject to which tiresome and long-spun paragraphs would be utterly meaningless and irrelevant.

I am encouraged, in laying this before the public, by the conviction that my conclusions have not been arrived at by unprofitable conjectures and high-flown theories; but by careful study of, and practical labours in, each branch treated of.

Perhaps some apology may be thought necessary for treating the veterinary portion of the subject so feebly: but I was less afraid of saying too little than too much, and have endeavoured to direct the course of treatment of diseases which would be the safest, and, if insufficient, at any rate not injurious.

It is impossible, without going more deeply into the veterinary art—which would have defeated the object of this work—to explain the nature and treatment of every disease; and, therefore, it occurred to me that, by setting forth as briefly as possible the nature of some of the diseases most frequently met with, and explaining the symptoms of each in sufficiently clear a manner to lead to their detection and treatment—previous to the services of a professional man being available—I should go as far as would be prudent in addressing the class of persons for whom this work is intended.

It has been my endeavour to explain in every instance the reason why the treatment recommended is desirable, in order that in simple matters those persons who may follow it may not be acting in the dark.

For the use of trainers or the veterinary student, no portion of this work is intended; since the one has access to men of superior practice and information to myself, and the other to works which treat of each subject discussed more fully and elaborately, but which would be at once both wearisome and unintelligible to the greater bulk of sportsmen and grooms.

RUGELY, STAFFORDSHIRE: *Sept.* 1865.

CONTENTS.

INTRODUCTION.

	PAGE		PAGE
Size	3	Race riding	65
Formation	4	After the race	67
The head	5	The steeplechase horse	73
The neck	5	Action	74
Shoulders	7	Further qualifications	74
The chest	9	Blood	75
Fore limbs	9	Size	76
Fetlock joints	14	Breaking	77
Pasterns	14	Riding	81
The foot	14	The character of the steeplechase horse of the present day as compared with the past	82
The trunk	15		
Ribs and back	17		
Loins	19		
Hind quarters	19	Hunters	89
The hock	22	Breeding the hunter	94
On breeding the racehorse	24	Jumping	99
Training for the turf	37	Condition	102
Training the two-year old	41	Work	111
Training three and four-year olds	49	Summering the hunter	117
		The riding horse	120
Training of five-year olds and upwards	49	The lady's horse	123
		The covert hack	12
Quick work	54		

CHAPTER I.

DISEASES OF NERVES.

Apoplexy	128	Paralysis	132
Tetanus—Lock-jaw	129	Megrims	132
Stringhalt	132		

CHAPTER II.

DISEASES OF THE ARTERIES AND VEINS.

	PAGE		PAGE
Accidents and wounds of arteries	134	Glanders	136
Aneurism	136	Farcy	137

CHAPTER III.

DISEASES OF THE RESPIRATORY ORGANS.

	PAGE		PAGE
Common cold	139	Chronic cough	144
Sore throat	140	Pleurisy	145
Influenza	141	Congestion of the lungs	146
Bronchitis	141	Inflammation of the lungs	147
Broken wind	142	Roaring	149
Thick wind or high blowing	143		

CHAPTER IV.

DISEASES OF THE ABDOMEN.

	PAGE		PAGE
Inflammation of the liver	152	Inflammation of the kidneys	156
Dysentery	153	Inflammation of the bladder	157
Diarrhœa	153	Spasm of the bladder	157
Colic	154	Inflammation of the intestines	158
Gastritis	155	Worms	158
Inflammation of the womb	155		

CHAPTER V.

DISEASES OF THE EYE.

	PAGE		PAGE
Simple inflammation	160	Cataract	162
Ophthalmia	161	Glass eyes	163

CHAPTER VI.

DISEASES OF THE SKIN.

	PAGE		PAGE
Grease	167	Surfeit	172
Cracked heels	169	Warts	173
Swelled legs	170	Saddle galls	173
Mange	171		

CHAPTER VII.

DISEASES OF THE SYNOVIAL MEMBRANES.

	PAGE		PAGE
Bog spavin	175	Wind galls	176
Thorough pin	176	Capped hocks and elbows	177

CHAPTER VIII.

DISEASES OF BONE.

Bone spavin	179	Ringbone	183
Splints	182	Ossification of the knee	183

CHAPTER IX.

DISEASES OF THE FOOT.

Corns	184	Navicular disease	190
Sandcrack	185	Founder, fever in the feet, or	
Thrush	186	laminitis	191
Canker	187	Pumiced feet	193
Quittor	189		

CHAPTER X.

ACCIDENTS.

Wounds from stubs, stakes, &c.	194	Strains	206
Injuries to the eye	197	Strain of the shoulder	206
Poll evil	198	Strain of the back and loins	207
Fistulous withers	199	Strain of the back-sinews, and rupture of the sheath of the tendons	208
Broken knees	200		
Fractures and dislocations	202	Breaking down, or rupture of the suspensory ligaments	209
Wounds of the foot	204		
Overreach	205	Curb	210
Speedy cut	206	Epidemic fever	211

CHAPTER XI.

ADVICE TO GROOMS.

On dishonesty, &c.	214	Care of clothing and saddlery	227
On driving	221	The purchase of horses	232
Grooming	224	Veterinary examinations	239

ON

THE THOROUGHBRED HORSE.

INTRODUCTION.

The Racehorse, perhaps, combines in the greatest degree perfection of symmetry and power with gracefulness of action, and therefore I propose first to introduce him to my readers.

To see one or two dozen three-year olds of the best blood in the world, in blooming condition, stripping for the great contest at Epsom, is a most impressive sight. Vivacity and courage mark every movement of their eyes and limbs as they lash out as if to feel their elasticity, while the head lads cautiously remove their neatly-made clothing.

There is something one may almost say supremely aristocratic in their whole demeanour as they step out of the enclosure, scarcely deigning to touch the sward, with their talented pilots looking neatness itself.

Without entering into any details as to the history of the present thoroughbred horse, I will merely say that it appears to me, from the information at my disposal, that we are indebted to the cross with the barb for the fine, speedy, and high-couraged animals to be found among our thoroughbreds. First-class barbs appear to have been animals standing 15h. 2in., not very strongly built, but having fine trotting and galloping action, and, moreover, possessed of indomitable courage and endurance, but at the same time inclined to be restive; or, in the phraseology of old writers, 'difficult of management.' It has been asserted by some that our thoroughbreds have been descended from Eastern mares and horses. But there is no evidence of this; and, moreover, there certainly are two or three gaps in the pedigree of Eclipse—that prince of the stud-book.

But, apart from this, we have evidence that in the early part of the seventeenth century racehorses, and successful ones, were bred from barb stallions out of English mares, and that such a cross invariably defeated both the pure-bred English, and pure-bred barb horse. This can readily be understood from the happy combination of the fine quality, action, and courage of the barb, with the finer size, length, and stride of the English mare.

There cannot be the remotest doubt that the characteristics of our thoroughbred stock have very materially changed since these days.

The fine pastures, liberal diet, and careful and judicious crosses have all tended to produce the noble thoroughbred that we sometimes see, with all the fine size, power, and action necessary for all purposes for which the animal horse can be required, combined with the finest quality of his eastern ancestors.

From this it will be, as a matter of course, utterly hopeless ever again to attempt to find a more fitting sire elsewhere than is to be found among the ranks of our stud-horses, and equally hopeless to attempt to introduce from any other lineage an animal capable of coping successfully with them on the turf. Since their quality must be about the same as their best rivals, and with the addition of so much size and length, the issue of such a contest could never be for a moment in doubt.

But were we as jealous of retaining our finest specimens of thoroughbred stock—save and except in the case of our colonies—as the Arabs were of old, we should not have to lament that dearth of sound, powerful sires that now exists in nearly all parts of Great Britain.

SIZE.

Most men have their peculiar fancies with regard to the size of the racehorse, and will hold out for some particular limit in the standard measure as perfection.

I am not prepared to take up either the high or the low limit very strongly, as I have seen about as many good little as big horses, and *vice versâ,* on almost every racecourse in the kingdom.

Take, for instance, the race between Stockwell and Teddington. The one was big enough to carry the other, yet the little one had the greatest weight, in addition to being a little amiss on the day; but nevertheless defeated his great adversary after, perhaps, one of the most severe struggles ever witnessed. We will also take Fisherman and compare him with Blink Bonny, and further say that he was not superior to either Saunterer or Vedette, and a host of other moderately-sized animals. We have seen how, when up to his hocks in mud, the then pigmy Daniel O'Rourke cut down his opponents; how Midas bore Lord Exeter's colours to the fore so often; how the Flying Dutchman had enough to do to get the best of Hotspur; how Rowton, the Hero, Sweetmeat, Euclid, Venison, Beeswing, Andover, Weathergage, Saucebox, Underhand, Saunterer, Blink Bonny, Vedette, St. Alban's, Caller Ou, Tim Whiffler, the Marquis, and Macaroni were careless of the weights they carried and the distance of ground they went over; while Charles XII., Sir Tatton Sykes, Fleur de Lis, Hetman Platoff, Bay Middleton, the Flying Dutchman, Voltigeur, Stockwell, Rataplan, Surplice, Wild Dayrell, Fisherman, Leamington, the *par nobile fratrum*, Lifeboat and Gunboat, Buckstone, and Dictator, have shown us about equal results. Whatever the weight may be, however, there must be size and length somewhere, and, in my opinion, the more size and length there is on short legs the better.

FORMATION.

Were we to cull six out of all the horses we have ever seen that we think most nearly approaching perfection, they would be Sweetmeat, St. Alban's, Saunterer, Fandango, Tournament, and Vedette, and we should place them in the order named.

I am especially fond of strong, muscular backs, loins, and quarters, added to great length and compactness, combined with well-moulded and short limbs. But, in my opinion, to pick out certain points in a racehorse and uphold them as outweighing all others, because such and such horses may have run very successfully with only this or that good point to recommend them, is the height of ignorance, and shows an utter want of careful consideration as to what constitutes the 'rule' and what the 'exception.' Unless this be determined, all discussion on the subject will be fruitless.

That certain forms do run the best I am confident, in spite of the hackneyed theory that 'horses run in all forms.' But I do not deny this; though I fearlessly assert that *in proper forms horses run most successfully*, which is surely the point at issue.

THE HEAD.

To begin with the head, I prefer a clean, blood-like head, but do not care what the size is so long as it is not out of proportion to the general frame; though I must confess to a decided objection to the small Arab head, which is generally indicative of more cunning and temper than is desirable.

Large, long ears I have long esteemed as a sign of gameness, and appreciate them accordingly.

THE NECK.

To the formation of the neck I am inclined, from experience and comparisons, to attach the greatest importance. The lower surface of the neck, or portion of the œsophagus or gullet perceptible,—i.e. from the larynx to the breast—cannot be too short. The distance or length from the top of the withers to the end of the cervical vertebræ should be more than double that of the former; because this formation presents the smallest possible distance for the air-pumps to work, and consequently renders rapid respiration more easy. Also, such formation is effected by the proper formation of other portions of the frame, and more especially by proper formation of the shoulders,—i.e. by the base of the scapula or shoulder-blade being pushed forward, and the apex being thrown back in a corresponding degree. Thus the apex of the scapula, being well inclined backwards, or thrown into the back or dorsal vertebræ, lengthens the superior surface of the neck, while the base of the scapula and apex of humerus, or arm-bone, being pushed forward, shortens the inferior surface of the neck—or, in other words, lessens the space between the breast and the larynx.

I have scarcely ever seen a good neck on a bad animal, or a bad neck on a good one. By a good neck I mean a strong, deep, broad neck running right into the shoulders imperceptibly, and formed as above described. I abhor either the weak thin ewe-necks, or the light tapering arched peacocky roaring necks, which indicate weakness, not only of this particular organ, but of the whole system.

This I take to be a rule. A well-developed muscular neck, properly formed, indicates strength, and a thin, and therefore badly developed, neck indicates weakness.

I have often been told that a good neck should be light, arched, long, and airy; but in answer, all I have to say is this: when it can be proved that a want of muscular development constitutes a good neck, I shall then, and not till then, alter my opinion.

SHOULDERS.

I must pass on to a point of all others the least understood, or rather the most misunderstood, by ninety-nine out of every hundred persons conversant with horseflesh. Among such it is very common to hear what are termed clean, or rather thin, weak, knify shoulders upheld as a *sine quâ non* of a racehorse; though how the Sweetmeats, Blair Athols, Fandangoes, Voltigeurs, Fishermans, Stockwells, Lifeboats, Touchstones, and numerous other notoriously muscular-shouldered horses, go to prove the correctness of such opinions, I am at a loss to comprehend; and if we are not to derive our conclusions from living horses, from whence can they be obtained? That the scapula must be properly placed,—i.e., in an oblique position, I think all must agree, though Teddington and one or two more come in as the exceptions; but why such formation should be unattended by a proper covering of muscle, is an enigma. The Touchstones can all stay, and we never heard it stated that they were deficient in speed; but if any one should be tempted to make such an assertion, the fact that Touchstone has some two hundred winners attached to his name in these days of flying handicaps should set this question at rest for ever. Yet almost invariably the Touchstones have strong and muscular shoulders.

And, moreover, what can thin and light shoulders consist of but so many bones with a paucity of muscle to work them?

Surely the trapezius and the antea and postea spinatus are not useless muscles; and, if not useless, why should there be so great an objection to seeing them well developed? Without these muscles the shoulder cannot move, for the scapula must remain motionless. Surely, then, if they are well developed, may we not expect quick and vigorous action?

There is yet another point that I must not omit, and which I consider of great importance in a racehorse, which is the inferior extremity of the scapula, or shoulder points. I like to see this point taper gradually, or fine down. That is, the two points of the scapula and humerus should incline towards each other, be well covered with muscle, and yet narrow perceptibly to the eye, as you stand in front of the horse; and immediately behind the scapula the fifth, sixth, seventh, and eighth ribs should appear to swell and bulge out boldly.

This formation does not render the chest narrow, but ensures more compact and vigorous action of the shoulders, since the points of the bones thus converging, if properly placed, are too far forward to interfere in any way with the capacity and formation of the chest.

THE CHEST.

Of the chest in a racehorse I need say but little, as the proper action of its organs depends more on the development of the contiguous muscles than on its own formation.

The chest should be of sufficient breadth to allow of the proper action of the respiratory organs; but I have no fancy for a wide chest as you stand before the horse, not seeing how, with such formation, the frame can be so compact and regular as is desirable, and even necessary for maintaining continued exertion.

FORE LIMBS.

In spite of continual opposition and assertions that forelimbs have little or nothing to do with racing, I nevertheless hold that a horse is unworthy of the name of a racehorse which does not possess properly-formed fore legs.

That a horse cannot race in good company with badly-formed fore legs, I will not attempt to prove, for the simple reason that I do not wish to offer decided opinions on what must be a great uncertainty, dependent on the nature of a particular course, &c. I do say, however, that I never yet saw such animals bring anything but disappointment and vexation on their deluded owners and trainers.

Pray watch the next racehorse you may chance to see in his gallop still more closely. See how, when fresh and well, the good fore legged horse sends out his limbs like darts from the shoulder points, and how the elasticity of the tendons bears the concussion harmlessly. Then look at a bad legged one. Here he comes stumping along, keeping his action as if in bonds, and evidently chary of letting his limbs get too far ahead of him. And why? Because he feels his weakness, that the muscles and tendons are unable to perform their duties as they should. Never shall I forget gazing at Saunterer's sweeping, straight, and grand action, as he cantered down previous to running third in the Cambridgeshire under the unprecedented impost of 8st. 12lb. Where, I thought, can such wonderful powers lay? At a distance, and looking at the whole animal, he seemed somewhat mean; so I waited patiently until he appeared on the Suffolk side of the Cambridge Road, and right well was my patience rewarded and my curiosity gratified. Where does it lie? that was the question. After scanning him from head to foot, from shoulder to tail, the result was this question, Where does it not lie? It is true that he was not big anywhere, but so truly balanced was his whole frame, that it looked like working at any rapidity and for any length of time!

I was satisfied and went my way, still worshipping 'formation' as something real after all, and with increased devotedness.

I have somewhat wandered from the dry formation details, though I think every one likely to be a reader of such very practical sentences must have justly settled what the true formation of a racehorse's fore leg should be. Imprimis, the arms should be broad and flat as you look at them sideways; the muscles going full into the knees. The legs should stand in a perfectly perpendicular position,—i.e. the elbows should be in a direct line with the stifle joints, and neither point inside nor outside the hind legs; if the former, the action will be jarring, stilty, and weak, owing to the concussion being more direct; and if the latter, it will be sprawling and ineffective.

Thus, if I were to choose between the out or in-elbowed racehorse, I should manifestly choose the latter as being the best adapted for racing, but nevertheless very far from being what is desirable. Were I called on to mention the best legged racehorse I ever saw, that one would be far and away Sweetmeat by Gladiator, my especial favourite.

From the knee downwards it is simple enough; since it is chiefly composed of tendons, it stands to reason that the space between the knee and the fetlock joint cannot be too short nor too broad; and above all, the tendons should appear to enter the posterior portion of the knee boldly. That I may better explain my meaning—as you look at the leg sideways, as a whole, it should not appear as if the leg were made up of so many different joints, but present a beautiful and gradual tapering all the way from the elbow to the fetlock joint.

If there appear—even to the casual observer—various indentations and abrupt lines, then there is an undue contraction of the muscles or tendons somewhere, as the case may be, and consequently their powers will be diminished. Once more let me advise the inexperienced to look at the whole fore leg, and not at parts and parcels of it, which are very apt to deceive them; inasmuch as they hardly know what fault to find, and if they feel the leg cool and hard conclude that they possess a valuable wearing animal. Alas! once round the Ascot course would very soon undeceive them. What secrets, what stable truths, has not this royal course revealed! How many owners are yearly cursing their luck, and yet how few profit by such untoward circumstances! Surely 'experientia docet' was only meant to be quoted in irony!

What is meant by an infirm horse but a bad fore legged one in ninety-nine cases out of every hundred? A naturally infirm horse,—i.e. one with improperly-formed fore legs, can never pull satisfactorily through a long course when the pace is good; though a good legged horse which has become infirm from over exertion may do so, when carefully patched up; though I confess I am dead against the experiment. If, then, there be any truth in these statements, do they not go to prove that, unless a horse has good fore legs *to begin with*, a man had better throw his money over a bridge than become the possessor of him, however many good points he may have, and, however well the stable may speak of his home performances. Keep him at exercise, with his tendons at a gentle tension, and all may be well, and he may show great speed and promise; but begin to try a weakly strung bow with your fullest force, and the tale is told. The brute will become more infirm every day; though his owner may and often does wonder at such an untoward result. He finally breaks down after having been first favourite for at least half-a-dozen good stakes, and never even having won a bad one,—and the next you see of the brute is perchance at a country market town, and ask, though not for information, but for the sake of something to say, 'how he broke down?' and you are immediately told with admirable candour, 'Struck 'is leg h'exercising one mornin';' and, pointing at the manifest decrepitude, 'that lost he the Derby, that did!' With such men argument is fruitless. Accuracy of formation is nothing to them: indeed I fancy that they harbour a sort of jealousy towards good formation and manners in the animal horse, being blessed with so little of either themselves!

Having said thus much on the formation of the fore leg, I will only add in conclusion, that a calf-kneed horse, or as the dealers have it 'back at the knees,' must be avoided most carefully for racing purposes, however well-proportioned the leg may otherwise be, since the strain on the tendons must be too severe to be long endured without serious consequences. On the other hand a horse rather 'over at the knees,' if naturally so (and by natural—I mean natural contraction of the tendons, and not contraction consequent on inflammation), will be able to undergo a more severe tension, and therefore it is that such formed legs invariably wear the longest.

FETLOCK JOINTS.

It is necessary that great attention be paid to the formation of this joint, badly-formed joints being the curse of many otherwise good racehorses.

First examine the joint laterally; the suspensory ligament should appear to go right unto the bone, clearly and well defined; the joint itself should be somewhat flat at the sides and posterior surface, but nicely rounded in front. The bones should feel clear and distinct, or what is termed clean,—i.e., free from all synovial or osseous enlargements.

PASTERNS.

The pasterns should be large, long, oblique, and not upright; which is occasioned by undue contraction of the flexor pedis perforans, which must consequently destroy that elasticity of action so essential to the success of a racehorse. If the pasterns are short, they indicate a want of speed, and tax both foot and leg unduly, and should therefore be avoided even if well-shaped otherwise. I recollect making a memorandum of some thirty thoroughbreds whose legs had given way, and the result was that twenty-eight out of the thirty had short pasterns.

THE FOOT.

The foot in a racehorse may not be of so much importance as in general purpose horses; but nevertheless, I have seen more than one race lost by weakness in this organ on hard ground.

The foot should be high at the heels, and indeed tolerably high all over; very concave underneath, and tolerably wide at the bars; for if not wide at the bars the frog cannot be well developed, and is more liable to disease, on account of which the chief support— indeed, the greatest protector attached to the action of the foot—is lost. The frog, being so elastic and yet firm, is capable of resisting the most terrible shock, and without injury to the foot. In examining the foot great care should be taken that there is no swelling nor enlargement on the coronet, and that the horn be of a healthy colour, and of an even regular form; if rings are evident, of a sort of dirty reddish hue, disease has been going on, and most probably an odd foot will be the consequence.

This has very frequently been the weak point in many of the Orlandos, good and racing like as they nearly all are. That grand mare, Melissa, used fairly to pick her way, avoiding every stone in the road about as carefully as an old maid's cat shrinks from the trap-like puddles in her path.

On a flat or slightly uphill course, a bad footed horse may run successfully, but when he is called upon to go down a steep pitch at the top of his foot on tolerably hard ground, nothing but sheer gameness can enable him to persevere.

THE TRUNK.

Great importance is generally attached to what is termed great depth of girth. Indeed, I have frequently been told that unless a horse be six feet and more, he cannot be considered a Derby or Leger horse. Yet how strangely did Teddington, who was nearer five feet six inches than six feet when he won the Derby, upset this theory! How also did Sweetmeat, Fandango, St. Alban's, and Saunterer, with comparatively light girths, support this theory!

But let us look into the formation of the girths, or true ribs, and ascertain how a very deep girth does or does not constitute strength. First then, in passing the tape behind the withers, and judging of the measurement, you should remark of what the measurement be composed. Should the true ribs be flat and deep, like those of some greyhounds, with an exaggerated development of the pectoralis magnus (as is often the case with such formation) no great object will be obtained.

Rather see that the horse has a properly formed girth, for the tape passes over muscles (serratus magnus) that alone extend and draw forward and outward the ribs that expand the chest, that move the shoulder blade in action (latissimus dorsi), that retract the humerus and brace the muscles of the back (pectoralis magnus), that aid the muscles of the haunch in propelling the body. It will thus be seen that great development of these muscles, or as the jockeys term it " thickness between the knees," is a great sign of strength of wind and limb. I know from repeated trials that this latter formation will not measure so much as the former. It was only the other day that I measured two thoroughbred hunters in the same stable, that fully exemplified this. One measured 5ft. 9in., the other 6ft. 1½in., both being in a fine condition. The former had more muscle, was thicker through, seemed up to more weight, and I was informed could stay longer than the latter.

Thus I conclude that these measurements, without proper formation and proper development of the lateral muscles, is utterly useless and inconclusive.

RIBS AND BACK.

The false ribs, or as they are more frequently termed back ribs, in a true made horse will form a beautiful and gradual decline from the girth. As you stand before the horse, the back ribs should not appear to swell out, which the jockeys justly call 'swill bellied.'

It may seem somewhat strange that I should speak of the back and ribs together; but they are, on investigation, so mixed up with each other, that separately their powers of action could not be described.

Between each rib, externally and internally, there are very powerful muscles (called intercostals) in connection with the diaphragm internally, and externally with the whole muscular formation of the back. The internal and external muscles of the ribs are most beautifully formed for action—their fibres running in adverse directions or crossing each other, which gives additional strength to their united action, which is to contract or draw closer the ribs, and thus acting in direct connection with the diaphragm—a muscle that extends from the chest to the termination of the loins by distinct fleshy fibres—the viscera are forced backwards, and inspiration is performed. The muscles of the abdomen then contract, and converging the ribs, push back the diaphragm, and expel the inspired air from the lungs. It will now be understood that jockeys and trainers dislike what they term 'a spare rib,' with some reason; as it shows a want of development of muscles which act on the respiratory organs, and consequently any deficiency here must gradually exhibit inability to perform extraordinary exertions satisfactorily.

The huge muscle along the dorsal vertebræ or backbone (latissimus dorsi), which is generally so conspicuous in the Touchstones and some of the Birdcatchers, is of importance, inasmuch as it is connected with the muscles of the loins, &c., bracing all the muscles of the back, as well as aiding in working the humerus. The proper formation of the loins is great width. The muscles of the loins being spread over the hind quarters are necessarily of the utmost importance; more especially in carrying weights, going uphill, or indeed in performing any extraordinary exertion. We must conclude, therefore, that a racehorse cannot be cursed with a worse defect than a want of sufficient muscular development in the back, and I think that living horses bear me out in this opinion; the two best-backed racehorses of these days having been the best performers —St. Alban's and Saunterer.

A roach-backed horse I hate most cordially, notwithstanding that some assert that it is a sure sign of strength.

I am, however, of opinion that it is a sure sign of cramped action, and consequently weakness. I never saw one of this formation that did not stretch out his neck and go blundering along over-reaching, most frequently tumbling on his knees and head, and not always ending there, without apparent cause. Such horses, however, stand, as the dealers say, 'all of a 'eap,' which most truly represents the badness of such formation.

I do not at all dislike a rather hollow-backed horse; they are nice to sit on, and many racehorses have proved that they can run well with this formation, of which, perhaps, Glencoe was the most remarkable example.

The back in a racehorse should be long, broad, and rather straight; but if slightly hollow it should not be objected to.

LOINS.

The loins in a racehorse should be very broad and well rounded, or curved slightly. Most of the best horses have been thus formed, and, perhaps, this point being thus exaggerated enabled Saunterer to climb the hill for the Cambridgeshire so successfully.

The bones of the loins should be broad for manifest reasons; for, in proportion as is the length of the spinous processes, so is the extent exposed for the insertion of the muscles and tendons.

HIND QUARTERS.

The hind quarters are, indeed, worthy of a great deal of study, both as to the structure and action of the principal muscles. In the first place, then, the hips should be wide though not ragged, and square, which proves that there is a grievous defect in the development of the gluteus muscles. Nevertheless, such formation is frequently met with in strong, dashing goers and great fencers, though very seldom in successful racehorses. Such hips, however, are generally wide and long, and therefore present an immense surface for insertion of the muscles; so that, if there be a paucity of development of muscle, there is nevertheless, also, an extended space for their action; therefore, although ragged hips are not, generally speaking, characteristic of great racing properties, they should not be condemned too hastily.

From the hip-bone to the setting on of the tail the length should be considerable, though the structure should never be level, or what jockeys term 'peacocky' and 'high setting on of the tail.' Most first-class horses, both on the flat and across country, have their tails set on low, with long and wide quarters—almost approaching what racing men term 'mean quartered,' from the circumstance, I believe, that most butchers' horses with such quarters are celebrated as trotters.

Possibly the two most remarkable instances of the extremes of this formation are Mr. J. Anson's two very successful mares, the Oaks and Derby, and the St. Leger victors, Blink Bonny and Caller Ou.

Still it must not be forgotten that there is no other reason, anatomically speaking, for condemning straight quarters, than that the angles being less, the hind legs are generally placed too far behind them in consequence.

From the tail to the thighs powerful muscles for locomotion are passed. The posterior muscle of the quarters is called the rotator tibialis, and, as its name implies, it rotates the tibia; the bone between the hock and thigh, or indeed what is generally termed the thigh. Next to this comes the most powerful muscle of all, the adductor femoris; it is easily distinguished from the preceding by the indentation or line called by grooms the 'quarter mark,' which is very evident in all horses in racing condition.

As these muscles are the most powerful agents in moving the hind limbs, it stands to reason that they should not only be large, but long, that there may be greater leverage.

A line drawn from the round bone and stifle joint should fall immediately on the centre of the loins. From the stifle to the hock the distance cannot reasonably be too great, nor the muscles too large, for there are not so powerful agents in the whole muscular system as the anterior and posterior muscles of the thigh. They are known to the anatomist as the 'gastrocnemii,' and almost in proportion to their development is the propelling power of the horse, great or small. I thought in 1858, that Arsenal's quarters and thighs were about as near perfection as possible.

It would seem, therefore, that a racehorse with thin and weak thighs or gaskins would be an utter anomaly, at least anatomically speaking; and practically I have seen no reason for altering the verdict, since not one first-class horse can I call to mind with this defect.

In spite of this, one frequently sees people who ought to be good judges overlooking this point in toto, and having to pay pretty dearly for their carelessness in consequence.

THE HOCK.

Scarcely less important than the thigh is the hock; for by reason of malformation and consequent weakness in this part, the muscles of the thigh will be deprived of the force of their action, or at any rate they will have to perform their action with unsatisfactory and feeble results.

The calcis or point of the hock should be a considerable distance from the other bones of the hock, inasmuch as the power of action or length of leverage of the tendons will be in exact proportion to the distance; therefore, to come to the point, the hock should be very broad as you look at it sideways. The hock should taper gradually into the shank, and not present a tied or wasted appearance at its inferior extremity. The hock should be free from all fleshiness between the calcis and the other bones, as well as behind and below the calcis. I have seen horses with rather full hocks (I neither talk of thorough-pins nor curbs) that always go sound and well; but still I have never found them to be remarkable as jumpers or stayers. Indeed, such formation must arise either from inherent weakness in, or incipient inflammation of the bursæ of the joints or ligaments, as the case may be. I am quite indifferent about the shape of the hock,—i.e. whether it be 'sickle-shaped,' as it is commonly termed, or 'straight'; but I think the greatest number of wearing powerful hocks that have come under my notice are rather straight than otherwise. Perhaps the most remarkable instance of this formation known to the public was 'Cassio,' a celebrated hunter which was knocked down for 640 guineas, to Mr. Joseph Anderson, at the Wynnstay sale in 1858. There was also a similar peculiarity in The Huntsman's hocks—that wonderful weight-carrying steeplechase horse by Tupsley; most of the Harkaway's have it to a very remarkable degree, and very wearing and good they are in this point as a general rule.

I have now gone through briefly the formation of the horse connected with the muscular action as determined by anatomy, and when practicable, illustrated by living specimens, that the force of my theories may be more easily comprehended. I must here, however, state that my conclusions are, that although horses may run well, follow hounds well, and perform other offices satisfactorily, though not shaped in accordance with my theories, I am convinced that horses so shaped seldom belie their looks.

I know of few instances where it has been in the power of any one man to test the superiority of certain formations in the racehorse; but this fell to the lot of one man well worthy of the opportunity. I allude to 'Lord George Bentinck,' that Prince of the Turf, who was amongst the first to reduce horse-racing to a science.

He was anxious to test the superiority (for of this he had been convinced) of horses with arched knees; and to effect this he tried several horses over different courses, and the result was that on level and inclined courses there was no perceptible difference; but over up-hill courses their superiority was most marked.

ON BREEDING THE RACEHORSE.

What sort of animal, asks every breeder, am I to choose to ensure successful produce on the turf? This must depend entirely on the description of course over which your produce will have to race.

If they will have to run principally in flying handicaps (which pay as well as anything in these days) and are not expected to be sufficiently good for the Derby, Oaks, and Leger; or, Doncaster, Goodwood, Chester, and Ascot Cups, then mere formation must be thrown to the winds, and the *character of the blood* be carefully weighed. But if the desired formation with the desired blood can be obtained, then you may be sure that, barring accidents, the produce will be a racehorse; but the one will never do without the other, nor the other without the one. The breeder must only estimate good looks and formation for just so much as they are worth. The folly of going for looks alone in breeding hunters has been the cause of so many sad disappointments that one wonders people do not turn over a new leaf. But the folly of it in breeding racehorses is so transparent that it is nothing short of madness to neglect that all important point, *character of the blood.* Without diving into the annals of the stud book to reproduce the celebrated stout and equally celebrated speedy sires, I will merely add that the produce of Bay Middleton, Birdcatcher, Harkaway, Sweetmeat, and Orlando, all have a fine turn of speed; while Voltaire, Venison, Emilius, Touchstone, and Melbourne appear to like a distance better. Thus if speed and stoutness be aimed at, a judicious combination of these bloods must be tried: but if speed alone be desired, the former strains of blood should be closely adhered to. I am persuaded, however, that a combination will pay the breeder better; for it will not do in these days that a racehorse be able merely to stay at his best pace for some three or four miles; but he must be possessed of a fine turn of speed as well, or he never can be anything but a second-rate horse. A very interesting and brief letter appeared in the *Sporting Gazette* a few days since under the signature of 'Philippos,' which so nearly embodies my opinions on the results of breeding from certain strains that I cannot do better than quote it. It runs thus:—' As you appear to encourage discussion in your columns on the subject of crosses in breeding, I venture to mention a few instances of successful " hits " which have occurred to my mind at different times. Now, in the first place, that the Sultan and Birdcatcher blood combine successfully we have two notable instances in the cases of

Stockwell and Saunterer. The dams of both are by sons of Sultan, viz., Glencoe and Bay Middleton, and whilst Saunterer is by Birdcatcher himself, Stockwell, as all the world knows, is by the Baron, one of Birdcatcher's most illustrious sons. And if we wished to go still further into their affinity we need not dip deep to discover that Ennui's great grandsire Woful, and Pocahontas's great granddam Web, are own brother and sister. The blood of Sultan, and son too, seems to have harmonised well as the latter's two sons, Tadmor and Wild Dayrell, taking Tadmor's dam Palmyra being by Sultan, whilst Ellen Middleton owes her patronymic to her sire, Bay Middleton.

'Again, Melbourne and Touchstone have crossed very successfully, West Australian to wit by Melbourne out of Mowerina by Touchstone, and Blanche of Middlebie, that *beau idéal* of brood mares, by Melbourne out of Phryne by Touchstone; whilst by sons of Touchstone out of Melbourne mares we get the first and third horses in this year's Leger, viz., Lord Clifden by Newminster out of the Slave by Melbourne, and Borealis by the same horse out of Blink Bonny by Melbourne; and to another of Touchstone's sons Orlando, that famous Melbourne mare Canezou, is indebted for Fazzoletto, the winner of the Two Thousand Guineas and other races. Nor will it be difficult to predict an equally brilliant future for her this year's produce by Newminster, now a foal in Lord Derby's possession. Pantaloon also and Camel do not seem to try conclusions vainly, as we find the Libel was got by

Pantaloon out of Pasquinade by Camel; whilst from the loins of Camel's son, Touchstone, sprang Lord of the Isles out of Fair Helen by Pantaloon; and reverse the parentage, and we get Windhound, Hobbie Noble, Elthiron, &c., by Pantaloon, out of the Touchstone mare Phryne.

'Alarm, Elcot, and Caractacus tell us how well the Venison blood has suited the Defence mares.

'In fact the examples of successful coincidences in breeding might be multiplied till they wearied my pen, and more than exhausted your readers.'

Young mares are to be preferred for many reasons to old ones. First and foremost they can adapt themselves better to change of food and temperature, but all thoroughbred stock must have corn and good food. They have been accustomed to it since they were foaled, and therefore their circulative organs require such treatment in a moderate degree, if they are to withstand the searching rains and piercing winds *sub Jove frigido* from October to April. In this climate the change from heat to cold, combined with damp atmosphere, are so great and so frequent that moderately good living is indispensable to health and stamina; and most of the dangers during the process of foaling are due to the feeble action of debilitated organs, not to mention a host of cutaneous diseases which may be traced to similar causes.

Nevertheless a caution may not be out of place in certain seasons of the year, when the grass is too luxuriant and mares fatten and eat too much, thereby frequently contracting plethora and inflammation of the bladder. I mean the autumn, when the foal has been weaned and the udder has not ceased secreting milk. At this period a poor pasture with plenty of clean water at hand, should be chosen. Some breeders are particularly favoured by having within their boundaries some moor land, which is particularly useful for all breeding animals at this season of the year.

It may be objected, and often is, that there can be no necessity for exposing the mare to cold and low diet, and that it is merely a false economy; but to any one really conversant with the generative system, such arguments will appear utterly opposed to reason.

A mare cannot be kept too cool either internally or externally. Anything that tends to increase excitement of the general system must in like ratio tend to lessen the chance of generation. Still it must not be understood that keeping a mare cool is half-starving her and exposing her to every inclement season without shelter; for this would be equally prejudicial, by causing great debility, which would most likely terminate in death both of the mare and her offspring, or, at least, render the constitution of both feeble for life: or, what is more common, the mare might contract a chill on the kidneys, producing violent inflammation of this and contiguous organs, the result of which would be equally fatal. Therefore, though the food should be of a cooling description, it should, at the same time, be good and nourishing; it should sustain the system, and keep up animal heat without creating anything like plethora. It should consist of good sweet hay, carrots, oats, peas, or beans, with bran or the like. But for mares, and indeed all horses exposed to the changes of atmosphere, I consider peas or beans and bran the best and most wholesome food. Of which two quarterns per day with a quartern of bran will be ample, commencing on November 1, and ending May 1.

The mare will thus be kept in fair condition, and should any untoward event present itself—such as slipping her foal, inflammation of the womb or udder—she will have sufficient stamina to contend with either the one or the other, with reasonable hopes of a favourable result, and will thus lessen the greatest risks of horse-breeding.

I consider that a good roomy shed with the east, north, and west sides well secured from wet and cold winds, affords ample shelter for both mares and foals.

Where there is convenience for bringing in every mare to a comfortable loose box every night, it should, no doubt, be adopted; though I am confident it is unnecessary, and greatly adds to the expense.

One thing, however, is indispensable, and that is, that each mare be tied up to consume her food morning and evening, or some will be sure to fare better than others.

One man can look after and feed twenty-five mares without help, if kept in the ordinary way, but when each mare is to be brought home separately, half this number would be as many as he could attend to properly.

TABULAR STATEMENT.

	£	s.	d.
Thus the cost of attendance at 14s. per week would be per head	1	2	0
24 bushels of beans at 5s.	6	0	0
4 cwt. of bran	1	8	0
2 acres of grass at 30s.	3	0	0
Hay chaff, half ton	2	5	0
Straw chaff, half ton	1	5	0
	15	0	0

Thus it will be seen that with liberal diet a mare may be kept in the ordinary way for the sum of 15*l*. per annum inclusive of good attendance.

The cost of foals will be nearly the same until they enter the training stable, and I consider from experience that about 30*l*. will clear both the mare and foal's expenses through the twelve months; and if we take 25 guineas as the average charge for the use of first-class stallions, we shall have a total of 55*l*. on the yearling's head at the time he is offered for sale or enters the training stable.

It is commonly asserted that to render breeding remunerative, yearlings should average at least 100gs. per head; still I think breeders might justly be content with some 25*l*. per head under this, unless the mares had been very high priced indeed.

The public, however, are very variable in matters of horse-flesh, and unless certain strains become fashionable, very low prices are obtained. It should always be remembered that although no animal commands so high a price as the thorough-bred colt if of high character, no animal is so valueless as the reverse. Therefore it stands to reason that a breeder must go for first-rate blood in both stallion and mare, or else leave breeding alone altogether. The market never flags (thanks to foreigners) for really good animals, and the latter have become such good judges that they will not only have blood and performances, but great size and power in addition, for their money.

Indeed, it appears to me that Frenchmen go more for a class of animal we should think best adapted for steeplechasing, if one is to judge by their stables, the prominent in which has been Cosmopolite, by Lanercost (who should have been left entire but for his light neck), than whom we have many a worse 2000*l.* customer at the stud.

It is far from improbable that ere long we shall have reason to wish we had gone on the same principles.

Thus it seems that size and power do represent money value after all. At any sale of yearlings the great upstanding furnished animals always make the most money, unless there chance to be a remarkably fashionably-bred one among the smaller division.

There are certain defects which I should not be inclined to pass over in either horse or mare, but if especially partial to either a mare or stallion with a serious defect, I should endeavour to counteract it to the best of my ability.

Many good horses have crooked fore legs, toes pointed out or in, &c., but in either case I should pause before breeding from such animals; but if determined to do so, I should look far and wide for the best and straightest legged partner I could find.

Thus the failing might be modified in the progeny, and a racehorse might be the result; but if careless on this point the offspring might, and most likely would, be well-nigh deformed and useless.

I utterly deprecate the system so ruinously adopted by many, of breeding from animals merely because they were good. If we consider the essential qualifications of a racehorse, we must see that an animal may be extraordinarily gifted in certain peculiarities: as temper, handiness, immense nervous action, and indomitable courage. These then may, and often do, outweigh some grievous defects in conformation; but unless we can be sure of such peculiarities being handed down to their progeny in equal ratio, we ought not to regard them more highly than their worth.

For this reason, I say that Bay Middleton and the Flying Dutchman, &c., have proved decided failures at the stud; yet no one will deny, I imagine, that they themselves were quite unsurpassed as racehorses.

To sum up then, I like a very long, low, and rather loosely built mare, in opposition to a compact closely ribbed up animal. They generally throw finer and more racing like foals, although Crucifix and Beeswing come in as the exceptions.

This is the only point on which I think the stallion should differ from the mare. He cannot be too compactly set, so long as he has freedom and length.

February is the best time to put the mare to the horse; and if only just out of training, she should have a dose of physic and cooling diet; and if then she shows no symptoms of being stinted, a few quarts of blood as a last resource should be taken.

She should on no account be allowed to see the horse again under three weeks, for I am convinced that many mares are rendered barren from the foolish notion of allowing the mare to see the stallion frequently, to ascertain whether she be really stinted. Some animals get so irritated by such excitement, that they rarely prove in foal.

The food should be cooling for another ten weeks from this point, when the sooner the mare is put to grass the better. Of all things it is desirable to avoid cooping mares up in sheds and yards in the day-time. Exercise is always necessary for the proper function of the digestive organs, and not more than six mares should be put together in one field, which should consist of at least ten acres.

Nothing renders animals so liable to mange, dropsy, water farcy, worms, &c., as a want of sufficient space for exercise. The secretions of the whole system become morbid, or, at best, enfeebled and inactive; which state of things is not very likely to render the process of foaling, when the time comes, more easy.

If any symptoms of the kind are apparent, rub the body with a mixture of sulphur and oil of turpentine, and give internally linseed gruel with half a drachm of iodide of potassium daily to increase the action of the absorbents, and continue this for a week. The mare cannot be left too much to herself when foaling, taking care that no dangerous place is at hand, such as a deep muddy ditch, pit, or the like ; for to such places mares invariably turn when their labours commence. Immediately after foaling the mare should be removed, together with the foal, to a well-littered roomy box, and have moist bran and beans, with a large supply of water always at hand, and all other liberal, but not heating diet. If the mare should be very weak, there is no better food than bean flour, linseed gruel, and old ale, given warm. If she prove an indifferent milker, which can be readily ascertained by the colt not filling himself, the best new milk should be given after the foal has dried its dam, and a soda water bottle will prove the most convenient feeder for this purpose.

After a little perseverance, a colt will drink milk as fast as a calf, and the future of a colt need in no way be despaired of, either because it had a bad mother or even if its mother die. The very names of Cade, Milksop, and last and not least the gallant little Saucebox, almost make one wish many a colt were motherless ! But, whether with a mother or without, the foal must have sufficient nourishment, or it will never come to early maturity ; and I cannot deprecate the absurd notion too strongly, that a colt should be left to itself. Left to itself, forsooth, when it represents a debt to us of something like 40*l.*, putting aside the loss of an object of one's wishes for the last twelve months !

Still, monstrous as this may seem, we daily hear men give vent to such a pitiable and imbecile thesis. Indeed, I am acquainted with one gentleman who goes to the expense of procuring some of the stoutest and best bred mares, and breeding rare animals, which are fatted on rich pastures till November, starved on litter till the following April (if they live so long), then fatted again, and so on until another year; and if they survive such treatment, are sold at five or six years old at no very great size or price, as may well be imagined. Yet the whole object of this gentleman's life is that of breeding blood stock—merely to starve them!

On remonstrating with him one day, he replied that 'It made them harder; at least, such as lived had done great things, and earned the character of being tough, wearing animals in every instance,' forgetting to add that for every one that lived through such treatment, three died; and that if an animal did live through it, he must of necessity have an iron constitution, and consequently would, under any circumstances, have proved equally good and sound, with the advantage of greater size. I tried to persuade him that nourishment tends to the formation of bone and muscle; want of it, emaciation and death. I might as well have endeavoured to persuade Mr. Lincoln that his slave emancipation Act was the act of a madman.

It is always true that no people are so obstinate in their theories as those who have neither reason nor facts to back them. Still, in these days of enlightenment one is astonished to witness such things. Colts should be weaned early in October and turned into a good fat piece of clover for another six or eight days; at the expiration of which they will have gained flesh, and be ready for a feed, both morning and evening, of some finely-crushed beans, bran, and hay chaff, in some home paddocks, on which there should be a good bite of grass.

If the colts can be conveniently separated from the fillies at this period, the condition of both will be materially improved thereby.

Colts intended for geldings should be castrated in April or the end of May, after which operation they should have one hour's walking exercise per day to prevent swelling and inflammation, and great care should be taken that no heating food be given at this period. Bran mashes and a little hay will be the most proper food for the week following the operation, after which, if the operation have been properly performed, the colt may be put to grass again.

The making up process will now begin in real earnest, for buyers like to see a big sleek-looking yearling inasmuch as it gives evidence of his having suffered from no serious illness up to this time; and very frequently are yearlings left unsold or absolutely begged, which give evidence, by the poverty of their condition, of having been afflicted with mange, worms, influenza, &c.

Therefore no means should be neglected to furnish their frames. Corn, linseed, beans, peas, Indian corn, or all mixed up together, and as much of them as they will eat, should be allowed; in addition to which they should be well dressed over, morning and evening, which will not only make them put on flesh the faster, but render them more healthy, and will consequently render the trainer's task a much easier one. No one but a practical man can imagine the anxiety and trouble attending the conditioning of a half-starved light-fleshed yearling. Some drugs must be used in addition to good food for many months, and then you only get an artificial soft brute, incapable of undergoing any real work. And in these days, when trainers have so much on their hands, it is doubly necessary that, so far as is practicable, yearlings should be properly prepared for them, previous to being consigned to their charge.

TRAINING FOR THE TURF.

In training for the Turf, the great object to be attained is the least amount of bulk combined with the greatest amount of muscular action, or, in other words, to reduce the system from a dropsical habit, softness of muscle, and consequent incapacity for severe action, to an active and healthy tone, as well as to increased vascularity of the whole muscular system; which will produce the required increase of strength, activity, and stamina usually designated by the simple word *condition*.

Having thus briefly explained the first principles and the objects in view, I will proceed to show how this condition is to be brought about.

In the first place, too great caution cannot be given as to too great anxiety in attaining this object, or what trainers term 'hurrying.' Consider what a change you have to effect—the change of the whole circulative organs, the secretions, absorbents, as well as the whole muscular and nervous system! Amongst the many difficulties you will be sure to encounter, let 'nil desperandum' be your motto. Commence your work slowly but surely—use gentle means—and to use Dr. Abernethy's words, don't begin 'by bullying your (horse's) guts into order.' It is true that I have witnessed two or three animals reduced in about three weeks from a state of Aldermanic obesity to fair condition for a country flat race. But in this, great care and experience was required, repeated stoppages in work, counteraction of nervous depression, and loss of appetite by means of tonics, &c., which is a course of treatment never to be recommended, I may say, always to be avoided, if possible.

As surely as a political revolution upsets the entire organisation of a state, so does a rapid revolution from obesity to condition upset and unduly stimulate the whole nervous system of the horse. In the first place, you must study the constitution of your horse very closely, and if you are not very gifted in that desirable faculty, 'diagnosis,' don't satisfy yourself too rapidly on the subject.

If you have ten horses in training and treat all of them in the same way, you will assuredly, unless they all have similar constitutions, which is not probable, have only a few of them in good condition.

Of all things throw routine overboard altogether, and use the intelligence that Providence has blessed you with, both as to the quantity and quality of the food, as well as the pace and duration of work, best adapted to the peculiar constitution of your horse.

Some horses require a great deal of physic to reduce their secretions to a healthy condition; others require next to none, and would be reduced to patients if physicked to a like extent. Some require to be sweated twice a week, others will carry no muscle if sweated once a month. These considerations will, in a measure. pave the way for a due consideration of this subject; and I must here state that in handling this subject, I do not for a moment intend these remarks for trainers or training grooms worthy of the name; who, if they would take the trouble to do so, could add to their greater experience far greater ability than is in my power to bring to bear on the subject.

But I have some hopes that those who, having the proper condition of their horses at heart, and occasionally try their hands at private training, and leave, in a great measure, their valuable animals to the ignorance and caprice of their 'grooms, who know no more of training than consists in physicking and galloping horses to death,' as I once heard an old and clever trainer remark, by which means a highly-bred and gifted horse is frequently brought to the post literally unfit to gallop, much less to race, the usual distance of from one mile and a-half to four miles; either in a puffy, feeble state, or else something like one's idea of a hunted devil; but, nevertheless, if he has been subjected to the prescribed number of nostrums, sweats, and ' go-downs of water' (hateful term), he is forthwith pronounced by his attendant faculty, with the utmost assurance, to be 'bang up to the mark.' The result is, that the race is run in which this poor creature is able to take no part, and his owner, who perhaps knows his horse to be a good and fast hunter, believes him incapable, notwithstanding, of performing successfully against horses of his own calibre, and attributes his defeat to want of pace, and more frequently to want of stoutness; when, in numerous instances, he is wanting in neither, but *terribly wanting in fitness for the task he was called upon to perform*; and thus frequently a good sportsman, not wishing again to figure so ingloriously, refrains from ever entering the lists on future occasions, and so the support of many honourable sportsmen (and they are sadly wanting in these days) is entirely lost, and the sport of hunt and welter flat races and steeplechases, which, whatever cavillers may say, encourage the breed of horses most universally in demand in all parts of the world, becomes sadly depreciated, and maintains only a flickering existence.

It is frequently urged that gentlemen have no business to train their own horses; that they can send them to trainers and have them brought to the post in as high a state of condition as skill and experience can effect. But the numerous huntraces in which horses that have been in training-stables are either excluded, disqualified, or penalised, must ever be an answer to this. I am, however, ready here to admit that any trainer of skill could bring a horse to the post at least seven pounds better than nine private individuals out of ten, even if the latter were gifted with the same skill and experience, which is not either probable or possible. In the first place, a trainer has the advantage of a good training ground, close to his stables, by which 'tramping for miles' along a hard stony road is avoided; and also, he has the command of horses equal to the task of testing his progress from time to time, both in speed and stoutness; and, moreover, can usually command the services of a rider of a weight proportioned to the horse's powers, which immense advantages are rarely ever within the reach of private individuals.

In addition, it is oftentimes inconvenient to part with a horse for the necessary time at a training stable, inasmuch as he can carry his owner, almost up to the day of running in a steeplechase, the greater portion of a day's hunting, by which means he is not altogether deprived of the use of his horse, nor compelled to make an addition to his stud which would be both inconvenient and expensive. Moreover, the value of such stakes do not often warrant the expense of a trainer's bill.

TRAINING THE TWO-YEAR OLD.

The colt should reach the stables somewhere about October, immediately after which he should be bitted, which should be performed by placing a roller on his back having a buckle to either side, to which is attached the reins, with a loop at the back through which to pass the strap of the crupper. This being accomplished, put in his mouth a smooth, straight snaffle attached to the head collar by buckles or spring clasps, and allow him to run loose about the box for two or three hours during the first three days, after which his mouth, having become accustomed to the pressure, reins may be attached, and at such a length as will cause him to bend his neck and give his mouth, so as to avoid pressure from the bit. Keep them thus for an hour a day during the next three days, shortening the reins a little each succeeding day.

A week will now have elapsed, after which attach the reins as before, and make him trot gently in a circle, attaching the reins just so as to keep his head in the right place; but carefully avoid distressing him. No animal at this age should be kept at work for more than one hour a-day. And severe work this is when they have their backs 'set' in a way to which they are wholly unaccustomed.

Continue this practice for another week, after which, at the termination of the sixth longe, let a light lad mount him and ride him back to the stable.

It will thus be seen that by this simple method, twelve colts can easily be broken by one man and a lad, at the same time, and that two weeks have elapsed previous to his being mounted. On the next day let the lad be in readiness to mount, after the colt has been longed gently for half-an-hour; then let him mount and ride out the remaining half-hour of the longe, walking and trotting alternately. All longeing should now cease, and the colt may be safely ridden out for an hour by any lad who can be depended on;

as his mouth will be tractable enough to be made sufficient use of to baffle any attempt he may make to turn restive.

If the colt show symptoms of restiveness, sit still! If you take tight hold of the bit and scold him, he may learn that most dangerous of all vices—rearing and tumbling back, which may irreparably injure both his rider and himself.

I may here as well state that I consider all dumb jockeys worse than useless; in short, very injurious indeed. Some are manufactured with steel springs, others with elastic gutta percha reins, which keep up a continual wearing pressure on the mouth; so that whether the colt behave well or ill; whether he give his mouth or no, still this irritating pressure continues.

Such treatment is at once senseless and cruel. What you want to do is to make the colt give his mouth, and so to supple and bend his neck. When the colt discovers that by bending his neck the pressure from the bit ceases, he soon learns to do so with a good grace. I speak feelingly on this point, as I had a very fine and valuable five-year-old colt almost ruined by the gutta percha reins, and it was not until I altered them that he showed any signs of amendment. His custom was to put his head out and hold it doggedly in this position, as he had found out that by so doing he could as easily bear the pressure, and at the same time avoid taxing the muscles of his neck. But the irritation caused by them was so great that he would knock his head against the wall, throw himself down and bruise himself from head to foot. Indeed he contracted scars which he never quite lost; and, in addition, his temper was so severely tried that he sulked and became jaded for weeks. In short, it was evident that had the use of the elastic reins been continued he would have been ruined irretrievably.

I have heard of several colts being fairly mouthed with these gutta percha reins; but that in no way affects the argument, for their tempers could not have been so sensitive, and moreover they would undoubtedly have been better mouthed with common leather reins, properly adjusted, for the reason above given.

I used to wish that every colt-breaker in the country had the money wherewith to purchase a dumb jockey, but now I am thankful that they have not got it to spare!

When the state of the weather and ground will admit of it, the colt should have one hour's walking exercise with a lad on him daily, and his food should consist of four quarterns of bruised oats per day; the last feed on Wednesday and Saturday evenings being varied by a linseed and bran mash. This work should continue until February, when cantering should commence—going about a quarter of a mile at a steady canter on some good soft turf, and if on rising ground so much the better.

This distance should be got over from eight to ten times, walking the remainder of the time, which should never exceed one hour.

DURATION OF WORK.

If this work be continued for two months, the colt should be fit at any time to have a trial over half a mile of ground, and could be got ready to run this distance within a month.

Two-year olds should never be sweated unless very gross, or very weak in their pins; and if ever they are sweated, only one light rug and hood should be put on, or the weight of the rugs and the debility caused by the sweating will make them slow, jaded, and utterly unfit to race. Had I the alternative of sweating or muzzling a two-year old to reduce flesh, I should adopt the latter practice most certainly, since sweating renders young ones very weak and faint, and causes their muscles to become soft and placid; or, in other words, they *train off rapidly.*

I maintain that one hour's work—cantering a quarter of a mile from eight to ten times (which would occupy, say five minutes) the remainder of the time (55 minutes) being consumed by walking—is quite enough for any animal that has to grow as well as work. For training young animals properly, the exercise should be quick and the time short. The cantering after the first fortnight should be done at a quick sharp pace. They should never be kept on their legs too long, since the muscles and sinews are not sufficiently matured to stand any lengthened strain without injury.

I need hardly add that a two-year old should have a nice airy roomy box, and be left quiet as long as possible, that he may rest at his pleasure: for at this age they require an immense amount of repose. Now, as at all other times when they are working hard, there should be no limit to their allowance of food. A craving for food will always induce a bad and irritable temperament; a sufficiency of food, contentment and good temper.

Unless the colt be within three or four weeks of running, a few carrots, a handful of vetches, rye-grass, &c., now and then, will stimulate the digestion and cool the system generally, as well as prevent the necessity of flying to drugs in all cases of slight derangement.

At this age there is no medicine so good to counteract undue astringency, worms, hidebound, &c., as one drachm of emetic tartar, given in a bran mash, every day for a week; but, on no account, to be continued longer. The safest rule is, whenever the use of this drug produces running of the saliva, sickness, or looseness of the secretions, to discontinue its use at once.

The shoes of a two-year old should be made as light as possible, and on no account be allowed to remain on over two weeks; and indeed at this age it would always be well if the walking could be done on dragged and harrowed fallows, where the whole of the foot could bear the pressure, instead of the mere crust, which is too weak to bear the whole of the weight with impunity.

Great care should be paid to the state of the mouth, as the teeth are far more often affected than is generally supposed.

PROPER LEANNESS NECESSARY.   47

If any roughness of the teeth (which may be ascertained by sores on the tongue, &c.) should be apparent, they should be filed level, or if inflammation of the gums be detected, means should at once be used to allay it, by using weak astringent lotions. Also when the teeth are loose they should be pulled out, as they frequently cause great uneasiness when feeding. At such times some chopped carrots or green food should, if possible, be given, on account of their being more easy of mastication, and also because there is always a slight feverishness flying about the constitution at these times.

As to the general appearance of a two-year-old when fit to run, my opinion is that it should not be nearly so light as that of an older and more matured horse. In the latter case the ribs should most certainly be apparent; but in the case with which we are dealing, the colt would be overdone and jaded, as well as his constitution materially injured, by being drawn so fine. Of course his frame should give evidence of sufficient leanness and the muscles should be '*out*,' to use a common expression; but to rob the constitution at this age of so much of its vital powers that he should present a spare rib would be most injudicious. In short, if the wind be clear, the sweat clean, and the muscles firm and hard; as much will be arrived at as will be prudent at this age.

At the same time I am quite sure that in all matured animals great development of muscle, with *a lean rib*, must be the *sine quâ non* of fine condition. For I am persuaded that, without it, neither a horse, foxhound, greyhound, nor stag can run up to their best form, neither can a man run, row, or fight without sufficient leanness in the ribs. Flesh here can be of no use, and therefore can be only a needless incumbrance. But I do not argue for this in either the two, three, or four-year-old, considering as I do that, unless violent sweats were resorted to, the colt would be jaded to death before such leanness were effected. Undoubtedly, then, the great art in training young horses is to get their muscles firm and bulky, and their wind clear; more than this is overtraining at this age, and moreover would be quite superfluous for horses that only have to run over two-year-old courses, which should never be exceeded; and how men can be found 'penny wise and pound foolish' enough to run two-year-olds in the 50*l.* Plate last three miles of the B. C. at Newmarket, Houghton, &c., I cannot imagine. I know of no sight more disgusting than that presented by the little lads and the two-year-olds during the last mile of this race, rolling about like a ship in a storm, from sheer distress! It is too much to ask of the most furnished two-year-old, and it is very easy to understand why animals that have run in this race invariably show so little speed afterwards.

It would be bad enough if it were limited to two-year-olds only; but to admit all ages makes it doubly bad, since 'the cutting down work' is the only method of taking due advantage of their pull in the weights.

TRAINING THREE AND FOUR-YEAR-OLDS.

In training three and four-year-olds very much the same process will have to be gone through as with two-year-olds, with this exception, that the distance of the canter should be increased from one quarter to half a mile, and the duration of work from one to two hours. And further it is desirable that the colt have occasional opportunities of testing his improvement in speed and stoutness by having a rough gallop with an older horse at a fair speed for one and a half mile *once every fortnight*, unless ill health or the state of the ground prevent it.

This gallop, however, should always be gone through with as light a weight as is desirable, and also *without any clothes*. Nothing makes horses slower than galloping under a weight of rugs. Well can I remember three racehorses in one stable being made incorrigible curs by being subjected to three brushing gallops in clothes in one week, with a view to presenting a 'semblance of condition' at the end of it; for the trainer in this instance was a man of too sound judgment and too much experience ever to imagine that anything more than the 'semblance' would be exhibited on the day. He satisfied his employer and his horses so fully that they both had *quantum suff.* for that season.

TRAINING OF FIVE-YEAR OLDS AND UPWARDS.

In the first instance we must consider the age, constitution, and previous work that the horse has been doing.

1. If he has been on the turf and in training.
2. If he has never raced but has been hunted.
3. If he has only been hacked.
4. If he has only been broken and has done no severe work of any kind.

We must of course take it for granted that the horse is sound in limb at any rate, and that, whatever ailments of the respiratory organs he may be afflicted with, that they do not interfere with his running very materially, for it must be understood that no treatment can give new legs or new organs of respiration; but all we can hope to do will be to alter and improve the present and not to generate a new system.

The only reason for which I have thought it necessary to separate the training of horses into four different classes is that the *amount of practice required will not be the same in either case*; though the *same condition of body* will be required in all.

1. Then the horse that has been raced. Do not imagine that because he has been raced he can race now, for he may be utterly out of condition for such a purpose; nevertheless this will not be nearly so difficult as the other three cases with which we have to deal; since the amount of *galloping practice* will be comparatively slight, and the time for getting the horse fit consequently more limited. All we shall have to do will be to reduce his body to a sufficient leanness and to increase the bulk and firmness of his muscles, to effect which two principles must be fully understood and acted upon. First, that slow and long work is

required to develope muscle; and, secondly, that quick work is required to increase the powers of respiration.

To effect this, then, sufficient time must be allowed, and the shorter the better commensurate with the undertaking, for it must be borne in mind that no relapse from work can on any consideration be allowed; but when once training commences, it must be *work and not exercise throughout*, and then, if in a fair state to begin with, from two to four months will be sufficient. From this it will be seen that, if the horse be stale when taken from his work, proper rest should be given to him *previously* to his being put under the trainer's care. It is absurd to put a stale horse into training; still more absurd to attempt to train a horse while in ill health. In either case training will make matters worse, and will most likely ruin the animal for life. Therefore if an animal is not in rude health (I care not from what cause), all ideas of putting him into training should be discarded.

First get your iron bar, and then you may reasonably hope to use it! First then get health, soundness both of wind and limb, and you may reasonably hope to refine them both by trying them in the fire. As I have said before, I will presume that the horse's legs are clean and firm, that no marks of humours are apparent, but that he is merely fleshy and short of work.

Your first step will be to keep your horse walking on turf for at least four hours a day; and if time can be spared to divide the time into two periods, so much the better; for the horse will be all the fresher, and feed all the better. His daily allowance should be three quarterns of moist bran with three quarterns of old oats, and about eight pounds of prime old hay. This exercise should be continued for the first week; when, in nine cases out of ten, you will perceive the legs getting rather full and soft, with possibly filling and tenderness at the heels. Immediately stop your work as well as corn and hay, and give bran and linseed mashes, and reduce the amount of work to an hour's walking on some sheltered spot, for at least two ensuing days, then muzzle him during the night, and physic in the morning; after which, give as much water as he will drink. But if you have any reason to think he will not drink well after his physic, give him as much as he will drink immediately before administering it, because the more the bowels are diluted, the less will be the required amount of aloes. Give the following ball:—

Barbadoes Aloes	4 drachms
Powdered Resin	2 ,,
Sulphate of Iron	2 ,,
Peruvian Bark	2 ,,

made into a ball with Castile soap and a syrup of some kind, and if the symptoms do not appear to abate within a few days, let the following ball be given on each Saturday night for four ensuing weeks:—

Barbadoes Aloes	2 drachms
Powdered Resin	1 ,,
Sulphate of Iron	2 ,,
Peruvian Bark	2 ,,

ACTION OF PHYSIC.

In this physic-ball the amount of aloes may seem large at first sight; but if (as in this case) the horse has previously been in training, a less quantity would, in nine cases out of ten, be insufficient, and if insufficient, utterly useless, as the purpose would not be effected, and valuable time would have been wasted. It is better to give a fair dose, or a dose sufficient to increase the action of the absorbents, than to bully a horse with two or three smaller doses, which would occupy more time than could be spared.

At least two hours' walking exercise should be given immediately after the ball has been administered, with as much chilled water as he will drink, and a loose bran mash, when he may be shut up and left quiet until the next morning, by which time, if no symptoms of purging are apparent, he should be immediately taken for a walk in the field nearest the stable, so that he may be taken to the stable immediately purgation commences; and if chilly, an extra rug should be thrown over him without delay, for be it understood that the action of physic is to *cause a determination of the secretions from the skin to the intestines*, through which they may be carried off, and therefore the skin will require additional protection from the effects of the atmosphere; consequently, the less a horse's coat is brushed during the action of physic the better. If the excrements are not very foul, purging for twelve hours will be quite sufficient; but if very foul and fœtid, twice that period will be required; and in the latter case, a little wetted bran and linseed should be mixed with every feed for four or five days after purgation has ceased, or a troublesome astringency of the bowels may ensue.

Begin immediately to give four quarterns of oats, and lessen the hay to 6lbs., and recommence walking two hours in the morning and evening during the ensuing week, when one fourth of your time will have expired without even a canter.

Never mind! Better go a-head slowly yet surely, than begin rapidly, undergo check after check, and finally end by nursing your patient a full week before running, and then give out that he has 'gone amiss,' which would be better interpreted has been '*hounded to a standstill!*'

Now then you have hardened your horse's muscles by long and repeated walks, you have cleaned his skin by good grooming; and, last and not least, you have relieved his overloaded system and removed the inflammatory symptoms produced by change of work and diet. And rest assured that there is something gained, that you have not been standing still, but have been rapidly preparing the whole machinery of your horse's frame for hard work; and hard work, without preparation, is not only worse than useless, but absolutely dangerous and cruel in the extreme.

QUICK WORK.

Now we have arrived at by far the most difficult part of our undertaking. When the horse is undergoing quick work, the eyes should be strained to discover the least downward tendency in the system. The hands should be frequently placed on the pulse, and passed down the legs to see how the constitution is standing the rough usage—for rough usage it must be, or *training* has never been entered on. There are, however, such a number of obstacles thrown in the trainer's path, when 'sending a horse along,' that it would be an almost hopeless task to recount them. Suffice it to say, however, that during extremes in the state of the ground—whether very wet or very dry—fast work cannot be pursued with advantage. In the former case, a bad over-reach or strain in the hocks and hind limbs, together with a severe over-reach in the fore joints; in the latter a breakdown, strain of the muscles of the shoulder, or inflammation of the knees, fetlock joints, laminæ of the feet, &c., may be expected; therefore, the state of the ground should be carefully considered before galloping at any pace, or absolute stoppage in work may be the result.

It is far better to allow a horse to get fleshy, and stick to walking exercise, than terminate his existence by impatient and unwise treatment. I must own that, in handling this subject, I feel that so little can prudently be laid down, further than general principles, that any direct rules, which I may consider adapted to nine horses out of ten, would lead only to a mischievous routine in treatment, which would entirely defeat my object.

First, then, the objects of quick work are twofold: to exercise and strengthen the organs of respiration, and to accustom the muscles and tendons to bear the tension resulting from the force and rapidity with which they must be put in motion.

Now the usual practice of training is to give horses continual walks and continual 'breathings' as they are termed,—i.e. walking down half a mile, and cantering back the same distance at a good pace, continuing this work for three hours every morning—*too long*, in my opinion, for any colt to be on his legs *at any one time*.

This system of training may be all very well when two year-old courses, or even mile courses are the objects in view; for which short spurts—the shorter the better —must be resorted to, as the only means of making a horse quick on his legs, on which acquirement nearly all his chances of success depend. But for such courses no animal should be kept out more than two hours per day, and this at separate intervals,—i.e., one hour in the morning and one in the afternoon; during which time, alternate walks and spins must be given. This species of training, however, is generally confined to professional trainers; so little need be said on this head.

The quick work must, as I have previously remarked, depend entirely on the distance to be run.

Should the distance be from one and a-half to two miles the horse should be lightly fed during the morning of galloping the distance, which should be gone over at his best pace from once to twice a-week, according to circumstances. The horse should be walked about for one hour, then stripped of all his clothes, whether summer or winter, and having as light a saddle and lad placed on him as is deemed prudent, he should be sent along over the whole distance at very nearly his top speed; always bearing in mind never to allow the horse to *run himself out*,—i.e., exhaust his powers; but still make him do his utmost, just keeping him *inside the mark*. Immediately it is over, let the girths be slackened, and the horse led about till he has done blowing (which will be in about ten minutes), then let his clothes be put on, his mouth washed out with nitre and water, and the sooner he is walked back to the stable the better. On removing the rugs the horse will be found to have sweated considerably, and, indeed, this is all the sweating either desirable or necessary, when the horse's skin is clean and his frame spare. His clothes should be removed immediately and his skin rubbed perfectly dry (which will take from twenty minutes to one hour), after which dry clothes should be thrown over him, and his legs and feet well washed, rubbed dry, and flannel bandages applied. This done, the rug must once more be removed, and the brush applied briskly all over him until every particle of dust, dirt, and scurf has been removed.

This brushing will take a full hour; after which his eyes and nose will require sponging, and his mane and tail combing, when his toilet may be considered accomplished. A feed of corn and some water may be given, and rest for four or five hours, at the expiration of which the exercising cloth and hood must once more be put on, and an hour's stroll on some turf gone through, when the ill effects of the gallop, if any, will be evident, and due precautions taken immediately. If all is well, on the next and two following days he should resume his two hours' walk, morning and afternoon, when the time will have arrived for another brushing gallop, the same as the preceding.

I have found from experience that not one horse in ten can stand more than two brushing gallops during the week, and many cannot stand as much; and therefore this must be taken as the rule, that no horse should be galloped a second time until the soreness and stiffness consequent on the previous spin has subsided. Galloping in this state would only produce what is termed staleness, and possibly permanent grogginess; at any rate, the horse would lose all speed, and consequently all chance of success.

Many horses will remain stiff and sore for days after a gallop of two miles; and even if they were to remain *weeks*, patience must be called into play, and time allowed *for the vessels to relieve themselves and contract on their contents.*

Unfortunately, however, time is rarely given, and the horse is pulled out on the next and every subsequent day (till he breaks down), to be galloped and walked, and walked and galloped, till he is little better than a jade, having lost all elasticity and dash, on which speed depends so much.

I am well aware how unfair it is to make disparaging remarks on the too frequent method of training horses, since trainers are ordered by their employers to bring a certain horse to the post, fit to run at a certain meeting (whether there be sufficient time or not), disobedience to which orders would only lose them the custom of their employers; therefore trainers should not be judged harshly when they bring a horse to the post manifestly unfit to run. In nine cases out of ten the blame lies with their employers, who engage their horses early in March, well knowing that, unless their horses are galloped on ice half their time, they cannot be galloped at all, save and except they be able to avail themselves of a 'tan gallop,' which is not always 'good going' in severe weather; consequently sweating, or more properly *wasting*, is the only method left open to them of ensuring even a *semblance of condition*.

But to return to the subject. We will suppose that the horse shows symptoms of puffiness and inability to hold a severe pace for any distance over a mile. It must not be supposed that he is therefore only *a miler*.

The correct decision can readily be arrived at by a practical observer. If the horse be only 'a miler' he will lose his muscular powers entirely after this distance has been got over at top speed. If he be able to go a greater distance, merely loss of the powers of respiration will be evident, which must be strengthened by exercise and general health, always bearing in mind that nothing tends more decidedly to relieve the organs of respiration than *great attention to the skin*.

In any case—from whatever cause the horse may feel distressed—he should be pulled up immediately such symptoms are apparent, which can be easily discovered by his pace becoming wretched, and his stride short and irregular. He should go through another gallop, with the same caution, on the next day but one, when he will doubtless improve on his former performance.

For many reasons, at this stage of training, it is most foolish to gallop a horse until he be distressed.

In the first place, it can be of no use to force or allow him to continue a *wretchedly slow pace*—all that could be got out of him—which could never win a race in any company. And in the second place, the effects on the system would be so injurious that it would be quite ten to one that the horse would have to be thrown by, perhaps for months.

It is only when you find that your horse is lean on his ribs, clear in his wind, firm and hard in his muscles, and high in his spirits, that you may venture on taxing his powers to the utmost; not until you perceive that he holds his pace from end to end with unabated vigour and freedom of action, are you justified in allowing him to be shaken along, or if lazy to receive a stroke or two of the whip during the last two or three hundred yards; when if he be really fit to run he will spring from the whip and increase his efforts tenfold; but if *unfit*, unless wonderfully game, he will die away immediately any additional call is made.

I know of no better symptom of good training than this, when a horse has sufficient vigour and freshness left in his constitution, after going at top speed for two or three miles, to make continual rushes when called upon.

It proves that the nervous system is by no means exhausted, and also that the system is quite free of any obstruction to its powers of action.

The time will now have arrived for a trial, but care must be taken that inexperienced hands are banished from participation in the performance.

The leader of the trial should be possessed of a cool head, a good knowledge of pace, and should never begin too quickly, which overexcites nervous horses, and makes them scramble along before getting fairly and gradually into their stride. As a rule, in a trial the first mile had better be got over slowly; it calms both horses and riders, and gives the latter time to consider how he can mend the horse's 'style of going.' It is always easy to mend a bad pace, but very difficult to preserve a clipper; therefore the *real trial* should not begin until one mile has been gone over; the horses being well together and going with a collected sweeping stride.

It is no trial to allow lads to burst off and chop one another down in the first half mile, or to allow one to leave the other some lengths in the rear at starting.

All such tricks—and they are nothing else—however satisfactory on the racecourse, when successful, must be entirely forbidden on the training ground.

Supposing the horse has to run two miles, mark out two miles and a half, and order the lads to come along slowly for the first mile, and then go the remainder of the distance 'a duster!' Never allow horses to be ridden out, and moreover never to be run away from;

nothing disheartens a horse so much as finding himself quite outpaced. He will be very likely to give it up as a hopeless task, and relinquish the contest ingloriously, unless forced to continue it by aid of whip and spur, which only makes matters still worse. Then, as a rule, the leader of the trial should be on the best horse, and he should ride the distance in favour of his opponent all the way, so that the latter has nothing to do but to sit still and keep with him.

If you were to allow each lad to ride his own race, one would generally outwit the other to such a degree that nothing correct could be made out of the trial. One would make too much use of his horse, and the other would lay too far away from the other ever to have a chance of getting up again, and therefore the only safe plan is to make them keep together all the way; at any rate never to allow more than two or three lengths to separate them. There are a great many persons who lay great stress on timing a trial in addition to ensuring its being run truly from end to end, considering that the result without accurate time is utterly inconclusive, and indeed liable to mislead; but as 'time' is so dependent on the state of the ground, atmosphere, and many other considerations, I cannot bring myself to accept its decision as conclusive either one way or the other. And, moreover, apart from the above reasons, I have no faith in timing a trial, inasmuch as I have never known either man or horse go over the same course in the same time, either twice in the same day or on two consecutive days.

Therefore, to time a trial and then make allowances for this or that discrepancy in time owing to this or that circumstance, would be a most complicated undertaking, and one which I should not recommend any one to attempt, unless for mere self-gratification.

It is frequently objected that time is always taken abroad with very great success, in determining the respective merits of racehorses; but I must object to this that the climate, state of the ground, atmosphere, &c., are all diametrically opposed to those of England; and therefore, that what may be a correct test in one country may not be a correct test in another.

It is a matter of fact that in America, India, Jamaica, &c., exported English platers can make better time than first-class racehorses are able to do in Great Britain over our very best and soundest courses, which I apprehend can only be accounted for by the rarity of the atmosphere in those countries; for no one will, I presume, hold for one moment that three stones would bring a Derby or Leger winner and a colonial plater on a par!

The trial over, the horses should be walked home with their rugs on, and after being well dressed, and made generally comfortable, should be allowed as much to eat and drink as they please, and then be shut up for three or four hours, after which they should be taken out for a stroll, when nothing more will have to be done for that day.

If they have been overdone, and appear languid, a slight tonic, such as equal parts of gentian and black antimony, or one ounce of 'extract of chamomile,' should be given without delay; but the less these remedies are used the stronger will the horse's constitution be.

It is well to allow some time to elapse between the trials, and also between the last trial and the race, and I consider five days between the final trial and the race indispensable. Five days then before the race is run the trial should take place over the same distance of ground as the coming encounter, and also at or nearly the same weights, at a strong pace all the way; as if the horse performs badly he can be scratched in due time: but if well he may, after the arrival of the next morning, be safely backed; since, if all appears right then, it may safely be presumed that all will be well on the day.

Now I must give the greatest caution as to treatment: *work must cease entirely*, and the horse must be allowed rest to enable him to recover the effects of his efforts in the trial, and may indeed, to make a long story short, be allowed to get fresh; or, to be more explicit, to allow him to get rid of his soreness and staleness, and for this he will have none too much time. He should stroll about in the fresh air for an hour or two daily on as soft ground as can be chosen, and be allowed as much water and corn, but less hay, than usual.

If gluttonous, he should be taken out at seven on the morning of running for an hour to allow him to empty himself and have a breather for two or three

ADJUSTING THE SADDLE.

hundred yards, after which one quartern of oats and a little water may be given, and the horse must be carefully secured, either by muzzling or racking, until taken out for the race.

In adjusting the saddle, &c., great care should be taken that the weights are level; that there be not a greater weight on one side than on the other; and, if there be no breastplate, that they be put on very forward; also that the girths are not drawn too tightly: 'if a horse cannot grunt he cannot gallop,' is a very old and very wise saying that many strong-armed grooms would do well to remember.

The practice of washing out the mouth, previous to the jockey getting into the saddle, is a very good one, since it prevents that dryness and harshness of the mouth which so frequently annoys both man and horse on suddenly commencing rapid inspirations, and moreover it renders the mouth more supple and sensitive to the rider's touch.

RACE RIDING.

Little need be said on this subject, since there is so much practice in these days, that, unless in the most remote parts of England, the services of a fair performer can generally be secured. No definite rules can be laid down, with the exception of the following general remarks.

1. The fitter your horse is, the more severe should you make the pace.
2. If you have reason to doubt your horse's game-

ness jump off with the lead, and keep it as long as you can.

3. If a horse pulls very hard, keep a steady pull on him, but *don't haul at his mouth*, which will prevent all regularity of respiration, as well as throw him out of his stride and injure his temper. These sort of horses should be calmed down gently; but this can only be done at, or very nearly at, the top of their speed.

4. Young and untried horses should never be allowed to jump away from the starting post too quickly, since they will only outrun or outpace themselves before three-fourths of the distance has been covered; neither should they be allowed to make the pace severe until fairly in their stride, when they must be sent along at as fast a pace as they can possibly maintain. This method will usually prevent their getting flurried and nervous, which takes more steel out of a horse than is generally supposed.

5. When about seven-eighths of the distance has been got over, unless a very expert hand at timing your horse's powers, do not attempt to draw it very fine; but, getting on good terms with the leading horses in the race and laying hold of your horse's head, try and leave them, and ride him calmly but resolutely home; and, of all things, sit quite steady; if you find your horse straining every nerve, let him alone; but if running sluggishly, take tight hold of the reins in your left hand, and taking a sharp pull at the reins, give him a smart stroke with the whip and two or three kicks with the spurs; but if you have

reason to apprehend your horse's swerving at the whip (as is often the case with bad-hearted ones), keep hold of the reins with both hands, and give him two or three sharp kicks with the spurs, which will tend to keep him straight and very materially increase his chance of success.

6. If you find you are beaten easily, pull up and spare your horse's useless exertions; and, above all, avoid that unsportsmanlike practice of flogging a beaten horse, without a ghost of a chance, all the way home. I am well aware that unless jockeys do so, the ring men will not credit an honest defeat; but their incredulity is no excuse for such cruel and disgusting exhibitions, which are getting far too common in these days.

AFTER THE RACE.

The horse should be led about in as warm and sheltered a spot as possible for fully one hour before being taken to the stable, that he may recover the distress of his lungs, heart, &c., before being shut up in a comparatively heated and unwholesome atmosphere.

The sooner he be rubbed, dried, and his toilette finished the better, after which he should be shut up and left quiet for some time; and, unless he has to run again within a week, some bran and linseed mashes, as being the best sedative food known, and two days' entire rest, should be allowed.

At the termination of this period the horse may be

walked about and be put through a gentle and short canter every other day, merely to keep him in wind, but nothing more. Any more severe work would only jade and depress him; or, in other words, make him 'train off.' Since you cannot hope to improve on the acme of perfection of condition, your only endeavour should be to keep as near to it as you can without endangering your horse's constitution.

It is, however, in all cases better to allow horses at this step to get a little jolly and big, giving *moderate exercise* only in the place of *hard work*, and putting them through a slight sweat two days previous to running, which will ensure a healthy skin and clear wind, without further taxing their already severely tried understandings.

There is no greater fallacy than the theory of 'keeping a horse in condition.' *It cannot be done.* A horse properly wound up for a race, will only be unwound if trained on. There must always be something to spare so as to stand the continual waste caused by severe exertion; and if there be no adipose or fatty matter in the system to supply the waste, as there will not be if the horse have been brought quite up to the mark, an injurious and continuous effect will take place in the constitution.

Therefore, after the horse has run his race, relaxation from work for a considerable time must be allowed, or the constitution of the horse will be severely impaired, and he never can be brought to the post in the same form again.

EVILS OF OVER-TRAINING.

These principles should be fully understood by every owner and trainer of racehorses, or cases of 'training off,' 'losing all form,' 'going amiss,' and numerous other verdicts, all arising from the very same cause, will be of frequent occurrence, and reduce the stable to little else than a hospital. And on this subject I cannot do better than quote the remarks published in the *Lancet* relative to the condition of the American pugilist, J. C. Heenan, after his defeat by Tom King, since it most vividly sets forth the insurmountable evil of prolonging training beyond its proper limits—i.e., to decay. It runs thus:—

'Four or five hours after the termination of the fight on the 10th inst., he arrived at a friend's house in London. Mr. J. F. Clarke saw him immediately. He was then suffering from great exhaustion. His face was considerably disfigured, and there was a cut on the right side of the upper lip, about half an inch in length, which required a stitch. There were no bruises of any consequence about the body, but there were a few scratches on the chest. The action of the heart was very feeble, and the pulse scarcely perceptible. Suitable medicines were resorted to, under the influence of which he gradually improved until the 13th. On the evening of that day he had a fainting fit. On the 14th Dr. Tanner saw him in consultation with Mr. Clarke. He was then weak, his nights had been restless, and there was considerable uneasiness on taking deep inspirations. On examining him, all marks about the chest had nearly disappeared, while the bruises on the face were evidently quickly fading. The cut in his upper lip had healed. The right nasal bone was loosened from its articulations; but there was no fracture. On carefully practising auscultation, the heart's action was found to be feeble, though there was no bruit—the valves acting efficiently. The pulse was weak, very compressible, and rather above 100. The left lung was healthy, but over the apex of the right there was dulness, with evident signs of congestion. On either side, at the back of the neck, there was considerable stiffness, which was ascertained to exist chiefly in the tendinous attachments of the trapezius muscle to the occipital bone, ligamentum nuchæ, dorsal vertebræ, and spine of the scapula. The immense development of the muscles about the shoulders and chest was very remarkable; they stood out prominently, and as little encumbered with fat as if they had been cleaned out with a scalpel. In firmness they resembled cartilage. The same conditions were also apparent in the recti muscles of the abdominal wall, the tendinous intersections (lineæ transversæ) of which were strongly marked.

'But with all this splendid development it was evident that Heenan had received a shock from which his system was only slowly recovering; though whether this loss of power was due to the punishment received in the fight, *or to the hard training which he had previously undergone,* may be a disputed point. As physiologists, it seems to us highly probable that his training *had been too prolonged and too severe.* When Heenan went into training on Wednesday 23rd

September, just eleven weeks before the match, his weight was 15st. 7lbs. As he stepped into the ring on the 10th inst. he was exactly 14 stones. At the same time King weighed 13 stones, though he was three quarters of an inch taller than Heenan, whose height is 6ft. 1½ in. Those who know what severe training means, will, perhaps, agree with us that *Heenan was probably in better condition five weeks before meeting his antagonist than on the morning of his defeat*, although, when he stripped for fighting, the lookers on all agreed that he seemed to promise himself an easy victory, while exulting in his fine proportions, and splendid muscular development.

' It is now clearly proved that Heenan went into the contest *with much more muscular than vital power.*

' Long before he had met with any severe punishment—indeed, as he states, in the third round—he felt faint, breathed with difficulty, and, as he described it, his respiration was ' roaring.' He declares that he received more severe punishment at the hands of Sayers than he did from King, yet at the termination of the former fight, which lasted upwards of two hours, he was so fresh as to leap over two or three hurdles, and distance many of his friends in the race. It was noticed on the present occasion that his *physique* had deteriorated, and that he looked very much older than at his last appearance in the ring.

' Without offering any opinion as to the merits of the combatants, it is certain that Heenan was in a state of very deteriorated health when he faced his opponent, and it is fair to conclude that that *deterioration was due in a great measure to the severity of training which he had undergone.*

' As with the mind, so with the body, *undue and prolonged exertion must end in depression of power.* In the process of the physical education of the young, in the training of our recruits, or in the sports of the athlete, the case of Heenan suggests a striking commentary of great interest in a physiological point of view.

' Whilst exercise, properly so called, tends to development and health, excessive exertion produces debility and decay. In these times of over-excitement and over-competition in the race of life, the case we now put on record may be studied with advantage.'

There will be no necessity for me to enter into the details of the daily training required for those horses which have not raced, nor undergone much galloping practice previously to being put into training, further than to say, that instead of being put through mere walking exercise they will have to go through alternate walks and spins, the same as the two and the three-year old, for at least two months, at the expiration of which they will require long slow gallops of three or four miles, at three-quarter speed, twice in every week for a month, so as to ensure their stride being even and measured, without which no horse can stay over a long course. For another six weeks they may enter on precisely the same work as that recommended for training the horse that has previously been raced. By this it will be seen that it will take just two weeks over double the time required for training the horse that has previously been raced, to get the hunter, hack, or untried colt fit to run; and the whole reason is, that the amount of galloping practice required for giving them action and supporting their muscles and joints will be more than double that of a previously trained animal, since you have nothing to teach the latter, and only have to arrive at a certain condition of body to fit him for his contest.

THE STEEPLECHASE HORSE.

As to conformation I have little more to demand than that stated as being desirable for a racehorse, with the following few exceptions:—

1. The withers should be higher and the shoulders longer.

2. The girth should be deeper, and the back or false ribs shorter and lighter.

3. The hips should be wider, and the pelvis broader.

The reasons are these: unless the withers be high and shoulders long, there will not be sufficient leverage to enable him to rise well at his fences; as well as to clear whatever obstacles may come across him when galloping, in the shape of ridge and furrows, drains, hillocks, &c.; and unless the hips and pelvis be broad, together with light back ribs and a loose flank, the haunches cannot be dashed under the body in the form required for a big jumper.

The only parts, then, in which I consider the steeplechase horse should differ from the racehorse, are the shoulders, back ribs, hips and haunches; otherwise, all else should be similar.

ACTION.

Unless the horse gets his hind legs well under him, and appears almost to balance himself on them as he walks, lifting his hind feet rather high, I should not consider it desirable.

In the gallop the style of going in the steeplechase horse should differ from that in the racehorse entirely. The former should seem to be a dashing savage goer, bending his knees well; while the latter should go gliding along with a straight reach as smoothly and calmly as a cutter yacht through the water.

FURTHER QUALIFICATIONS.

A quick eye, a determined spirit, and great activity are essentially necessary in the steeplechaser,—i.e. he should have a foot always to spare, and a quick eye to direct it in every emergency, without which he will never be safe to ride or back.

These are the great attributes of the steeplechase horse, and very frequently do they render a very bad racehorse a fair performer over a country. Pace and action alone will never make a steeplechase horse, and a *coward* should always be discarded; for if the horse be taking every opportunity of cutting it, he will assuredly succeed in either doing so, falling, or being cleverly defeated. Such brutes are unworthy of the name of steeplechasers, and the sooner they be consigned to cabmen the better, for it is utterly useless to train them on, as bad-hearted ones generally become worse instead of better the more they have of it.

BLOOD.

The thorough-bred horse of five or six years old is the only animal a man would be justified in putting into training as a professional steeplechase horse.

Time was when the half-bred hunter was supposed to be the only animal capable of carrying high weights over a country. This, however, has been quite upset of late, and we see that a veritable half-bred one is hardly ever placed for a big race.

There are still some good pseudo half-bred ones, to wit, Medora, Bridegroom, and Wee Nell, being the best of them. If all these three are really half-bred ones, it certainly goes far to establish the theory that a stain in the pedigree is desirable, since no one can deny that at high weights and over long and severe courses it would, at this time, puzzle any one to find three superior horses. Still only in the letter, but not in the spirit, are these to be considered veritable cocktails, since their pedigrees must be considered about as good as that of Eclipse, if not quite within the pale of the stud book.

As to the choice of blood, many strains run well— the Tupsleys and Sir Hercules's being the most successful, and the Bay Middletons and Touchstones the least so.

SIZE.

Careful analysis of steeplechase winners does not favour any particular size in the standard measure, and I think that living horses go to prove that want of size is no bar to a good one's success in the very best company. The invincible and wearing Brunette by Sir Hercules, was a small one, so also was Brunette by Rochester. Lottery was not oversized, nor was The Huntsman. Abd el Kader, Odiham, Little Charley, Anatis, The Dane, for the small division have quite as many trophies to show as the larger division, Peter Simple, Bourton, Sir Peter Laurie, British Yeoman, and Jealousy. But at the present moment, a little one bears the palm, the long, low, and symmetrical Emblem, by Teddington, who, from her pace, made a terrible example of some large fields in 1863, during which year good races were won by horses of all sizes, from Victress 14h. 3in., and Wee Nell 15h., to Penarth 16h. 1in., and Bridegroom 16h.; the medium size getting the best of it with Lincoln, Medora, Emblem, Sinking Fund, Yaller Gal, and Oliver Twist.

It seems, then, that a first-class steeplechaser under fifteen and over sixteen hands is not impossible, but is nevertheless an exception to the general rule. Nevertheless I must admit that size is one of the many good points we must look for, though it must not be considered (as it often is) to outbalance all others.

BREAKING.

Now suppose you have a horse that has just come out of a training stable, solely for flat racing, where a turf with as smooth a surface as a bowling-green has been his exercising and trial ground, and where he has never been obliged to keep a sharp look-out for holes, grips, mounds, and a thousand and one other stumbling-blocks.

A strong, steady, and experienced man with good hands should be put on him, with orders to ride him at a walk over a ploughed ridge-and-furrow field for an hour, and then to trot him over the same until he sweats. The extensor muscles of the arms and shoulders will have been sufficiently called into play for the first lesson, by this exercise, which should not exceed one and a half hour. He should be then walked back to the stable as soon as possible.

Continue this daily for one week, at the expiration of which time a change may be adopted with advantage. Choose a flat meadow full of hidden grips and water-courses, and letting the horse have his head loose, ride him at a walk all over it for about the same time, and continue doing so daily for about a week.

His eye and foot will now have adopted the regular workmanlike action so desirable, of avoiding obstacles carefully in whatever shape they may present themselves. Therefore, he should be made to avoid them at an accelerated pace, which should be done by walking over the ridge-and-furrow field until you think he has had enough of it (the time should not exceed an hour in any case), when he should be taken to the water meadow, and trotted sharply all over it with a loose rein for about ten or fifteen minutes at the outside. This will test the quickness of his eye and foot to the utmost, and make him cool and clever in difficulties without having time to consider their nature. On the next day resume this exercise, and have a big tree of some sort drawn across the gateway after the horse has entered, and after trotting about the water meadow as before, let him scramble over it on his way home. And the next and three following days make him jump the tree into the meadow as well as out of it. It will be ten to one, unless very temperate and clever, that he strike his legs hard, and this will make him clear them after a day or so; but he should not be stopped in his work on this account; cold water bandages will be sufficient to relieve the vessels and prevent injury, and whatever soreness and stiffness there may be will be of use in preventing a recurrence of such carelessness or clumsiness, as the case may be.

If during this week he have performed well, either a hurdle gorsed, or some thorns, may be placed on the other side of the tree on his return from the water-meadow on the next five following days. The tree will ensure his rising properly, and prevent his running through the hurdle or thorns, as many horses are very apt to do. Be quite satisfied with this exercise for a fortnight, after which, the horse should follow hounds as soon as possible and opportunity presents itself.

He should not be played with now, but ridden smartly at the very tails of the hounds, in the front rank during the first two hours, when the sooner his head is turned homewards the better; which will generally be reached after a sharp walk of about two hours, which will be none too much to cool him down and enable him to enter his stable in a calm and healthy condition. He should now be allowed two days' rest, and then should be ridden with hounds as before; carefully avoiding riding through deep muddy rides, through woods, &c., which only strain and make horses slow. Continue this for one month, during which time he will have had eight lessons in the hunting field, which will make him, if properly ridden, quite clever enough for a trial. About one mile of country, with fair fences, should now be marked out; and a good, strong, and very resolute horseman placed on his back. Let an old horse lead him at a strong pace for the first time round, then let the old one be pulled up and take no further part in the trial until the next time round, when he should again join in, and they should have a friendly gallop over the course for the third and last time, neither taking any advantage, but keeping close together.

This distance (three miles) is as much as it will be prudent to put him over at this stage; since the severe shocks, &c., from jumping and galloping over rough and uneven ground, will sooner tell their tales on the frame than is generally supposed. He should now be indulged with a quiet walk for about four days, when he should be put through the same ordeal as before; and if he perform creditably, he should be forthwith put into training the same as for flat racing—having two brushing gallops during the week, and varying the work on alternate days by going over eight or nine gorsed hurdles in his gallop. He will require this training for four weeks, when he may be safely entered for a steeplechase.

It will thus be seen that with care, attention, and opportunities, three months are sufficient to prepare an *untried* horse to run in a steeplechase.

The training of the steeplechase horse, who knows his business, should be different from this; for it would be a needless risk to hunt him, since a horse can but know his business, and knowing it, should be put over fences which are not likely to cause any injury, such as bangs, cuts, stakes, &c. A gallop once a fortnight over gorsed hurdles is all the jumping he will require; and in every way, with this exception, he should be prepared the same as for a flat race.

As to the distance of ground over which a steeplechaser should be put, there will always be a variety of opinions; but I am persuaded that they must have long gallops, both for the sake of their muscles and wind, for no horse, unless his muscles and respiratory organs have been well prepared, can by any possibility be expected to perform successfully in a steeplechase. The concussions, &c., from jumping are so severe, that he would soon be hors de combat, unless his joints, muscles, and organs of respiration had received a proper preparation. No horse can hope to cross a country at any pace without wind. Few clever horses fall until deprived of the powers of respiration; after which, they generally go down a terrible burster, through not having sufficient power to contract their frames and rise at the fences, or else they refuse altogether.

This should teach any one who attempts to train a steeplechase horse, how hopeless it is for a half-prepared horse to stand a chance in a steeplechase, where everything tends to knock the wind out of him. I never yet saw a fat horse run to the end of a steeplechase that was run at a fair pace.

RIDING.

There are several nasty tricks that steeplechase horses usually contract, such as swerving, rushing, pulling, and not rising sufficiently at their fences. These vices cause fully seven-eighths of the accidents both to man and horse that occur in steeplechases, and they are all of them more or less brought on by the rider being unable, through the want of sufficient physical strength, to collect and pull the horse on to his hind legs, and so shorten his stride before reaching the fence.

Sometimes—and more frequently—they are brought on by that hateful practice of holding the reins in the left hand, and throwing up the right hand as the horse is rising at the fence, for the purpose of balancing the body; this necessarily causes the horse to swerve to the left, and allows him to run into the fence just as he pleases; and thus refusing, swerving, not rising, and rushing, are all engendered by the most ungainly practice that any horseman can be guilty of.

Until men learn that horses, having two sides to their mouths, require an equal pressure on each side to keep them straight, and an unequal pressure to make them turn, there will be no fewer refusers, rushers, swervers, &c., than there are at the present time.

THE CHARACTER OF THE STEEPLECHASE HORSE OF THE PRESENT DAY AS COMPARED WITH THE PAST.

In choosing a steeplechase horse, it is often a matter of extreme difficulty what class of animal to select from among the ranks of flat racers; and indeed, the running of certain horses on the flat and across country seems so utterly opposed, that no just conclusion appears attainable.

Some horses which cannot get a mile on the flat, often prove invincible over thrice this distance across country, and defeat their former victors with such ease, that it would seem well-nigh absurd to suppose that they could be brought on a par at any kind of racing.

If, however, these facts are looked into more closely, they will not appear so startling as they seem at first sight. In the first place, on the flat a horse must be able to go at his best pace throughout, without a moment's pause for gathering his wind, collecting or altering his stride, or any other action for easing the tension of his whole frame. Every nerve, muscle, and tendon must be at their fullest tension; and this tension we find many very brilliant horses unable to preserve beyond a mile, but at a slightly reduced speed they can keep it up—so to say—for ever.

But it may be objected, 'why cannot also the Queen's plater do precisely the same and in an increased ratio?' The answer is this, he would undoubtedly do so, if equally possessed of the same qualification for steeplechasing, viz., action, formation, a quick eye and foot, and indomitable courage; but if he does not possess these, he will assuredly suffer an inglorious defeat at the hands of his inferiors in racing over smooth turf, but his superiors in getting over uneven and unsound ground, and consequently his superiors *in action*.

It does appear then that *action* must be the one qualification, and that the horse must be thoroughbred I have already stated as my firm conviction.

It is also a matter of moment with some to consider what importance attaches to any distinct strain of blood; whether the very stout or the more speedy strains are to be sought; but these are questions, for the reasons stated above, on which I must decline to offer any decided opinion; but this much I think it safe to assert, that if a horse can be found of the stoutest blood and performances together with the desired shape and qualifications, undoubtedly he is to be preferred to an animal of more speed but inferior in stoutness; but if stoutness be his only recommendation it will avail him little in steeplechasing.

For these reasons I admire the steeplechaser and flying hunter more than any other class of horse living; because they are possessed of more admirable points than those of any other class.

They have more power, courage, and action than the flat racer, and more blood, speed, and activity than the common hunter and hack. Truly a first-class steeplechase horse of the present day is a magnificent animal. I have often heard it remarked that the steeplechaser of late years is but a racing weed—a mere cast-off from the racing stable, and utterly unfit for coping with a good honest horse of his own class; but such conclusions are the result of superficial investigation. The truth is, that the steeplechaser is a cast-off from the training stable, not because he is not a magnificently-bred and shaped animal, but because he cannot cope with his fellows successfully in *a particular performance*. And to assert that the steeplechaser of these days is inferior to that of the past, either in blood, size, power, or performances, is truly monstrous.

If blood, power, and qualifications be carefully weighed, where have there been seen in any age such fine specimens of the steeplechaser as Bourton, Emblem, Emigrant, Lincoln, The Huntsman, and Flyfisher, not to mention such weight-carriers as Penarth, Bridegroom, Medora, Acrobat, and Express, *cum multis aliis?*

Surely persons capable of judging of a horse's merits in the smallest degree must be joking when they view such animals and assert that *they are not capable of carrying weight!* For not one of the above-mentioned horses, at the lowest computation, could be considered overweighted at from twelve to sixteen stones with hounds. Then, may I ask, do men above this weight expect to ride horses of high pedigree and performances in the front rank in any county in Great Britain? And if so, let me further ask, at what period and on what horses they ever did so? I can only say that when I look at our top-weighted steeplechasers I feel proud of the magnificent action and calibre of my country's champions. Indeed it would be hard to say for what purpose, had they undergone different training, they would have been unfitted, from drawing a ton to racing on the flat!

What were Lottery, Vanguard, Discount, and Cigar, in point of steeplechasing capabilities, when compared with Bourton, Emigrant, The Huntsman, and Emblem?

Or what were the Clinker, Grimaldi, Vivian, and Gaylad in comparison with such horses as Penarth, Flyfisher, Lincoln, and Bridegroom?

To any judge of horses, acquainted with both these periods, I willingly leave the issue without further comment.

Were I called upon to mention the best steeplechase horse of late years, I should not hesitate to mention my predilection for Bourton by Drayton (who himself never appeared, and was got by Muley out of Prima Donna by Soothsayer). He was, perhaps, the biggest animal that was ever a first-class race or steeplechase horse, standing fully 16 hands 2 in. high, with immensely long and strong shoulders, and rather knify withers, a strong neck, and rather plain head. His back ribs were very light, and his loins very slack, set into very wide hips and haunches. He was a coward on the flat, but nevertheless a horse of immense capabilities, which will readily be accepted when I say that his trainer (and there are few better judges) always held that he was as good as that great horse Defiance, and actually beat him in a trial on the flat at home. It therefore may be reasonably doubted whether in any age we shall see a match for this prince of steeplechasers: for, owing to his immense length and fine action, any ordinary fence was no obstacle of importance to him, and his fine turn of speed always reduced the racing part of the performance to a certainty; and I have heard good judges assert that when he carried off the Grand National Steeplechase, with the heavy impost of 11st. 12lb., he could have won it, in their opinion, with 3st. more on his back.

It is rarely ever that a horse of his size has the activity and speed to render him first-class; but, as is frequently the case, the exception comes in with great brilliancy in the case of our hero. I may further remark, as another of his peculiarities in formation, that the fore legs were excessively arched, or what is called 'over at the knees,' and is another proof of the correctness of Lord George Bentinck's theory of the superiority of this formation.

It is very often objected with some degree of plausibility, ' If there are all these magnificent horses, why are they not more readily procured?'

The answer is this,

1. Such horses cost a large sum of money to breed.

2. They are so highly appreciated by liberal purchasers from all countries as well as our own, that the demand is far greater than the supply.

3. That they can be obtained, but not without considerable cost; for, like every other article deemed by the [public to be really good, be the commodity land, timber, carriages, or whatsoever else, the money value will be in exact ratio to its worth. Nevertheless, how frequently do we hear men vowing that there are no horses of blood and power left in the country, merely because they cannot find them at their own preconceived ideas of cost, or at the same price at which they themselves or their forefathers in times gone by used to obtain them, forgetting that in those days they only had a home market to contend with, for the simple reason that the merits of our thoroughbred stock were neither appreciated nor known by foreigners generally, owing to the meagre means of international intercourse that then existed, but which has since been entirely removed. It is now an easier task to send a horse from York to Vienna than it was in former days to send one from York to London.

Therefore it is no matter of surprise that we find such a staff of foreigners at all our principal fairs, more hungry buyers than dealers of our own country.

Of steeplechasers both the French and Germans are especially fond, and are always ready to give a high price for a highly tried horse capable of carrying a high weight over stiff fences; and if the taste for steeple-chasing maintains its rapid growth in these countries, we must put our shoulders to the wheel in earnest and produce more powerful thoroughbred horses. There are, on an average, some fifteen hundred thoroughbred colts and fillies bred every year, out of which there are about three really first-class racehorses, or one in five hundred, and some twenty or thirty moderate race-horses, or about one in fifty worth keeping in training for the Turf.

The others are scattered about all over the world as hunters, hacks, cab horses, steeplechasers, and for breeding purposes.

Then, as only about one-fiftieth of the number of thoroughbred horses are ever kept in training more than two years, it is of the deepest importance that sound-ness, power, and action should be the careful study of every breeder in the land, or assuredly foreigners will soon establish better markets in their own countries.

It is now a matter of fact beyond all doubt that by a fair competition in exhibitions and on the race course, by the encouragement of a public, and the direct sup-port of a government, the British thoroughbred horse is capable of being produced in any country in Europe in almost the same perfection as in the warm paddocks at Hampton Court.

The Emperor of the French was the first to fully comprehend this, and by purchasing thoroughbred stallions of fine size and power the French govern-ment has rendered great service to the country in aiding her in the production of animals which formerly were only to be obtained in another land.

This conception has been followed by similar efforts in other countries, such as Russia, Prussia, and Austria; and, no doubt, when Victor Emanuel finds the inhabitants of the Italian nation sufficiently awake to the clear loss they sustain by purchasing, instead of producing, the noble animals that are yearly despatched from this country to the royal stables at Turin, at an immense cost, he will be first and foremost in lending his subjects substantial aid in their efforts to compete with the breeders of this country.

No unprejudiced man can shut his eyes to the high calibre of the American horses as stout racehorses and steeplechasers; and should they select another of the Glencoe stamp, it is very probable that the blue riband of the Turf may ere long fall to their lot.

HUNTERS.

The hunter may or may not differ from the steeplechaser very widely in proportion to the description of country for which he is intended.

The make and shape of the hunter must be precisely the same as that of the steeplechaser, whether he be full-blooded or no, save in one particular, viz., his back ribs. These certainly should be deeper and of greater expansion to enable him to go through the many hours of severe labour without food.

In other respects all should be the same, and whether the horse has to carry ten or twenty stones he must in no way be a coach-horse.

The neck must be strong, the shoulders long, compact, and well covered with muscle. The hips wide, quarters long and muscular, and the legs flat, clean, and straight.

His action should be rather more correct than I should demand in the steeplechaser, from the roughness of the ground over which he must go at all paces.

But again must I caution my readers against mistaking coaching for hunting action. The hunter's action must *not be knee but shoulder action*, or it never will be safe. Without shoulder action the very best hind leg action will be useless, for this reason, that unless the shoulders are capable of throwing the weight of the forepart of the body back to the hind limbs, that weight can never be thrown back by any other agency. This is what is meant when a horse is said to ' *bend himself*,' which he cannot perform if he has bad shoulders without breaking his back into two pieces.

A hunter with bad shoulders is dangerous in the extreme, for he will always lean against instead of rising over his fences, and unless they give way, over he must come; consequently such horses should never be ridden at timber with impunity.

The hunter must have good feet. Big platter feet can never be anything but fatal to him, for he must run the risk of bruising his feet some dozen or more times every day he goes out.

In addition to which he will be more liable to hit his legs and pull off his shoes—two of the worst and most troublesome faults with which a hunter can be afflicted.

I am well aware that it is frequently asserted that the hunter must have big feet to enable him to go through the dirt without sinking up to his knees; and undoubtedly he should have big feet if he be a big horse, but on no account must his feet be out of proportion to his legs; and, if this be the case, the merest tyro in horseflesh can determine at a glance, if he will take the trouble to look.

Whether, then, the horse be big or little his feet should be in proportion to the weight they have to carry. I have a partiality for high and strong, but a great objection to low and weak, heels.

It must never be forgotten that the foot is the foundation of all a hunter's exertions, and unless the foundation be good the whole frame will have its action materially weakened. Small feet are only objectionable in that they do not afford sufficient surface to support the weight in soft ground; otherwise, high and rather small feet are no doubt possessed of greater wear and tear than larger ones, but either extreme is very objectionable in the hunter.

In shoeing the hunter great care should be taken that the shoe exactly fits the foot in every part, and also that it is not a heavy shoe; for, inasmuch as the extra weight of a shoe, however trifling, from the fact of its being at the end of the lever, will very materially embarrass the action. 'An ounce on the foot is a pound on the back,' is a very old and correct axiom, but one which is nevertheless very little attended to. Many persons will persist that the hardness of the roads demand heavy shoes; but this is a very vulgar error. They demand, undoubtedly, shoes of better quality—of more steel in them—but in no way heavier.

As to the number of nails to be put in the shoe I am inclined to place but little importance in either the many or few nailed principle. The exact fitting of the shoe is the point. It must neither be too long nor too short, but should exactly fit the bars, and should, with the bars, incline and converge to the heels, and not go out straight from the lateral angle of the hoof as some very simple people think proper, considering it probable that the hoof will, by a sort of magnetic attraction, oblige them by following the same course as the shoe; which is, of course, utterly ridiculous, as is proved both by theory and practice.

Unless the shoe exactly fit the foot there cannot be an even pressure; and if there be not an even pressure, the weight must be borne unduly by some particular part which is only able and intended to bear a certain proportion of that weight.

The consequence of such shoeing must be patent to every one. If the horse cut his ankles, either before or behind, the only preventive will be a double piece of leather encircling the ankle, and not a patent thing intended to fit on the precise part interfered with, but which, as every horseman must know who has tried them, does not keep its position, but is hit round and generally pulled off after the strap has made a sore place above the ankle.

VICES CURED.

Patience and improvement in condition must alone be depended on for a cure; but the shoes must not be interfered with in any way, or they will, being set on one side, render the ankles weaker than ever.

Horses that have to gallop over fields that are literally sown broadcast with sharp flints, should always be shod with the best and toughest leathern sole; which will also be proper in cases of thrush, severe corns, &c., but which will be most improper in cases of laminitis, since the exciting cause of the disease will be increased, owing to an additional strain being put on the crust.

All horses of proper action stop themselves for leaping or any other purpose, with their hind legs; therefore, over slippery stones, down steep hills, &c., one or both of the heels of the hind shoes should be turned up or the horse's hind legs may go from under him, and he may strain his loins very severely, as well as injure himself by the fall.

During frost also no horse should be suffered to go out of the stable without being first shod with 'calkings,' which should be sharpened or renewed as occasion requires.

If the horse be a violent kicker while being shod in his hind feet, the best method is to put a noose on the fetlock of the hind foot required to be shod, and to attach this to the headstall.

This will cause him to wrench his neck and head severely, whenever he lashes out or endeavours to drag it out of the hands of the smith.

This is a much better method than 'casting' him,

which is always attended with extreme danger, and places the horse in such a position that no smith can put on a shoe properly.

BREEDING THE HUNTER.

In breeding hunters, it is most desirable to keep in view the style of horse required.

1. The twelve to fourteen stone hunters over a flying country.
2. The fourteen to twenty stone ditto.
3. The twelve to fourteen stone hunter over banks, hills, and walls.
4. The fourteen to twenty stone ditto.

First, then, we will suppose that a man is desirous of breeding a horse up to from twelve to fourteen stones over a flying country. Blood there must of necessity be, and plenty of it; and substance or muscular development there must be, and plenty of it; and *length* there must be on short legs.

Then we must choose a mare as much like what we want as possible, and with almost more length and breadth—length as we stand at their sides, and breadth as we stand behind them.

Without this all the make and shape in the world will avail nothing in carrying weight over a flying and big country. As to height it is of little consequence, so long as it is over 15 hands and 1 in., but under this standard I do not fancy a horse for a big country, unless possessed of extraordinary length, which is very seldom met with.

2. To carry from 14 to 20 st., a little less quality must necessarily be put up with; but still a great deal of breeding there must be, or the horse can never live the pace at which hounds go for any distance.

I cannot, however, see the necessity for demanding greater height. A horse standing 15 hands 2 in. is high enough to carry any weight, supposing he be wide enough. The fastest and best 16 st. and a-half hunter of my experience was barely 15 hands 2 in. and a half, but was very broad and muscular, and not very long. In my opinion the heavier the man is, the greater the breadth and the less length he should demand.

One principle in the matter of weight-carrying is quite clear, and that is, that the horse must first prove by his action that he can carry his own weight, and then there will be some chance of his carrying some considerable addition to it.

I have often seen horses bought at high prices as hunters supposed to be up to great weight, but in reality mere tall swill-bellied brutes, not even able to carry their own weight correctly and evenly, much less any addition to it; in short, only fitted to lean the front of their ponderous carcases against a collar. Such horses always die away in about two miles.

3. As I have demanded the hunter's standard for flying countries to be over 15 hands and 1 in., so do I demand that of the hunter intended for banks and hills and walls to be under that height.

For carrying from 12 to 14 st. over this description of country, a full-blooded cob, varying from 14 hands

3 in. to 15 hands 1 in., with plenty of depth and width, but not so much length as is desirable in the former cases, is the best description of horse.

For carrying from 14 to 20 st. over this description of country, a thicker cob of from 15 hands to 15 hands and 1 in. is the best adapted for the purpose.

In short, the great difference between the description of horse for the different countries is this: For the flying countries you necessarily require more size, length, and range; for close, hilly countries, more shortness and compactness of frame generally, great length and range being utterly useless. It is a very great, though very common, error to suppose that a badly-bred horse is capable of getting over the hills and banks better than a finer bred one. There can be no greater mistake. Unless a horse be a very highly-bred one he can hardly wag his tail, much less gallop, on arriving at the summit of a steep hill at a good pace, as every hard rider must have experienced. Badly-bred ones soon choke themselves if violent exertion is forced on them, and they then become dangerous whatever the nature of the fence or country may be.

The stallion should be chosen of the same stamp as the mare in every way; and they can, with care and judgment, easily be found, notwithstanding it is so confidently asserted that strong, compact, and moderately-sized animals, suitable for banking and hilly countries, cannot be procured from the racing stable.

I presume that Midas, Daniel O'Rourke, Saucebox, Wardermarshe, Rogerthorpe, and Underhand could hardly be found fault with for such a purpose, however much they may be considered undersized for purposes where greater size and range are desirable.

For hunters adapted for the flying countries, the most successful stallions of late years have been

    Birdcatcher and his sons Augur and Newcourt. } from Sir Hercules.

    The Steamer, Pompey, and Theon } sons of Emilius.

    The Libel and Windhound, } sons of Pantaloon.

    Harkaway.
    Catesby.
    Cranebrooke.
    Tupsley.

In rearing the hunter, the same caution must be taken as in rearing the racehorse for the first twelve months, during which period about the same quantity of corn, &c., should be allowed.

After which he may be suffered to live a little harder. It is, however, essentially necessary that all animals should live well during the first year, for bone and size cannot be obtained afterwards.

The hunting colt should be kept in a good roomy and dry straw yard during the winter, and always have a plentiful supply of clean water at hand. Great care should be taken that they be all tied up to feed, or they will rob each other of their corn. At four years old breaking should commence, and if any symptoms of curbs appear the colt should be bitted and longed, but on no account ridden. And if, after a fortnight's breaking, they do not seem inclined to disappear, a pair of high-heeled shoes should be put on, two doses of physic given with entire rest, and a cold wet sponge encased in a bandage of oiled silk placed immediately over the curb. Continue this treatment for a fortnight, during which time give no corn, but merely bran and hay or grass. He will now be in a fit condition to fire, and if the operation can be performed *without casting* so much the better, since very frequently a great deal of inflammation is caused. And sometimes a great curb is thrown out through struggling, when of course firing merely adds to the mischief by increasing the inflammation, and a permanent enlargement and blemish may be the consequence.

Firing should always be performed for curbs at this stage, since it saves much trouble, expense, and disappointment. He will require, after the operation, at least three or four months' run at grass, the expiration of which will bring us into August, when he should again be taken up, bitted and longed quietly for a week; and after having been well prepared for and had a dose of physic, the sooner he is ridden the better.

He should be walked and trotted about through September for about two hours daily, after which he should commence longer walks and stronger work generally through October, so as to be prepared for one day a week with hounds from November 1st, which after two months' careful preparation he will be well fitted for, if he be a highly-bred one. Badly-bred ones require more time to make them hard and strong, their bones being more porous and their muscles less dense. I have known two instances of half-bred ones being soft bad brutes for two years, utterly unable to live with hounds at a good pace, and then prove extraordinary horses in every sense of the word. Of one thing I am certain, and that is, that half-bred ones are not more fitted for work at seven years old than thoroughbred ones are at five.

If the colt have good hocks and no ailments, he will have all the better chance of being in good condition for the hunting season, as he should have been ridden quietly about during the whole summer.

JUMPING.

Unless hounds meet at a very long distance from the stables, colts had better not be taught to jump at home unless the services of an experienced and temperate man can be obtained. They are very often spoiled by this kind of tuition, and frequently learn to be refusers, jades, and swervers in consequence; whereas a colt once taught to jump in the hunting field generally does his utmost to keep with the other horses and hounds, and gets over everything in as clever a manner as his experience will admit of, without being forced *against his will*, as is the case nine times out of ten in larking.

Whatever the horse's temper may be, great care must be taken that he does not run up to his fence, *dwell*, and then 'pop over all of a heap,' *instead of spreading himself.*

This is a most incorrigible habit, and is altogether the fault of the breaker.

On this account I have the greatest objection to horses being led over any description of fence with a longeing rein, *excepting banks and walls*; for they contract that hateful habit of leaning over and then jumping the fence. On this account so many Irish horses are spoilt, and I know of no fault so difficult to conquer as this. A rusher in clever hands can easily be calmed down, and brought up to his fences collectedly and well; but a doubling, dwelling brute, can scarcely ever be persuaded to have sufficient confidence, even by the most accomplished horseman, either in himself or his rider, to come boldly and straight up to his fence and spread himself without a bungle.

I have a great objection to what is called 'playing with' colts in the hunting field for the purpose of making them clever and handy.

It is a bad and senseless practice, and can never teach them how to cross a country resolutely and quickly, but very frequently makes them careless and indolent. A colt fit and well should be ridden as near the hounds as possible, and should be made to take his fences as they come, at whatever pace hounds go, and not at the pace at which he wishes to take them.

He will then learn to do a little place as well as a big one, and at a glance to estimate the effort by aid of his rider which each will require.

Great care should be taken that the colt do not have too much of it.

When he begins to get shorter in his stride, or to exhibit any other symptoms of distress, he should be pulled up immediately, and taken home quietly. *Of all things he must not be overdone.*

The unusual excitement, shocks, strains, &c., from galloping and jumping must, before his muscles become trained to bear them, take a deal of steel out of him; and further, it must be borne in mind that the shorter the time he is out the oftener will he be able to come, and the greater his practice will be. No doubt in banking, and perhaps in stonewall countries, it is desirable to have a high-mettled colt led over some fences with a leading rein previously to being ridden over them.

When this is done, however, it is highly desirable that he be not allowed *to dwell*, and to prevent this, the best plan is as follows:—Let one man take the leading rein at full length and proceed over the fence, and let another hold the colt by the check-strap, about ten yards from the fence, and getting him straight let him send him at the fence, giving the colt at the same time some encouragement. If he goes at it readily, do not urge him; but if he shirk it or dwell, touch him gently with the whip, and speak harshly to him; but on no account suffer him to come back to his former position, but force him over there and then. He will be sure, if forced over in this way, to do it in a bungling clumsy manner; but it will show him that when once sent at a fence he must get over it, be the manner in which he does so what it may. This will soon ensure his going straight at his fences, and he should be taken on to the next fence as soon as possible, and have his ten yards' run at it as before, and so on over succeeding fences until the colt seems to have had enough of it.

Teaching young horses to jump should generally be left to experienced, patient, good-tempered, and determined horsemen, and then there need be no fear of their turning out indifferent performers, if properly formed. Jumping, however, is such a bugbear to the generality of hunting men in these days that they would as soon entrust themselves to a horse's tender mercies that had never been jumped, as to the car of an experimentalising balloon; therefore, jumping should certainly be included in the hunter's education and breaking, or he cannot be considered to meet the present demands of the public.

CONDITION.

Nothing tends more to the comfort, health, and consequently condition of the hunter than a good airy, and more especially, a *thoroughly dry* stable. Whether it consist of boxes or stalls matters little, so long as horses have regular exercise; but no horse should be allowed to stand in a stall all through the day and night. If he does so, he will lose his action and contract inflammation of the feet. Therefore, where horses are suffered to remain in the stable for a day or two together, they should be stabled in boxes or other loose places where they can move about and prevent the circulation from becoming dormant in their extremities, as well as in any other part of their bodies.

The temperature of the stable, as I have said before, should be *dry, but never hot.* A free current of air should be allowed to pass through the *top* of every stable. Nothing is so injurious to a horse's wind, or more correctly lungs, as heated and impure atmosphere.

If the horse seem to feel cold, give more beans, and put an extra rug on him as a preventive, but do not shut up the ventilators in consequence.

There is no rule with regard to the temperature of the stable that can be adhered to with safety.

Some hold that 50° Fahr. is the proper temperature for the stable, others with quite as much reason stickle for 70° Fahr., *whatever the external temperature may be!* The consequence of such treatment is, that whenever the door of the stable is opened and the natural temperature admitted, up goes the horse's coat and he gets chilled from the fresh current of air being so much colder than that which had, up to that time, been circulating around him. Food, exercise, and warm clothing are the only safe methods of preserving the system from the effects of cold.

Good drains should always be run through stables, and kept carefully open; but draining is now so perfectly understood that nothing need be said here on this head.

The best pavement, in my opinion, is that formed by the best blue bricks filled in on the narrow side, which gives a better foot-hold, and is therefore a matter of great consideration, and though more costly, will prevent many serious injuries through horses getting cast, and slipping when endeavouring to get up.

Flannel bandages should always be in use. An extra set or two for warm or cold applications will prevent many troublesome disorders such as cracked heels, swelled legs, &c. During the autumn and winter—from September to March—every horse intended to hunt should stand in dry flannel bandages, bound moderately tight, when in the stable. But with the aid of all these appurtenances, little can reasonably be expected without good grooming and exercise. The horse must be well brushed and rubbed from head to foot every morning and afternoon—both before and after exercise—until every particle of dust and dirt be removed.

It is seldom now that one sees a horse properly strapped. Grooms now-a-days are mere fine gentlemen, and the good old strappers who used to open their shoulders and strap a horse with a will until they had brought a beautiful hue on the coat, have well-nigh passed away. Patent braces, a well-starched collar, and a fashionable waistcoat are now deemed proper attire for the stableman, in which he may make as much use of his limbs as he can. Consequently, physic, alteratives, hot stables, and the singeing lamp are called into play *vice* elbow-grease, and with very manifest results. Not that I condemn either physic, alteratives, or the singeing lamp as auxiliaries to condition; but *hot stables* I do condemn most emphatically. The former are all very well in their way, and scientifically used, are great preservatives of health as well as powerful promoters of condition, though they should not in any way take the place of grooming— this is the abuse of them; but go hand in hand with it —this is the use of them.

Physic should never be administered unless absolutely required; it causes great debility, and consequently unfits the horse for hard exercise for a considerable period.

Where a horse has been resting in the stable for some time on high feeding, and his secretions have become foul, physic—preceded by a course of bran-mashes —is absolutely necessary, to prevent a determination of inflammation to parts most excited by exertion, which would generally ensue, were the horse put to work without it. Strong doses should never be given, as they are injurious under all circumstances, and time is not so precious with the hunter as with racehorses. Moderate doses repeated as often as necessary will be found more effectual. After three days of bran-mashes give a ball composed of four drachms of aloes, two of Peruvian bark, two of resin, and two of ginger, continuing regular exercise.

After the action of this ball has discontinued, it will be well, unless the horse seem thoroughly clean and healthy, to give a ball composed of Barbadoes aloes, Peruvian bark, sulphate of iron, and powdered resin, of each two drachms, on every Saturday night, together with copious bran and linseed mashes, until the desired effect is attained. This treatment will prevent all astringency of the bowels, and a return to that morbid condition of the digestive organs which is so much to be feared. The use of this ball need rarely ever be extended beyond a month, if the horse have regular and sufficient work.

If the horse's appetite fail, and his muscles fall away, the best mixture as a powder undoubtedly is Peruvian bark and aniseed, of each two drachms, and emetic tartar one drachm, put into the last feed on alternate nights. No alteratives or tonics should be continued for more than one week without intermission, or the constitution will be unable to perform its proper functions without their aid. The best plan is to give them on alternate weeks, until the desired result is attained.

Very little physic is required by horses which are regularly exercised, and are allowed a bran and linseed mash every Wednesday and Saturday night. I am very much opposed to the use of sulphur and nitre as alteratives, since they cause great debility of the system generally without in any way stimulating the digestive organs to increased action.

Where horses are kept in the stables day after day and week after week, they may require a gentle dose of physic once a fortnight, but it is to be hoped there are few (save dealers') stables, where horses are thus treated. I must here caution my readers against the ignorant and mischievous practice of physicking a horse *because his legs fill.* Physicking in this state can only add to the evil by causing greater debility, and thus lessening the power of the circulative organs. A mild tonic and alterative, such as bark and antimony, with the use of dry flannel bandages—*bound tightly and tied loosely*—round the legs, is the proper course of treatment.

I have seen many cases of swelled legs produced by over-physicking; and they have taken months of liberal treatment before the vessels had sufficient power to contract duly on their contents.

If the horse's coat be long, it must either be shaved, clipped, or singed. Shaving, which was in great vogue about the years 1854, 1855, and 1856, has now quite gone out of fashion again. It leaves the horse too bare of covering, and makes him unsightly for a fortnight, and unless skilfully performed he will be scratched and scarred all over.

Clipping, without doubt, is the safest and best method that can be adopted for removing a horse's coat; for frequently the skin is materially injured by being scorched by the flame in singeing; so much so, that for a time the absorbent vessels of the skin are paralysed. This causes that dry, unhealthy, and rough appearance on the horse's coat after he has been singed, which is a marked contrast to the glossy and bright look after scientific clipping.

It is on account of this injury to the skin, that clever stud grooms invariably sweat their horses immediately after singeing; and sometimes it does succeed in exciting the absorbent vessels to a healthy action.

If the horse carries a short, thick, and bright coat, it would of course be madness to interfere with it; but a long coat must never be suffered to exist for an instant on the hunter. If he meets with a shower of rain going to cover, he will remain wet until a sharp gallop dries him by evaporation. He then sweats, and will remain wet, dirty, chilly, and miserable during the rest of the day; and it is at least twenty to one that he is found not more than three-parts dry at six o'clock next morning. During which time, active evaporation must have been going on, which will leave him as flat as dishwater. This treatment is only killing the horse by inches; is an injustice to the groom, and a disgrace to the master. It is truly strange that masters can be found in these days so short-sighted, prejudiced, and ignorant, as to prohibit clipping and singeing in their stables.

All of a piece with this is the practice of hunting horses from the grass field, in which a long shaggy coat is necessary. I was once induced to try this practice, and the result was that the subject of the experiment—a very hardy excellent horse—was sacrificed on the altar of foolish credulity.

He always got beat after going well over about a dozen fields, and turned roarer, and went blind to boot! Yet this system was recommended to me as *healthful and economical* by its votaries.

Every system, however absurd and unreasonable, will always have its apologists. And whenever 'Mr. So-and-so always does it, and finds it answer,' is brought forward in the place of argument to support a system, depend upon it there is rottenness at its foundation.

That every man may have his horse well clipped, I should recommend him—no matter how expert the clipper may be—to demand that at least twenty-four hours be occupied by one man over the operation, for it is utter folly for men to pretend to clip a horse properly under this time.

I am acquainted with a professional clipper who maintains that 'he can clip a horse as well in seven as in twenty-four hours,' the truth of which statement I am not in a position to dispute, not having witnessed any of his 'twenty-four hours' work;' but that his seven hours' clipping is a most disgraceful performance, I can faithfully certify. That a horse should be taken extreme care of, and not be allowed to move outside the stable for a week after clipping or singeing, is quite an exploded doctrine. He is far less likely to catch cold after than before the operation, and the only difference in his condition will be, that he may be ridden at a much faster rate without the same fear of injury.

It is a practice, now very common, to leave the saddle place unclipped that the horse may be less liable to saddle-galls; to which I have only to say, that I have found such a practice most productive of the very evil it is supposed to prevent.

It is, moreover, only reasonable that this should be so; for in proportion as the skin is saturated with sweat and filth, so will the irritation caused be great or little. It was also a fashion, happily now well-nigh exploded, of leaving the long rough hair on the hunter's legs for the purpose of warding off injury from thorns, bangs, cuts, &c.; but how the hair on the horse's legs can have the power of warding off either the one or the other, I have yet to learn.

One thing it certainly does very effectually ward off, viz., that of the groom being unable to discover thorns, stubs, or cuts, which when hidden beneath the mass of wet, matted, and coarse hair, are impossible to feel; so that the poor beast can only be rid of these extraneous and painful substances by means of the tedious and irritating medium of inflammation and suppuration; and further, if his heels crack, all healing applications will be useless, so long as the 'cracks' are continally irritated and 'kept open' by the presence of long hairs.

That there is much art in removing the hair from the leg, I must admit; but with care, any one can do it. The only point of importance is the long tuft or lock of hair at the posterior part of the fetlock joint. On no account must the scissors be suffered to interfere with this. Above and below, it may do its work; but every hair in this tuft must either be '*pulled*' or suffered to remain according to its dimensions, for it is this tuft that presents the desired formation and flatness of the cannon bone and fetlock joint, and if cut off, the whole symmetry of the fore leg is destroyed.

In cutting tails, all should depend on the style of horse to be operated on. Short, thick, and rather high horses, should have their tails cut up just so short as that they can carry them '*with a fall.*' If they do not carry them thus, but hold them out straight, with an ungraceful stiffness, they will require docking. But on the other hand, horses of fine length on short legs, should never be docked; but the tail should be suffered to reach within a few inches of the hocks.

Manes and tails should never be combed after they are once clean and free from matted locks. The free use of the dandie brush, followed by the water brush, is alone desirable, and these are the only proper tools for this part.

Nothing looks worse than a scanty mane and tail, through improper use of the comb or from the horse rubbing himself.

When the horse rubs his tail it should always be kept cool and damp with the water brush during the day, and at night a cold and wet flannel bandage should be rolled around the part rubbed.

If it be a very bad case, apply the following lotion as often as required: chloride of lime, 2 drachms in half a pint of water; and, between the applications, nothing is so beneficial as glycerine applied with a feather. A good groom will always be careful to take this habit in time.

I may here state that horses in blooming condition never contract this habit, and that it generally is a sign of feverishness consequent on shortness of work.

WORK.

After the hunter has been through his physic and alterative treatment, the sooner he commences work the better, and, like the steeplechaser and racer, he must *begin by degrees*.

To train the hunter properly, however, without injury to his legs, is a great art, and one to which it would be well were gentlemen to pay greater attention than they generally do. It is a great art for the following reason, that you require all the wind, activity, and stoutness, though not, perhaps, quite the same speed, which is required in the racer or steeplechaser; and the greatest difficulty is that you must arrive at all this *without stripping him of his flesh,* as is not only proper but necessary in the two latter cases.

How then can clear wind, a clean skin, with freshness on the legs, and without loss of muscle, be obtained?

The answer is, by time, by hard and long-continued, but not quick work, and by hard and often-repeated food.

The hunter's food should be strong and substantial. He should have fully as many beans as oats, with some good and sweet hay chaff, and as much water as he will drink. His work, from September 1st, should not be less than five hours' walking exercise daily, which should be gone through at two different periods—viz., morning and afternoon.

The question will then arise, 'How are you to keep him in health—by alteratives, physic, or sweating?' The answer is, by both the former and latter process.

In the first place, it should be fully understood that a horse can be sweated without being reduced or weakened in any way; and at least once a-week from September 1st to November 1st, he will require to be put through a sweat or plethora will sooner or later ensue.

On the night previous to sweating the horse should have no hay, and on the following morning one feed of corn and a few mouthfuls of water will be sufficient; after which put on the sweating rug and hood, which should be of double thickness to the ordinary clothing, and take the horse to the softest field near to the stables. Here he should be walked about until he has emptied himself, after which begin to trot him round and round the field for twenty minutes, then bend him well and make him canter for about ten minutes, not exceeding at any part of the time from ten to twelve miles an hour.

I say 'canter' instead of 'trot' at this pace, for the reason that horses are very apt when trotting round and round a field either to strike their legs or overreach, when going at the rate of from ten to twelve miles an hour.

He will by this method have been trotting and cantering for about half-an-hour, during which time between four and five miles will have been got over.

He should now be taken back to his stable without delay; on entering which about six rugs should be thrown over him, and should remain thus for about ten minutes, when he should be stripped, scraped, and rubbed dry; and after having a feed of corn and three or four hours' rest, he should be put through his afternoon's walk as usual.

It will now appear that the horse's muscles and

general health have been carefully attended to, but that his wind has been neglected, and, indeed, so far this is the case. His organs of respiration should be exercised and strengthened by the following means:— At the end of every afternoon's walk—when the horse must be sufficiently empty to prevent any injury arising from quicker work—he should be sent along at nearly full speed up about three hundred yards of a steep ascent, which will not make him sweat, but merely exercise his respiratory organs, and send him back to his stable a stronger horse than he was when he left it.

More cantering or galloping than this is not only unnecessary but injurious to the hunter, since nothing pulls off flesh so fast as quick work, and therefore he should only have enough quick work to clear his wind, and no more.

Every experienced sportsman reasonably expects his horse to stand *the process of wasting* from November to April; and it is therefore necessary that the hunter should commence the season with enough and to spare of good hard material on him, that will readily supply the waste without injury to the constitution.

From the moment hunting begins, or say from the first day of November, the sweating rugs will no more be needed, and the horse's walking exercise should be reduced from five to three hours daily, which should be gone through morning and afternoon; and, as the days get shorter, the time should be divided into two hours in the morning and one in the afternoon.

It will thus be seen that training or conditioning the

hunter is almost *diametrically opposite* to training the racer and steeplechaser. Nor is it so wonderful that it should be so, when it is considered that the latter classes of animals bear off the palm of victory in a period not exceeding from one to ten minutes, whereas the hunter's labours cannot be reckoned at a much less duration than from seven to ten hours!

A celebrated writer, early in the present century, considered training a horse for a Queen's Plate and for the hunting field one and the same thing; but had he studied the animal economy of the horse still more closely than he did he could never have fallen into so palpable an error.

But so far I will agree with him, *on the last day of the season* the hunter's condition should resemble that of the Queen's Plater as nearly as possible.

Great attention should be paid to the feet of the hunter. They should be well stopped every night, and the hoof dressed so often as any cracks or dryness are apparent. With the proper use of alteratives, bandages on the legs, and the above-mentioned work, there need be no fear of thrushes, inflammation of the laminæ, or any other inflammatory attacks in the feet and legs; but if they do appear they should be treated as is hereafter described.

As to the time required to condition the hunter, I consider that if he have been well summered and is healthy when taken up, from three to four months are sufficient.

With regard to the quantity of food, if the horse is doing five hours' walking exercise per day, not less than five quarterns, half oats and half beans, with a bran and linseed mash every Wednesday and Saturday night, should be allowed; and if the horse will not eat this quantity his *work should be still increased*; and if after this he refuse it, he should be discarded from the hunting stable, and take his place with the hacks or harness horses.

A horse that cannot eat cannot work without losing muscle, and becoming weak and washy, or utterly useless as a hunter.

With regard to water, there should be no limit as to quantity. There is no better sign of health than a regular and large consumer of water. Since water is the only cooling as well as diluent material that enters into the form of diet given to the hunter, it is absolutely necessary that a sufficient quantity be allowed, and if he have water always by him, so much the better.

On this account, then, it is almost needless to add that great care should be taken to avoid disgusting the horse by putting *messes*, such as nitre, &c., with his water, as also by chilling it too much, and thereby causing great nausea.

I know from experience that both these filthy and careless habits will invariably make shy drinkers, and consequently shy feeders, of otherwise very hearty and strong horses.

There is very frequently adopted in hunting stables the cruel practice of stinting horses in their water, which happen to be afflicted with roaring, a chronic cough, or any other affection of the respiratory organs. This ignorant practice is the cause of much suffering, since any irritation of the mucous membrane, bronchial tubes, or any other part of the system, gives rise to greater thirst, which if not satisfied will produce a feverishness and irritability of the whole system, which will necessitate a resort to cooling diet, physic, and a stoppage in work; or, in other words, will aggravate the state of the disease.

SUMMERING THE HUNTER.

The hunting men of the present day are apt to run into the opposite extreme to their forefathers, and confine their horses in such small and close places that they have not sufficient room to move for the proper performance of their functions. Exercise horses must have, after a time, or they will *lose their muscle.*

About one month's or six weeks' rest on some fresh tan in a cool box is all that can be required for the purpose of refreshing the system; after which all horses which are not suffering from disease, the effects of an operation or accident, will be all the better for a little walking exercise on some fallow ground and soft turf.

It is preposterous nonsense for men to assert that 'the horse does not lose condition in the box without exercise, *if on hard food.*' Every man of experience must know that the horse which has been running at grass is by far the stronger animal of the two during the first two or three weeks; though, of course, the flesh of the former is looser, and therefore is more quickly shaken off, and consequently he will require more time to put on a sufficient quantity of good material than the former. If horses are kept standing in boxes without exercise, and on strong food for three or four months, it stands to reason that plethora must have taken possession of their systems, and will show itself on the first excitement of the system in a most baneful way.

Let the hunter be rested for six weeks in a good roomy and cool box on fresh tan about eight or ten inches in depth, which will allow of his shoes being taken off without injury to his feet; and at the expiration of this time let him be taken up and walked for an hour every morning on the dewy grass, and continue to give enough grass to loosen the dung—in short, to take the place of physic.

Let this food and this work be continued until September 1, when the food and general preparation for work, as previously described, should commence in earnest.

I am well aware of all the arguments brought forward for and against the in and out-door system of summering the hunter; but I think that the votaries of both have overshot the mark entirely.

The great point is that neither the one nor the other system should be continued too long; but change and absolute rest for a short period will always bring about the desired freshness and vigour.

Another important consideration is to avoid all sudden changes and shocks to the system. The organs of respiration are always affected more or less seriously

CHANGE NECESSARY. 119

by sudden changes of diet and atmosphere, which are the most prolific causes of inflammatory attacks at all seasons of the year.

The sure signs of a horse requiring rest or summering are these: loss of appetite, dullness of the eyes, a sort of nettle-rash all over the body and legs, cracked heels, falling away of the crest, harshness of the skin accompanied by a hitching cough, excrements most frequently hard and voided with difficulty, with ears wet and cold after exercise. When any or all of these symptoms present themselves all work should cease immediately, and entire rest, with mild alteratives, given, if the future of the horse be in any way regarded.

If work be continued only for a fortnight after such symptoms have set in, so much injury will have been wrought on the constitution that it will take at least four or five months of absolute rest before the vigour of the constitution will be restored; but if taken at once, before a morbid condition has taken hold of the system, a month or six weeks' rest, with change of food, will be found amply sufficient.

Should this morbid condition of body show itself during the winter or early in the spring, when no green food is obtainable, the food should be changed by giving swedes, peas, Indian corn, oilcake, &c., in the place of oats and beans, with newer hay than that to which he has been accustomed, and if carrots can be procured so much the better. Some change of food and rest must, under all circumstances, be resorted to.

This condition of body is generally produced by

over-training and continuing work after the appetite has failed; or, in other words, calling on the system for that which it has not, wasting when there is nothing to waste, drawing water when the spring is dry!

Absurd as this may seem to the inexperienced, it is no less the truth. Horses are often called upon to exert themselves whether their muscles are full or wasted, whether their appetites are good or bad, and sometimes whether their health is good or bad; and according to their performances in either of the above-mentioned conditions, so are they unreasonably and unjustly judged.

In former years it was thought necessary to bleed previous to resting the hunter which became thus overworked; but in the present day the excessive folly of robbing the system of the small amount of its vitality left is well understood and admitted on all sides, save and except among the ranks of farriers, who fortunately are not often called upon to treat horses of a superior grade than the cart horse

Where the hunter is thus overworked it will be well always to give the tonic and alterative powder every day for the first week, after which discontinue its use entirely. Physic, sulphur, nitre, and resin, should all be carefully avoided in this case.

THE RIDING HORSE.

By the term riding horse, I do not mean the cover or galloping hack, but a riding horse suitable for the park or ordinary use.

His height should range from 15 hands to 15 hands 2 in., and in extreme cases, where the length of the rider necessitates it, 16 hands will not be too high.

His head and neck should be lighter and more handsome than that of either the racer, steeplechaser, or hunter. His shoulders should be long and oblique, with high withers, and his back, unless the weight exceed 14 st., should be long; his hips neat and rounded, and indeed the quarters may be more straight and peacocky than can be suffered in animals which have to undergo much wear and tear.

The feet must be especially good, with strong pasterns, which must be very long or the action will never be easy and graceful; and if the hind legs are not placed very much under the body it matters little.

His action must not be so high as to be rampant or gaudy, but must be longer and not so round as is desirable in driving horses. Great attention should be paid to the way in which the feet are put to the ground. As he walks along his feet and legs should appear to be *slung* from the shoulder straight before him, with the heel downwards. If this be not the case all the action in the world will only make him the more dangerous. A riding horse that thrusts his toe into the ground as he walks along cannot be suffered for an instant.

If the horse roll or waddle in his walk or trot, he has not the proper use of his shoulders, and must be discarded at once for this purpose. Nothing is more ungainly in appearance, and nothing more uncomfortable to the rider.

Irishmen have aptly designated this mode of progression by the expressive appellation of '*bog trot*,' which fully expresses the common and vulgar carriage of such horses. Many very excellent hunters and covert hacks are afflicted with this defect in their walk, but in the riding horse it is a most unpardonable fault.

In the riding horse there is yet a most important qualification, viz. *manners*, without which a riding horse is next to useless.

A good mouth, elegant carriage, and tractable temper, in addition to make and shape, must all be fully developed.

It will now appear clear why it is so difficult to obtain a perfect riding horse; and why, when procured, so large a sum is demanded for him. Some persons who are really in want of a good riding horse, and are prepared to give a fair sum for him, nevertheless very frequently miss the chance of being possessed of one, through a thousand and one prejudices which are of no importance whatever. Among the number the following are frequently urged:—A particular height, colour, age, sex, &c., and are most frequent causes of a life-long disappointment in failing to procure a good riding horse.

I would advise such persons to forsake without delay running in so narrow a groove, and whenever they see an animal that suits them—no matter of what colour, size, age, or sex—to seize the opportunity of procuring it without delay. A really good horse, with good action and manners, always looks well and handsome, no matter of what colour or size he may be.

It is desirable that the riding horse be able to walk at the rate of five miles an hour, for if he be unable to do this, and should chance to go in company with a fast walker, he will be compelled to 'jog,' which, however gracefully performed, is but a slovenly performance. And if in company with slow walkers, he will carry himself in no way worse by walking well within himself.

The riding horse should never be allowed to trot at a greater rate than eight miles in the hour, so that he may go collectedly and well, and have time to place his feet just where he or his rider may think fit. Nothing looks more plebeian and butcher-like than to see a riding horse over-trotting himself, and reaching along with his head out, like a pig on a spit.

The riding horse should always be nicely bent and collected when in motion, or he never can present an aristocratic or graceful appearance.

THE LADY'S HORSE.

The lady's horse should resemble the gentleman's riding horse in every particular save in the trotting pace; at which pace, for many reasons, no real horsewoman would condescend to ride; therefore trotting in the lady's horse should not be suffered for an instant; but he should start from the walk to the canter, and return from the canter to the walk without a break. To see a horse jolting in a trot before settling down from the canter to the walk, tells sad tales of the horse's education, at any rate, to say nothing of the rider's. Therefore it will be understood that a lady's riding horse will not be nearly so difficult to obtain, and accordingly not so expensive, as a gentleman's, inasmuch as a graceful canter is not nearly so difficult to attain as a graceful and proper trot.

Whatever the weight of a lady, her horse's back must not be short, or she and her habiliments will completely cover the horse's frame, and render the outline ridiculous, and something approaching that of a slim young lady set off with a huge carriage umbrella.

Most ladies are heavy in the hand, and therefore an irritable mouth is not to be suffered, since nine ladies out of ten will make it worse. For this reason I cannot too strongly condemn the use of strong bits by ladies, and I am persuaded that most of the bad accidents that have occurred may be laid to their charge,— such as running away, tumbling over, &c., which are most frequently occasioned by the improper use of sharp bits on high-couraged horses, and are the most frequent causes of fatal accidents to female equestrians. Another very important point in female horsemanship is that the seat should be perfectly straight and square, since nothing so fatally destroys the effect of the appearance of both the lady's horse and his rider, as the saddle being pulled over on one side.

Nine ladies out of ten ride too long, and so keep coming over on the near side for the purpose of reaching their stirrups.

This also gives rise to at least nine-tenths of the severe saddle-galls, sit-fasts, and warbles that one is so frequently called upon to treat in ladies' horses.

In ninety-nine out of every hundred cases they are met with on the off-side in the lady's, and on the near-side in the gentleman's horse, thereby proving that for the most part the seat is not straight and square in either.

No one but a saddler of the very highest reputation should be trusted to manufacture a lady's saddle, or continual annoyance will be the result, by the saddle being fully six months out of the first twelve in the unscientific hands of the maker, for the purpose of undergoing a thousand and one alterations, the causes for which should never have existed.

Two good saddles are sufficient for any lady—one for a broad and round horse, and the other for a narrow and flat-sided one.

Great care should be taken by the lady that the proper saddles be put on the proper horses, or mischievous results will be sure to follow, both with regard to the horses and saddles. This is, of course, the proper business of grooms, but they are too apt, when full of work, to put on whichever saddle happens to be cleaned and properly adjusted at the time, without the slightest consideration or reference to its suitability to the horse in question.

THE COVERT HACK.

Most men expect the covert hack to take them from five to twenty-five miles to meet hounds, at from ten to eighteen miles an hour, and at this pace he may have to go up to his hocks in mud, or on a road as hard as adamant. Both the walking and trotting paces are superfluous, and a good, even, and moderately high gallop is all that is required in the covert or galloping hack. He should be a pocket edition of *a first-class steeplechaser*, both in make and shape and action, and every other particular save size.

He should not exceed 14 hands 3 in., or he will not be so quick in his stride as is desirable for getting safely over uneven and rough ground, in which he will require the fine shoulders of the steeplechaser to enable him to preserve his pace without tiring to nothing under the weight.

When I say that the covert hack must be precisely similar in breeding, make, shape and action to the steeplechaser, I must not be understood to mean every galloping hack for every weight, from twelve stones to twenty, but from ten stones to fourteen. Above this weight a more coarsely-bred animal must be put up with, and the pace must decrease from eighteen to thirteen miles within the hour.

For such weights a fast-trotting cob is the best description of animal for going to cover at a quick pace; and a cob that can be found to accomplish fourteen miles over rough ground within the hour, under from fourteen to twenty stones, will always command a high price, and is very difficult to procure.

The best covert hacks for galloping are to be found in little cast-offs from the racing stables, which, when possessed of sufficient thickness and action, invariably obtain the greatest character for pace and stoutness.

In either case it is necessary that the hack have good sound legs and feet; but blemishes matter little, such as cuts, scars, and being blind of an eye. Manners, also, in the covert hack are of little or no importance; indeed, to please most hunting men, they should do everything short of actually running away; and even this is not always objected to, but is sometimes deemed an advantage by sportsmen who are a little too fond of their beds on a cold morning.

CHAPTER I.

DISEASES OF NERVES.

APOPLEXY.

Apoplexy, seldom makes its appearance in the stable; but when it does show itself, it can generally be traced to bad management, such as improper feeding immediately preceding quick work, bad ventilation, &c.

It is usually fatal, and the symptoms are marked by extreme drowsiness, the respiration at the same time becoming unusually slow.

The disease consists in lesion of the vessels of the brain, the effusion of which causes pressure. The effusion in nine cases out of ten consists of blood and not serum.

Immediately the symptoms are apparent active measures must be resorted to, as being alone likely to be of the slightest avail. An aloes drench, of a strength of at least seven drachms, and one scruple of calomel, should be administered, and the horse should then be freely bled, and the mane and poll cropped closely, and an active blister, consisting of cantharides, applied all over the head and neck.

If the horse show any signs of recovering, gentle exercise and a spare diet, with the occasional use of alteratives, will be the best course of treatment for some time.

TETANUS—LOCK-JAW.

Tetanus can only be properly described as a *permanent* and not a periodical spasm; but whether the extreme rigidity of the muscles is caused by a portion or the whole of the nervous system being in a state of extreme irritation and tension, seems uncertain.

It does not appear that the horse loses his powers of sensation in this disease.

Properly speaking lock-jaw is limited to the muscles of the jaw and throat; but when a more extensive contraction of muscles takes place, it is termed tetanus.

In the horse tetanus is generally of the acute and not chronic nature, and, consequently, is usually fatal.

I have heard of a case of tetanus caused by a stub in the foot terminating fatally in two hours, but generally the fatal advances of this disease are more gradual.

The symptoms are readily discerned by stiffness in the neck gradually increasing, which renders any attempt at movement of the head very painful. The difficulty of mastication and swallowing soon follows, and, in acute cases, becomes almost immediately utterly impossible. Very painful convulsive efforts attend any attempt at swallowing.

The spasms around the neck soon become violent, and the head is for the most part retracted, and the

K

muscles of the lower jaw are contracted with immense force.

As the disease continues more muscles become involved, and intense pain appears to be suffered. So violent sometimes are the contractions, that I have heard of muscles being lacerated, and very frequently the teeth are injured by the violence of the spasm. As the spasm reaches the abdominal region, the urine is frequently discharged with sudden jerks. It is, however, as frequently retained, as well as the contents of the rectum. At the last stage of this disease the eyes become fixed in their sockets, and the ears tense and rigid, which symptoms are soon followed by a violent convulsion, which terminates in death.

In dissections after this disorder, a great extent of inflammation is evident, but this is most probably caused by the violent pressure of the muscles.

Tetanus is usually caused by wounds of the joints, and more especially of the feet, where the nerves are lacerated, and it frequently follows the injury very rapidly; but occasionally it does not set in until the injury has been healed and totally forgotten. Exposing wounds in the course of nerves to cold air is an exciting cause in many cases.

All rusty nails and other instruments likely to cause a wound in the foot should always be removed from the stable.

It has been remarked that wounds from which the suppuration is very scanty, or what are termed dry wounds, are frequent precursors of tetanus.

TETANUS.

The treatment of this disorder is involved in great obscurity, since it is the consequence of a cause which has ceased to act; and, therefore, the existing cause cannot be attacked. Chloroform has been exhibited with great advantage in some cases, while in others it has entirely failed to produce any alleviation of the pain or convulsions. The Cantharides blister strongly recommended in the treatment of apoplexy, should be used in a similar manner, and continued down the spine; and if a strong dose of physic, such as three drachms of calomel and three of emetic tartar, can be placed at the root of the tongue, so much the better. Constant use of the enema will aid in the treatment, and the injection should be composed of turpentine and hot gruel. Some pin their faith on aconite, others on digitalis, opium, &c.; but chloroform seems now the favourite remedy.

In cases, however, where the disease has followed some direct injury or operation, it will be well to excise a portion of the nerve beyond the injured or lacerated part.

This cannot well be done where the disorder is the consequence of castration, but in docking, nicking, &c., it is easily accomplished.

Should the horse show any symptoms of recovery, good nourishment, chiefly in a liquid form, should be administered, and tonics will be found useful, but should always be combined with emetic tartar, as is recommended in all other cases where their use is desirable.

STRINGHALT.

This, like the preceding disease, is spasmodic, but does not appear to follow any direct or external injuries. It as frequently occurs in both legs as in one, and may be described as a spasm of the flexor muscles of the hind leg. Some consider it to be caused by irritation of the sciatic nerve; and since it is never met with in the fore legs, this conclusion may be a correct one.

It is generally and most unwarrantably considered as unsoundness, but I am not aware that a horse is incapacitated for any purpose thereby. This disease, if it can be called one, is quite incurable, and therefore I shall not waste time by putting forward any fanciful mode of treatment.

PARALYSIS.

This disease usually attacks the hind limbs, and is the consequence in most cases of violent injuries to the vertebræ of the back and loins, caused by blows, wrenches, and falls, giving rise to tumours, which press on and irritate the spinal chord. In numerous cases, however, it is occasioned by chronic affection of the liver and kidneys; and in others the causes cannot be traced.

The treatment should be similar to that recommended in tetanus.

MEGRIMS.

This disease is easily defined and distinguished from apoplexy, &c., since no convulsions attend it. It is usual amongst over-fed horses, which are suffered to remain for days together in the stable, and then driven fast up hill with a tight bearing rein or small collar, both of which aid in preventing the free return of the blood to the heart. In this case congestion of the vessels of the brain will take place, while in others there is evidence of a diseased heart.

This disease cannot be mistaken: the horse, after proceeding about one mile from the stable, will shake his head and ears, as though flies were annoying him, or as if some extraneous substance had got into his ear; if stopped immediately, he will rarely fall; but if not, he will stagger, hold his head aloft and on one side, and drop: the attack usually lasts about five minutes, when the horse will resume his journey as before, with no apparent inconvenience, though he will very frequently break out into a sweat. The treatment should consist of the following ball once a week for a month, and given with a bran mash: two drachms of Barbadoes aloes, one drachm of emetic tartar, and two drachms of ginger. The horse should be fed very lightly previous to work.

CHAPTER II.

DISEASES OF THE ARTERIES AND VEINS.

ACCIDENTS AND WOUNDS OF ARTERIES.

IN all cases of accidents or wounds of arteries, where the punctured artery bleeds profusely, the only means of stopping the bleeding will be by ligature. Such cases admit of no delay. Sending for the veterinary surgeon will be of no avail, since his services will not be available in time. Loss of life must take place before many minutes are over in such cases, so that it behoves the stud groom, if he values his master's property, to avail himself of what knowledge lies in his power on this subject, and to make an effort, though a clumsy one, to save the life of his charge.

I shall only here allude to superficial vessels, since it is not to be supposed that any but the professional man can with safety attempt the operation of tying an artery situated beneath a mass of muscles; for even if he arrived at the artery, he would most likely injure and tear the coats of the artery, or else apply the ligature round the sheath, and thus involve the nerves and vein—in either case, creating additional pain and mischief.

In all external arteries, although it would not be prudent for the non-professional man to attempt to effect stoppage of bleeding by means of ligature, for fear of involving nerves, &c., he should, nevertheless, immediately attempt to check the flow of blood by *compression, both above and below the wounded part.* The best means known of effecting the stoppage of bleeding operate on the principle of pressure, and the following will be found the most simple :—

Tie a cord or band round the limb, or neck, or body, as the case may be, about six inches above and below the wound, so as to check the flow of blood; then endeavour to bring the edges of the wounded artery together; then take square pieces of lint and fold them into compresses, soaking the lower compress, previous to application, in cold vinegar; put compress after compress on, taking care they increase considerably in dimensions as they are further removed from the wound; then take a flannel bandage and roll it round and round the compresses and tie it securely. This done, remove gradually both the external cord, ligatures, &c., and keep the horse as still as possible; after which, if no further bleeding take place, the case may go on well.

The veterinary surgeon should at once be sent for, and should the artery require tying, he will be able to perform the operation with every chance of success; and he will be able to lessen or increase the pressure of the compress, as occasion may require.

ANEURISM.

Aneurism is a tumour formed by a dilatation of a part of an artery, and is also occasioned by a swelling arising from a collection of arterial blood effused in the cellular membrane, brought about by a rupture of the coats of the artery. It is a disease rarely met with in the horse; but occasionally it presents itself, and the horse is pronounced by the faculty to be labouring under some other disease. It first shows itself by causing intense pain, and consequently lameness, if situated, as is generally the case, in the hind limb. If carefully examined, distinct throbbings or pulsations will be felt, and as the disease progresses, the leg will fill as though the animal was labouring under dropsy; and for this reason, whenever aneurism occurs in the hind limbs, it is at once confounded with dropsy or water-farcy, and even when the aneurism bursts, it is seldom detected.

The only treatment is to endeavour by means of medicines to lessen the action of the heart, and thus retard the formation of the tumour. For this purpose use digitalis of the strength of two drachms to the dose, and enforce strict rest and low diet, and bind the tumour tightly with a compress and bandages; but avoid bleeding, which induces a dropsical tendency.

GLANDERS.

Glanders is evidently a diseased state of the blood, or rather the existence of some poisonous matter in the blood.

It is frequently produced by great debility, but most frequently by bad atmosphere, which irritates the air passages, and gradually developes the disease.

The first symptoms of glanders are a thin glassy discharge from one or both nostrils, which, after a time, becomes purulent. It is also to be distinguished from other discharges by its stickiness and tenacity; and, according to the intensity of the inflammation, the discharge presents a green or dusky yellow hue.

This condition may last for months, and I once hunted an animal affected with glanders for two months previous to discovering its existence.

The *sympathetic glands* will be found to be much swollen, and *fixed closely to the jaw bone.*

The nostril will become ulcerated, and the inside of the thighs will fill and become dreadfully sore to the touch. Small ulcers will now break out all over the body, resembling bladders in the first instance, containing a purulent clear fluid.

As no course of treatment has been of any avail up to the present time, I will here leave the consideration of this disease, hoping that I may have explained the symptoms with sufficient clearness to lead to its detection.

FARCY.

Farcy is merely a modification of the previous disease, and may and frequently does terminate in glanders.

The hind limbs are usually the first affected, chiefly,

no doubt, because they are furthest from the centre of circulation.

Pimples, or as they are termed *Farcy buds*, usually break out on the inside of the thighs, and send forth purulent matter; but in slight cases the discharge resembles healthy pus. The absorbent vessels become hard and cordy in all cases, though farcy buds are not always visible; but a sort of dropsical and uneven swelling of the hind limbs, which comes and goes without apparent cause, is the most common symptom; and may be distinguished from dropsy by the *intensity of the pain*, as well as the *unevenness of the swelling*, on being touched.

Debility, neglect, and foul stables are the chief causes of this disease. Therefore the best course of treatment is, to open the buds with a knife, and either cauterise with the red-hot iron or dress with chloride of zinc. Give also sulphur, bark, aniseed, and emetic tartar with the food, which should be very liberal. Beans, oats, linseed, and carrots should be given unsparingly, and if the case be a bad one, give one scruple of blue vitriol night and morning.

CHAPTER III.

DISEASES OF THE RESPIRATORY ORGANS.

COMMON COLD.

By a cold is meant, simple inflammation of the membranes of the nose, which is first discovered by the presence of a thin discharge from the nostril, and in most cases from the eyes.

A slight feverishness generally attends the attack, and the mucous membrane soon becomes more largely involved, and begins to secrete a flow of mucus which may last for some time. A cough also usually attends this attack, and the pulse is somewhat deranged.

It is produced in most cases by being exposed to cold air when the pores of the skin are preternaturally susceptible or open, which is produced by increased action of the system, brought about either by heated temperature or exercise of the muscles.

In either case the treatment must be the same, and only modified by the intensity of the attack. A cool stable, plenty of clothing, moderate exercise, and cooling food *ad libitum*, must be alone depended on for bringing about the desired results in slight cases. In cases, however, of greater severity, linseed gruel, antimony, and nitre should be given with an unlimited supply of water.

SORE THROAT.

Sore throat is a frequent attendant on a common cold, or in other words, it is an extension of the former disease.

The first symptom of sore throat is a gurgling sound in the larynx, with inability to swallow anything harsh without causing great irritation of the mucous membrane, which will call forth a subdued hitching cough, the performance of which gives evident pain.

It will also be perceived that he is unable to swallow his water without considerable effort.

The treatment should consist of immediate change of food, and a paste formed of mustard and vinegar should be rubbed on the throat and under the jaw, and should be repeated every two days, until the attack yields to the treatment.

Physic is highly improper in this case. The food should be cooling, but nourishing, consisting of linseed, boiled barley, or malt dust, with bran mashes, or the horse will soon fall off in his condition, which will necessitate his being eased in his work for some time to come.

INFLUENZA.

Influenza is generally included among the list of epidemics, and must be considered as a most severe disease, and is always attended by great prostration of strength. The symptoms are much the same as those attendant on common cold, accompanied by an increased degree of fever, total loss of appetite, and consequently intense weakness. The pulse becomes quick and feeble, and a painful cough attended by increased respiration is soon apparent.

The mucous membrane becomes greatly inflamed and enlarged, and is somewhat tender to the touch.

The treatment should be similar to that recommended in the previous case, using mild aperients, tonics, and cooling yet nourishing food, which should be continued during the attack, and for months subsequently, on alternate weeks, or the constitution may never quite recover its wonted vigour.

BRONCHITIS.

Bronchitis consists in inflammation of the bronchii, and is attended by a great obstruction in breathing, which causes a wheezing sound during respiration. There is a thick discharge of mucus from the nostrils, attended by a very severe cough, which evidently causes great pain.

This disease very frequently leaves behind it an altered structure of the air passages, which produces chronic diseases, such as thick wind, whistling, &c.

The treatment should be the same as in the preceding cases, with the exception of the blister, which should be continued from the larynx to the sternum.

BROKEN WIND.

Broken wind is marked by a double act of respiration, which would seem to be caused by the admission of air into air-cells unfit for its reception, and from which it cannot readily nor entirely be expelled without an extraordinary muscular effort of the chest and flank.

The appearances of the lungs of a broken-winded horse, on examination after death, differ to such an extent that it is difficult to assign any general cause of this disease.

Sometimes there is no structural change evident, the only remarkable condition being increased bulk and a crackling sound on being pressed by the finger, from their being distended with air. However, in most instances, rupture of the cells of the lungs will be discovered.

From what has been said, it will be clear that all attempts at a cure of the disease will be fruitless; since we have not the mechanical power of creating new air-cells nor of repairing the old ones. Alleviation of suffering, then, is only to be attempted, the best means of accomplishing which will be by attending strictly to the horse's diet, limiting him to a certain quantity at any one time, so that distension of the stomach may not aggravate the difficulty of expanding the lungs.

Very slow work may be performed without additional inconvenience, but I have seen the effort of drawing heavy weights at a slow pace make the horse stagger and fall in a terrible state of distress.

Much has been said of the efficacy of arsenic, in doses of 12 grains per day, given for three weeks or a month; but this must depend on the *cause* of broken wind, for neither arsenic nor any other drug can have the power of creating or uniting the air-cells of the lungs.

THICK WIND OR HIGH BLOWING.

Thick wind generally succeeds an attack on the bronchial tubes or lungs, which has left a thickening of the membranes, thereby contracting the space or dimensions of the bronchial tubes.

It is easily perceived by an experienced horseman through the horse blowing freely without sufficient reason,—i.e. when he is not undergoing violent exertion, is not fat, and has not been eating or drinking largely immediately before leaving the stable. It is most commonly met with in under-bred animals of very full habit. The symptoms are utterly unlike those attendant on broken wind, the inspirations and expirations being similar, but very much accelerated. The treatment, however, should be similar to that recommended for broken wind, avoiding overloading the stomach at any time, and more especially previous to exertion.

CHRONIC COUGH.

A chronic cough is always the consequence of some previous affection of the air passages, which remain in a state of irritation. Bronchitis, if improperly treated, usually leaves behind it an irritability which causes chronic cough.

Coughing takes place immediately after drinking cold water, without any symptoms of the horse having caught cold; indeed, the cough is of a different nature and sound, being a dry harsh sound utterly unlike that existing in inflammation of the respiratory organs. Immediately after leaving the stable also, the horse usually coughs three or four times, and then is free from it perhaps for the rest of the day. The treatment of the cough must depend on its nature, which is so obscure, that the general health of the horse should be the careful study of the groom, who should never allow him to become either in very high or very low condition; and should give emollient food when practicable, such as boiled linseed and bran mashes.

All manner of balls and drenches are recommended in chronic cough, many of which serve to flatter the expectations of the owner for a time, but which all fall short of effecting a cure. The favourite drench consists of spirits of turpentine, mucilage, and laudanum, the favourite ball being composed of tar and powdered squill, of each one and a half drachms.

The ball is most preferable of the two, since it is the most harmless.

Chronic cough must not be confounded with a stomach cough, usually attendant on the existence of worms. The sound of the cough, as well as the condition of the horse, are sufficient to prevent any but the most careless observer being misled.

PLEURISY.

Pleurisy consists of inflammation of the pleura, a serous membrane that lines the cavity of the chest, giving a covering to the lungs. It may be caused by external injuries, or exposure to cold, &c.; and may be distinguished from other diseases of the chest by the unusual tenderness of the sides when pressed by the hand. The respiration is quick, and the pulse accelerated. Sometimes one side is attacked, and at others both are involved. One side should be immediately blistered with cantharides or mustard, and a mild physic ball given, consisting of emetic tartar, digitalis, and nitre, of each two drachms, to be given twice daily, until the symptoms appear to have changed for the better.

If violent sweats break out, the case may be viewed with considerable alarm, and dropsy or water in the cavities of the chest may be apprehended, caused by a serous effusion secreted by the pleura. This disease is termed hydro-thorax. The symptoms are, inability to hear the sound of respiration, and dullness of the sound on striking the side.

No treatment but tapping can be of any avail, and

unless it be performed without delay, the animal will die from suffocation.

CONGESTION OF THE LUNGS.

Congestion of the lungs is most frequently caused by the horse being galloped until distressed, when in an unfit condition of body. It consists of stagnation of blood in the lungs, which causes exhaustion and suffocation, and the horse at once assumes a distressed look; the eyes and nostrils likewise assume an appearance of congestion and stagnation, the breathing is accelerated and painful, with laborious heaving of the flanks. There is usually a cold sweat on the body, with great coldness of the extremities. It can be distinguished from inflammation of the lungs by the difference of sound on applying the ear to the horse's sides. In congestion the sound will be almost precisely similar to that heard in healthy respiration; whereas in inflammation, there will be heard a grating, crackling sound which is unmistakable.

The treatment should consist of endeavouring to bring about a determination of blood to the skin. To effect which, since neither the vapour nor hot bath are within our reach here, we must have recourse to hot blankets applied to the body, hand rubbing, and hot bandages to the legs; and a free current of air through the stables, together with the free use of hot cordial drinks, such as spiced ale, given at intervals of half an hour.

Bleeding must be carefully avoided, as it would only

increase the debility and, consequently, congestion of the organs of circulation. Good grooming and tonics, with moderate exercise and a cool stable, must be the mode of treatment during convalescence.

INFLAMMATION OF THE LUNGS.

The symptoms of inflammation of the lungs are similar to those of the preceding disease in every particular save *the pulse and the sound of the respiration.*

The pulse will range from sixty-five to ninety, and the membranes of the eyes and nostrils will present a deep red colour.

The coat, generally, is staring; the cough very short and painful, accompanied by expectorations of bloody mucus, the respirations being distressed and accelerated, with heaving of the flanks performed with great irregularity, and the nostrils are expanded. If he lies down, he will soon be on his legs again.

The horse will frequently give a distressed look round to his body, and will appear sore all over; and, as the disease progresses, the extremities will feel yet more cold and icy, with continual cold sweats on the trunk.

The treatment should consist of prompt bleeding, allowing the blood to flow until the membranes of the eyelids and nostrils give evidence of a reduction in the inflammation. These can be the only true guides as to when the vein should be pinned up. The same ball as that recommended for pleurisy should be administered, and the food should consist of bran and linseed mashes, carrots, and hay, attending strictly to the free ventilation of the stable; and if mustard poultices be applied to the sides, they will considerably lessen the poor animal's sufferings.

If the symptoms gradually subside, and the horse's appetite appear to be good, danger may be considered to have passed off.

But if continual reactions take place, and the colour of the nostrils change to a fixed leaden hue, with a cold chilly breath, and convulsive flutterings of the heart, death may be speedily apprehended, which is usually immediately preceded by the horse walking round and round his box in a delirious and vacant manner.

Horses rarely recover a severe attack of inflammation of the lungs, however skilfully the disease may be managed, for it leaves the system in so debilitated a state that a recurrence of the attack is more than probable within a few months, or congestion may take place, and, what is more to be dreaded, *suppuration*. Therefore, for weeks and months *all exciting causes* must be guarded against most sedulously.

A cool, roomy box, with cooling and nourishing food, combined with some active tonic, such as bark, aniseed, and emetic tartar, given on alternate weeks, must alone be depended on for a cure.

The horse, however, will be utterly unfit for any sort of work, exceeding mere exercise, for many months. It will, nevertheless, be unwise to turn him out to grass for fear of broken wind or roaring being the consequences. Patience must be called into play with this assurance, that as his condition improves with good grooming and gentle exercise, so will his powers of respiration increase in due ratio. Sudden changes, both in diet and atmosphere, must be carefully avoided ever afterwards.

ROARING.

Roaring may be the consequence of one or all of the above-named diseases, or it may arise from causes unconnected with them. Its existence is most difficult to ascertain in slight cases, and the most experienced are very frequently misled.

Most of the low class of dealers and grooms give horses several sharp and severe digs or blows in the side, or cough them by squeezing the windpipe; and if the horse grunt or wheeze he is at once pronounced to be a 'piper,' 'roarer,' 'whistler,' or 'grunter,' according to the judgment of the faculty, who thereupon looks knowing, alters the position of his hat, and struts off to perform on as many other unlucky brutes as happen to come within his unmannerly inspection.

In this way many horses are rejected as unsound which are perfectly sound, and many that are unsound are passed as sound.

The only way of judging accurately as to whether the horse really roars, is to take him to a ploughed field, and have him cantered round it until he blows freely, when, if there be any obstruction in the organs of respiration, it will be easily detected by any experienced man.

On a road the clatter made by the horse's feet is so great that it will drown, in many cases, the lesser noise of roaring; and it is not proper to examine their expirations when they are pulled up, as many bad roarers cease making a noise immediately they are stopped.

There is a rattling gurgling noise in the throat, however, which must not be mistaken for roaring. Many of the clearest winded horses will do it when very passionate and excited, or when pulled severely with a sharp bit.

I have known horses rejected by veterinary surgeons of limited experience, and others, for this cause, but I have never known one of them turn roarers. The usual causes of roaring are these:

1. Thickening of the bronchial tubes.

2. Paralysis of the left recurrent nerve and the muscles amongst which it ramifies.

3. Thickening of the tracheal tube, caused by inflammation or abscesses.

4. Exostosis of the cartilages.

I have thought fit to name the usual causes of this malady, not that the knowledge of them can in any way tend to effectual treatment, but to show that the causes of the disease are more or less occult during life; and, therefore, that when men undertake to cure this or that case of roaring by such means as firing the larynx, the use of blisters, caustic, &c., with doses of strychnine, they undertake what they cannot perform, and unjustifiably raise the hopes of the owner, which must sooner or later be blighted, as well as put the poor horse to unnecessary torture.

That roaring is quite uncurable there can be no doubt, notwithstanding the many instances in which various modes of treatment are said to have been successful.

And when I make this assertion, I allude merely to *chronic*, and not to *acute* cases of roaring. Acute cases are frequently the consequences of swelling in strangles, and, causing an obstruction, make the horse roar lustily. These causes can undoubtedly be cured by proper treatment, such as giving emetic tartar in doses of two drachms daily, for a week, and applying repeated blisters composed of iodine and mercury to the larynx.

Roaring is hereditary, in my opinion, in nine cases out of ten, and in predisposed constitutions (or constitutions which have a tendency to irritation of the bronchial tubes) will show itself sooner or later.

The only mode of warding off this disease is by keeping such animals as are predisposed to its ravages in good condition and regular work all the year round, carefully avoiding all exciting causes of inflammatory attacks, both in and out of the stable, which should be cool, airy, and well drained.

CHAPTER IV.

DISEASES OF THE ABDOMEN.

INFLAMMATION OF THE LIVER.

This is a very painful disease, and may be ascertained by the horse holding up one or other of his fore legs during the spasms, and turning round to look at his side very frequently, and especially after feeding.

Sometimes, though seldom, this disease assumes an acute form, and the horse seems to be suddenly attacked with gripes, and to be suffering intense agony.

All food should be removed, and small doses of calomel given morning and evening, until the symptoms show signs of abatement. It will be well to unite with the doses of calomel the same quantity of powdered opium.

Chronic cases of diseases of the liver are unfortunately of very frequent occurrence amongst horses which are very highly fed and worked severely, such as horses in training, &c., and its existence is rarely ever discovered until revealed by post-mortem examination. I have found in this case one ounce of extract of chamomile, given daily for a week, with change of food, the only certain remedy.

DYSENTERY.

Dysentery consists of inflammation of the mucous membrane of the intestines, attended by an increased secretion, which is discharged with hard and stringy fæces accompanied by perpetual straining.

The treatment should consist of a quart of linseed oil every six hours, until the intestines be cleared of their contents. Bran mashes, carrots, and hay should be the sole food for a week subsequently.

DIARRHŒA.

Diarrhœa is easily distinguished from dysentery by the evacuations being loose and watery, without the existence of mucus. It is most commonly met with among horses of a weedy washy formation, by means of which the peristaltic action is unnaturally increased, when it is a primary affection; but it is usually occasioned by superpurgation from over-physicking. Active measures in the latter case must speedily be taken. One ounce of laudanum in a drench of rice water and chalk should be given every three hours during the first day; after which, boiled starch allowed to get moderately cool should be administered, with the same quantity of laudanum, every six hours. If the symptoms do not lessen within twenty-four hours, a fatal result may be expected.

In all cases which have been allowed to go on for three or four days, danger is present. Where the discase is the result of primary affection give opium, powdered catechu, and chalk of each half an ounce, morning and evening, with bean meal and rice water as the sole variety of diet.

During convalescence give Peruvian bark and aniseed, half an ounce of each, with an increased quantity of beans, on alternate weeks for a month.

COLIC.

Colic consists of a spasmodic contraction of the muscular coat of the intestines, and it is most frequently confined to the small intestines; but sometimes the large intestines as well as the bladder are involved. When it is accompanied by great inflation of the abdomen it is termed flatulent colic, and should be treated by copious injections of warm water with the enema, which will be sufficient to cure the attack in most cases; but occasionally the case will demand the operation of puncturing.

In the case of spasmodic colic, stimulating medicines must be used, such as spirit of turpentine and laudanum, of each two ounces, in a drench of hot ale, given every half hour until the pain lessens. Give on the next day a mild physic ball. Horses of certain strains of blood are very subject to colic and should be avoided, for it is sure to terminate their career sooner or later, and frequently when in the most blooming condition and highest state of usefulness. Gross feeders and horses with great swill bellies are generally subject to this disease.

GASTRITIS.

This disease is very rare, excepting in stables where grooms think fit to poison their masters' horses with arsenic. When gastritis or acute inflammation of the stomach takes place, the existence of poison in the system may safely be apprehended. The existence of arsenic may be discovered by purging of a bloody nature, and the flow of saliva from the mouth, which take place.

The only treatment likely to be of any avail, is the frequent and liberal use of thin starch both as a drench and clyster, which may tend to allay the violent inflammation of the mucous membrane.

INFLAMMATION OF THE WOMB.

This is one of the most dangerous diseases with which the horse-breeder has to contend. It attacks mares usually immediately after foaling, and is marked by the following symptoms—delirium, acute fever, laborious breathing, great prostration of strength, as well as by the flow of a dark and very offensive fluid from the fissure. The treatment must be very active or it will be of no avail. Blisters must be applied to the loins, the milk veins must be bled freely, and a ball composed of digitalis, opium, and calomel, of each one drachm, administered every two hours until the bowels operate freely.

I have taken as much as eight or nine quarts of

blood from the milk veins in this disease with most satisfactory results.

The best injection into the womb is a solution of chloride of zinc of about the strength of a scruple to a pint of water. The food should consist of linseed and bran mashes, and an unlimited supply of water until the disease has abated, after which give tonics and a liberal diet.

This disease is fatal in at least seven cases out of ten, and therefore the most active measures should be taken immediately. It is frequently occasioned by ignorant violence during foaling, as well as by the mare being in too high a condition.

INFLAMMATION OF THE KIDNEYS.

This is a very painful disease, and is commonly attended with extreme danger; it can easily be distinguished from inflammation of the bladder by the pain occasioned by touching the loins with the hand. The general symptoms are the passing of dark-coloured urine in small quantities, with excessive pain and groaning, the pulse small and quick, with a straddling position of his hind limbs. Apply mustard poultices, and give a drench of linseed oil, and an ounce of opium every four hours. The horse should be bled freely at once. His food should consist of linseed gruel for some days, or other glutinous food.

This disease is produced most frequently by the ignorant use of diuretic balls, improper food—such as

INFLAMMATION OF THE BLADDER.

mowburnt hay or oats—exposure to cold, heavy horsemen addicted to short stirrups, and a violent strain, all of which causes are easily avoided, save the last.

INFLAMMATION OF THE BLADDER.

This disease, like the previous one, is often caused by the improper use of diuretic balls, cantharides, &c. The symptoms are the same in every particular as in inflammation of the kidneys, save the extreme tenderness on the loins. However, if there be any doubt on the subject, the hand after being thoroughly greased should be passed up the anus until the bladder is felt, when, if the mischief lies there, it will be very hot, tender, and contracted; but if not, it will not be more tender than might be expected from the existence of inflammation in contiguous parts. The treatment, however, will be the same as that recommended for the preceding disease in every particular.

SPASM OF THE BLADDER.

In this disease, caused no doubt by irritation, the neck of the bladder is closed, and consequently the urine is retained. The only treatment of any avail will be that of evacuation of the contents of the bladder by means of a catheter, which should be directed by a competent person. It will be well at the same time to give opium in one-and-a-half-drachm doses, every morning and evening, until the urine is passed readily.

INFLAMMATION OF THE INTESTINES.

This disease, generally known by the name of 'enteritis,' consists of inflammation of the membrane covering the viscera.

The symptoms are—alternate shivering and sweating fits, pulse very quick and small, the lining of the eye-lids and nose of a black-red colour, kicking at the belly, a fixed glazy eye, frequent attacks of delirium, together with tenderness of the belly. The only treatment of any avail will be prompt and free bleeding, and frequent drenches of linseed oil and opium; mustard poultices should be plastered all over the abdomen, with frequent injections of thin starch.

If, however, the horse be really labouring under this disease, there is not much hope of recovery; for mortification will soon set in and put an end to the poor brute's sufferings. It may readily be distinguished from colic, by the exquisite tenderness of the belly.

WORMS.

The existence of worms is marked by a rough coat lying in the wrong direction, a very irregular craving for food—sometimes accompanied by costiveness, and at others by scouring—with extreme itching of the anus; the belly also becomes pendulous and distended, attended with extreme leanness of the ribs.

The treatment of worms is fortunately now not confined to mechanically irritating substances, such as pounded glass, pewter, brass and iron, which frequently caused a state of irritation not easily allayed.

Emetic tartar given in two drachm doses daily, for a week, in bran mashes, seldom fails to weaken the worms so much that they can be carried off by means a purging ball composed of six drachms of aloes, two of ginger, and two of emetic tartar. I have never known this treatment fail. Much caution must be used in administering emetic tartar. Its action should be carefully noted, and immediately any irritation is apparent the quantity must be lessened, or its use prohibited entirely. This, however, may be taken as a rule, that when any irritation is caused by the use of emetic tartar, it may safely be concluded that the object for which it was given has been effected.

CHAPTER V.

DISEASES OF THE EYE.

SIMPLE INFLAMMATION.

Simple inflammation of the eyes is caused by external causes in nine cases out of ten, such as a blow, chaff falling within the eye-lids, &c., and must be treated according to the cause of inflammation. If any foreign substance be the cause, it must be removed immediately; and I have found a leaden pencil the best instrument for such a purpose. If the inflammation be very severe, the facial vein should be copiously bled, and all corn removed until some symptoms of abatement are evident.

It is very rare to meet with a case where the injury is more deeply seated than the cornea in simple inflammation. Great care, however, should be taken to remove the cause before ulceration of the cornea has taken place. It is difficult for one unacquainted with diseases of the eye, to distinguish between this disease and ophthalmia by whatever distinctions may be drawn. The chief difference is, that in the former disease the cornea alone is affected, while in the latter the inflammation extends to the internal parts.

OPHTHALMIA.

This disease is divided usually into two distinct classes by professional men—Specific and Purulent Ophthalmia; but, since the symptoms and treatment will be the same, I do not think any object will be gained by treating of them separately.

The symptoms are marked by closing of the eyelids, distended vessels, general muddiness of the iris and cornea, with an almost total loss of transparency, as well as by profuse weeping.

The treatment should consist of darkening the stable, lowering the diet, and putting a linen compress, soaked in a solution of sulphate of zinc of about the strength of one scruple to the half-pint of water, over the eyelids.

The horse will assuredly go blind sooner or later, if subject to periodical attacks of this disease; therefore, copious bleedings, large doses of physic, &c., are utterly inadmissible, inasmuch as they add to the evil by incapacitating the horse for work for a lengthened period.

The best way is to dispose of a horse after having recovered from one of these attacks, unless intended for double harness, when blindness will not be of much inconvenience either to the horse or his owner. In this case, however, great care must be taken to remove the exciting cause, which I take to be plethora. It is most common in coarse underbred horses of the hackney breed, probably because their circulative organs are less perfect. Such animals generally are possessed of a distended haw and sunken eye, and should always be avoided. One eye is generally more frequently affected than the other; but when one goes the other is not long in following suit. All kinds of wild statements are put forward with reference to this disease; the existence of a wolf's tooth is considered by many as a certain cause of ophthalmia, and its removal as a certain cure of the same. Others hold that only those horses which are subject to the pressure of a collar— thus retarding the circulation of the blood—are afflicted with it! All of which goes to prove that the direct causes are frequently indiscernible in the majority of cases. Overnight the horse's eye will be as well as usual, but on the next morning it will be, without any apparent cause, closed and inflamed.

I must, therefore, conclude that predisposition of the constitution is the chief cause of this disease; though, no doubt, plethora and foul stables aid and abet in the work.

CATARACT.

The previous disease frequently terminates in cataract or opacity of the crystalline lens.

A cataract usually commences in the centre of and behind the pupil, and is marked by no symptoms of pain or uneasiness during its formation. When a primary disease, all treatment is useless and cruel, and can be attended with no good results.

GLASS EYES.

This diseased state of the eyes is technically termed amaurosis, and consists of loss of sight from diseased condition of the optic nerve and retina. The eye, to all appearance save the imperfect functions of the retina, is healthy and sound. It may be caused by increased or diminished sensibility of the retina. This disease very rarely attacks both eyes at the same time. It is said to be the frequent consequence of staggers and immoderate bleeding. It may be discovered by the timidity and uncertainty of the horse's action, by the fixed size of the pupil, a shrunken iris, and insensibility to the light of a candle if placed close and opposite to the eye in a darkened stable.

The cause of this disease is irritability of the retina, consequent on a determination of blood to the head in some cases, and in others is the result of ophthalmia. I had a horse in my possession affected with this disease from the latter cause, which took place while riding to meet a pack of fox-hounds only six miles distant, so rapid is its progress at times. I first discovered it by his continually putting one or other of his feet into the grips and gutters alongside of the road, a thing that I never knew him do previously. He then went much as usual, until arriving at a water ditch, into the middle of which he went without an effort to save himself, and, on coming to the stable, he walked straight up against the wall, being evidently unaware of its existence. He was stone-blind from that moment, and never appeared to regain the power of sight afterwards. This horse had been subject to severe attacks of specific ophthalmia for two years previously, for which he had never been subjected to bleeding or large doses of physic. His age was six years, and he was subject to frequent attacks of plethora. In this case no treatment is of any avail; but its existence may be partially guarded against by strict attention to the digestive organs, atmosphere of the stable, regular food, and exercise. Violent exertion should be avoided where this disease is feared, but moderate riding and driving will materially aid in warding it off.

CHAPTER VI.

DISEASES OF THE SKIN.

A moderate knowledge of the action of the vessels of the skin is indispensable to all persons having the care of horses of value, for by it alone can the unprofessional man determine the state of the horse's health committed to his charge. The bloom on a horse's skin is like the ruddy and healthful complexion of the human being, and is of equal importance.

It will be necessary, then, to make some mention of the anatomy of the skin, in order that the treatment and nature of the diseases to which it is subject may be fully comprehended.

The skin is composed of three parts, says Mr. Percival, differing in appearance, texture, and organisation from each other.

The cutis or real skin ' is of a fibrous texture, tough but supple, elastic, very vascular, and highly sensitive. . . . The skin abounds with absorbents. In places where it is thin, the superficial lymphatics, which are supposed to take their origin from its areolæ or pores, are comparatively large, and their trunks in the subcutaneous tissue are readily found and injected.

'Of the infinity of pores the skin exhibits upon its surface, probably the greater number transmit hairs, but there are crowds of others, which are denominated the *perspiratory pores*, from their being known to emit an imperceptible vapour, distinguished as the *insensible* perspiration; that which is sensible being the ordinary *sweat*.

'. . . Again, there is another set of pores of larger size, more discernible in some places than in others, which are the mouths of follicles (or glands), from which issues a waxy matter, and those parts of the skin subject to friction are in particular beset with them; in fact, the unctuous matter furnished by them preserves the skin soft and supple, and in some places keeps up a constant greasiness of the surface.

'The skin at the bend of the knee and hock has a secretion of this nature, which, from irritation now and then becomes augmented, and, from want of cleanliness, grows inspissated, and collects about the parts, and, if the incrustation be not disturbed, will generate a foul ulcerous sore. Lameness, of course, must result from this as soon as pain or stiffness is felt in flexing the limb.

'The skin of the heel of the horse possesses very many of these glandular pores, through which oozes an unctuous secretion having a peculiar smell, and this it is that gives the well-known softness, suppleness, and greasy feel to the part. An unusual flow of this matter, somewhat altered in its nature, is what gives rise to *grease*.

'The cuticle (or outer skin) is a thin, tough, inorganic membrane, serving as an envelope to the true skin. It is everywhere pierced with holes, corresponding in size, situation, and number, to those of the cutis (or real) skin.

'First, there are the pores for the hairs; secondly, the perspiratory or exhalent pores; thirdly, the absorbent or inhalent pores; and fourthly, pores of a larger size, through which unctuous secretions in various parts are emitted.'

It will be seen from the above extracts that, unless the external skin be kept thoroughly clean by good grooming, the pores must become clogged and unable to perform their functions, which consist in carrying off the corruption of the system through the perspiratory pores, thus relieving the blood of a large quantity of water, saline, and animal matters, which, if confined, are dreadfully injurious to the system.

I will now proceed to consider

GREASE.

Grease consists of a morbid secretion of the glands or pores of the extremities.

In slight cases the skin becomes inflamed, swelled, and subsequently cracks, and presents numerous small fissures in the heels of the fore or hind legs, but in more severe cases ulceration, and then fungous tumours or 'grapes,' take place.

Debility is the chief cause of this disease, which is proved by its frequent occurrence among coarse, half-starved, and severely worked horses in an exaggerated form. Plethora and standing in the stable are also fruitful causes of it, for, by standing still, the vessels become inactive, enfeebled, and distended. It very frequently shows itself in young horses, when first brought into the stable, and put to hard work too rapidly.

The treatment must consist in first removing all hair and then thoroughly cleansing the part with hot soap and water. It should be rubbed dry, and dressed with an astringent lotion, consisting of one scruple of chloride of zinc and one ounce of laudanum in half a pint of water. This should be repeated three times daily, applying some glycerine after the last dressing at night.

The general habit must now be attended to, and the supposed cause of the attack removed, whether it be too much or too little exercise, plethora or debility, or the presence of cold.

Physic should rarely be given in any case, but when depletion is necessary, the purpose is better served by giving alteratives, such as sulphur, nitre, and black antimony, of each half-an-ounce, given in bran and linseed mash, every alternate day, and changing the food to carrots, malt dust, &c.

When debility is the cause, the tonic powders, consisting of one ounce of bark and aniseed, with one drachm of emetic tartar, given daily during alternate weeks, with liberal diet, should be persevered in until the desired effect takes place.

In the exaggerated form of this disease, the use of the lotion above recommended will be useless. The grapy excrescences must be removed with the knife, and then seared with a hot iron sufficiently to stop the bleeding; and if the case seem very hopeless, it would be well to try the effect of arsenic, in doses of from five to eight grains per day, which has performed wonderful cures when all else had failed. It should, however, be used carefully, and not be continued too long.

CRACKED HEELS.

Cracked heels are well known in every stable in the land as one of the greatest banes that horses in work are afflicted with. It consists of cracks in the posterior and inferior parts of the pastern immediately above the heel, from which flows a watery, and at times, a greasy discharge, which is sometimes accompanied by bleeding. There is nothing more painful, for when the horse is in action the old cracks open, and new ones are very frequently caused, unless the skin had been previously saturated with some emollient application, of which glycerine is by far the best known. The most frequent cause of cracked heels is *unprepared for exertion*. If you take a colt up and work him hard, his heels will be sure to crack in spite of the best treatment and grooming. It is the fashion to attribute its existence to want of rubbing the heels when drying or evaporating, after being washed. Indeed, I have heard one of Her Majesty's officers assert that every man having a horse under his charge with cracked heels should be sent to the guard-room; but it is to be hoped that he did not carry out his threat in every case, or some worthy and careful men must have fallen victims unjustly to his capricious and illogical mind.

This disease is most frequently rather general than local, and must be treated by due observance to the causes—giving tonics if the horse be overworked, and liberal diet, with sulphur, nitre, and sweating, if plethora be the cause.

SWELLED LEGS.

There are different kinds of swelling, resulting from divers causes. In some cases there appears great swelling, accompanied by a serous discharge, for which the blame is invariably attributed to the kidneys, which are irritated violently by various diuretics until the swelling disappears. Most frequently the horse's legs 'fill,' and are remarkably hard and round; exercise of about two hours' duration usually fines them down, they nevertheless resume their former condition after being in the stable for a few hours, and the swelling, unless the cause be removed, becomes more obstinate with time.

Overworking and underfeeding, as well as overphysicking, and the too constant use of diuretics, are very prolific causes; but the two latter are by far the most difficult of removal, since the kidneys have contracted a diseased habit, and the system become so weakened, that very frequently change of food and absolute rest for months are essentially necessary.

Flannel bandages should be applied and bound tightly, immediately after the horse has returned from exercise, and the legs bathed from time to time in warm salt and water, and *exercise* should take the place of *work*, until the swelling disappears. Tonics may also be used, as recommended in the previous disease.

There is yet another form of swelled legs very prevalent among thoroughbred horses in the autumn, which can readily be distinguished from the foregoing by its inflammatory nature. It usually sets in on the inside of the thigh, which is dreadfully painful to the touch, and when the horse turns over in the stall he will lift up the leg affected and hop on the other. Give bran mashes at once, and otherwise prepare for and give physic, and give alteratives for a week after the setting of the physic; and if it shows no symptoms of disappearing give another dose of physic and begin to give harder work after its operation.

MANGE.

The disease known as mange is occasioned by the existence of an insect which, no doubt, owes its existence to the accumulation of a mass of scurf and other filth on the skin. It occasions unbearable itching, which causes the horse to gnaw and rub himself from head to foot, and he will lose his condition irretrievably if the disease be not treated in time. Use the following ointment, and rack up the horse during its action, so that he cannot lick himself:—

   Corrosive Sublimate . . . . ½ ounce
   Soft Soap . . . . . . 3 pounds
   Mercurial Ointment . . . . ½ a pound.

Rub in this ointment three times a week, washing the body all over with warm soap and water on alternate days.

SURFEIT.

This disease presents itself by a mass of broad and flat pimples breaking out all over the body. Sometimes the eyes are completely closed from the swelling.

I was once called to see a thoroughbred mare which had undergone a severe clothes sweat when over fat, and in about six hours she was one mass of eruption, which had been carelessly mistaken by a pseudo-practitioner for farcy, and the mare's death warrant was nearly sealed. I ordered her to be led out in the fields without any clothes during the cool of the evening and have no food for twenty-four hours save bran and water, with two ounces of spirits of nitre. In two days all the eruption had disappeared, and the mare resumed her work without further treatment. It may be as well to state that the lumps produced by surfeit are easily distinguished from farcy buds by the most inexperienced if they will take the trouble to examine them.

Surfeit lumps are broad and flat on their apexes, and are not in any way tender to the touch; whereas, the farcy buds are conical and very tender.

In all cases of surfeit have the clothes taken off altogether for twenty-four hours, no matter at what season of the year the attack presents itself.

WARTS.

Warts are unsightly but not dangerous, unless they occur on the penis, when amputation is often necessary. In the generality of cases warts should be cut to a level with the skin, when some caustic, such as acetic acid, should be applied in very small quantities, but as frequently as they rise above the level of the skin.

SADDLE GALLS.

When the pressure of the saddle has inflamed and galled the skin of the withers or elsewhere, immediate attention should be paid to the injured part. If the gall be large, and many vessels of the cutis appear to have been ruptured, which can easily be ascertained by the dark-coloured and bruised appearance of the skin, cooling and emollient applications must be at once used; and suppuration must not be hurried on by poultices or irritating applications, or a terrible abscess may be the consequence. A slight suppuration must invariably take place, which is best treated by placing over the wound a piece of dry lint, subsequently to a water dressing, twice daily until it heals, which will vary from two to six weeks.

If granulations or proud flesh is thrown out, damp the lint in a lotion consisting of chloride of lime of the strength of one scruple to the half-pint of water. No saddle can be suffered to be put on until the wound has healed.

CHAPTER VII.

DISEASES OF SYNOVIAL MEMBRANES.

Synovial membranes are given for the purpose of lubricating joints, and other parts of the frame subjected to friction. These membranes are plentifully furnished with nerves and blood-vessels. They are, therefore, as may readily be supposed, subject to inflammation, which is always accompanied by an undue secretion, which, occasionally, by pressure on surrounding vessels, causes partial lameness.

BOG SPAVIN.

Bog spavin is occasioned by inflammation of the synovial bag; it presents itself at the inner portion of the hock, or where the joint is fixed, and blood spavin is occasioned by the obstruction to the circulation of the blood passing through the superficial vein of the hock, consequent on the enlarged synovial capsule—or bog spavin, as it is usually termed.

These capsules used to be opened and their contents evacuated; but the operation more frequently killed than cured the patient.

When they first appear give cooling diet and a mild dose of physic, with entire rest, and resume work gradually. But when once the capsule has become seriously inflamed no treatment will be of any avail. Repeated blistering and firing are commonly recommended, but are both utterly useless in effecting a cure, and only add to the horse's sufferings.

THOROUGH PIN.

A thorough pin consists of an enlargement, consequent on inflammation of the bursæ, situated between the tendons—above the hock. Sometimes the swelling is of an enormous size, but very rarely causes lameness, and usually becomes partially absorbed. No doubt pressure, where feasible, is the best treatment, and a well-made truss just adapted to the size of the leg could be easily manufactured, and would well repay the cost. Generally, however, a little rest and a dose of physic will be sufficient. They rarely recur a second time on being once reduced.

WIND GALLS.

Wind galls are generally met with in horses whose legs have been subjected to severe concussions, and more especially where they have been ridden hard along the road. They consist of an enlargement of the synovial capsules of the fetlock joint.

A dose of physic with cold bandages bound tightly round the joints will reduce them; but they will recur again as soon as work has been recommenced; therefore, no further treatment should be adopted than that of applying a cold flannel bandage with two wet compresses of linen placed immediately on the swellings. Happily, the old practice of puncturing the cysts has long since been condemned as most dangerous and mischievous, so that I need give no warning on this head.

CAPPED HOCKS AND ELBOWS.

Both these enlargements are produced by a swelling of the bursæ mucosæ, and are usually consequent on a bruise or severe blow.

Kicking in the stable is the most prolific cause of capped hocks, and when they become of a great size they are very unsightly.

The treatment consists in allaying the inflammation, and afterwards reducing the swelling by applying biniodide of mercury, as well as preventing a recurrence of the mischief by the application of a common buckled dog collar around the pastern joint, and attaching thereto about twelve inches of a heavy iron chain, which by bruising the legs when the horse kicks will prevent a recurrence of the habit.

A lotion consisting of tincture of arnica of the strength of two ounces to the pint of water will be found beneficial; but a lotion composed of equal parts of white wine vinegar, spirits of turpentine, and olive oil, is generally the most efficacious application in severe cases. It should be rubbed in morning and evening for about two minutes, and persisted in until the enlargement is reduced. This reduction may, and often does, take a considerable time, and occasionally baffles all the skill of the veterinary surgeon; but these are only extreme cases, and are not sufficiently numerous to deter owners from giving the above-named treatment a thorough trial.

CHAPTER VIII.

DISEASES OF BONE.

Bones must be considered as a living texture, being well furnished with all the adjuncts of vitality. Some anatomists have denied the existence of nerves, but the existence of pain in bones is a sufficient proof of the existence of nerves; accordingly, bones are liable to various diseases, such as inflammation, suppuration, and mortification. The former leads to an increased and morbid growth of bone which leads to various complications, such as union of bones in joints, undue pressure on ligaments, nerves, &c., both of which cause lameness.

BONE SPAVIN.

Low-bred horses which are accustomed to draw or carry heavy weights are usually afflicted with this disease. It consists in increased growth of bone on the external surfaces of the inner side of the bones—usually the scaphoid and cuneiform—of the hock. It is generally met with in horses which stand with their hocks close together, which no doubt arises from their being subjected to greater strain.

The symptoms of spavin are an unnatural formation of bone, usually in one of the hocks, a stiff dragging action of the hind leg—the toe generally being dragged along the ground, instead of being lifted boldly over it, by which means the toe of the hind shoe will be found to be worn unduly. The greatest care should nevertheless be exercised before determining the existence of spavin. Both the hocks should be carefully compared —each from precisely the same site—and this examination will occupy a long time; since it is most difficult to get the horse to place both his legs in the same position, and unless they are both in the same position the most experienced eye often fails to detect the existence of a spavin, and far oftener succeeds in detecting an imaginary spavin; which has ruined the reputation of more professional men than any other false prognosis. Unfortunately, when the case is a difficult one to decide, many professional men adopt the phrase 'incipient spavin,' as a sort of umbrage for their ignorance; but such cunning rarely ever has the effect of satisfying an intelligent owner.

Very many hocks are formed with bones having an excessive protuberance, which is perfectly natural, and will be found to exist equally on both hocks; but nevertheless hocks with this formation are rarely ever passed by the military veterinary surgeons, whose singular judgment on this head has frequently caused much disappointment and annoyance.

Some of the soundest and best hunters have been thus formed; and, therefore, unless lameness exists at the time of examination in one or both of the hocks, it is most unjustifiable ignorance to reject the horse as unsound.

Dealers have a very expressive phrase for small spavins—'*rough hocks*'—which most clearly defines the existence of *unnatural* and *uneven* growths of bone.

The treatment should consist of cooling diet, a dose of physic, and absolute rest for two or three weeks; when, if the spavin appears not to have increased, and if no inflammation exists, which will be discovered by the horse going sound when led out, a second dose of physic may be administered, and the hocks fired as soon as the action of the physic has subsided; after which a rest of at least three months must be allowed.

I do not mean to assert that this treatment will be sure to effect a cure or anything of the kind; for I do not believe that more than one case in ten is ever cured; but such treatment has the merit of being humane, since it abates the inflammation, and checks the deposit of bone.

All manner of barbarous remedies for spavin have been called into play, such as the insertion of a seton under the skin, and immediately over the exostosis, so as to produce irritation and sloughing of bone; the application of sulphuric acid; and some of the old school of farriers have gone so far as to chip off the spavin with a chisel. All these courses of treatment have more frequently produced inordinate inflammation and anchylosis of the joint, than they have been attended with successful results; and no treatment has up to the present time been found equal to firing, when the irons have been properly heated, and the system properly cooled.

SPLINTS.

A morbid growth of bone from the canon bone is termed a splint, and is most frequently met with inside of the fore leg, and on the outside of the hind, which fact has led many to assume that disease of the artery must be the predisposing cause; but be this as it may, there can be but little doubt but that concussion is the exciting cause. If the growth of bone be extensive, and form too rapidly to admit of the periosteum being able to adapt itself to the distention, great pain and inflammation will be the result, or, if the splint interfere with and press on any of the ligaments or tendons, the inflammation will be sufficient to cause lameness. In these cases cooling and lowering treatment must be adopted, with entire rest until the inflammation has ceased, when the hair should be cut off immediately above and around the splint, and biniodide of mercury rubbed in, and the dressing repeated, if necessary, once a fortnight.

In slight cases of splint, where the growth of bones forms slowly and causes little or no inflammation, no treatment is necessary.

RINGBONE.

Ringbone consists in a morbid growth of bone round the circle of the coronet, involving very frequently the pastern bones as well.

It is usually apparent to the eye, and very tender when touched. It is caused by concussion, or by some external injury, such as in double harness one horse occasionally stepping on the other's coronet when turning. Ringbones are met with in the hind as well as the fore legs, and if the growth of bone is extensive, it renders the joints anchylose, or causes unition.

The treatment should consist in reducing the inflammation as quickly as possible by means of cold swabs applied to the coronet with the addition of cooling treatment, and after having sufficiently removed the inflammation, and otherwise prepared the horse for firing, the operation should be performed and the horse thrown by for three months.

OSSIFICATION OF THE KNEE.

This more frequently occurs than is generally supposed, and when forming causes intense pain and lameness. It usually occurs on the lateral border of the inferior head of the radius or forearm. No treatment is advisable, since joints are very liable to take up violent inflammation, resulting in anchylosis, if subjected to powerful blisters. A little rest and cooling diet will be sufficient to allay the inflammation.

CHAPTER IX.
DISEASES OF THE FOOT.

The foot of the horse is subject to numerous severe diseases, and, indeed, this is not to be wondered at, when it is considered that the foot has to bear all the weight and concussion of the whole frame on hard and unyielding roads, at all kinds of paces. They have, too, to withstand the injurious effects of bad shoeing, in addition to which, they are frequently defective in formation naturally.

The effects of standing throughout the day in the stable, whereby the vessels of the feet—which are not furnished with valves—become inactive and well-nigh congested, are very injurious, and very frequently lay the seeds of acute diseases.

CORNS.

Corns are the result of pressure on the sole of the foot, whereby the blood-vessels are ruptured, giving rise to a morbid secretion, which, if allowed to continue, will render the corn well-nigh incurable.

The treatment will consist in removing the pressure and stimulating the sole to secrete a healthy deposit of horn, by means of the application of oil of turpentine and spirits of wine—equal parts of each, after having cut out the corn with the buttress.

This dressing should be applied for three consecutive days, when the horse should be shod with a leathern sole of the strongest hide, and the hoof should be stuffed with tow, saturated with the above dressing. This will enable the horse to resume moderate work without injury to the corn. Corns most frequently arise from shoes being left on too long, whereby the inner heel of the shoe works in and presses on the sole between the crust and the bars.

SANDCRACK.

Sandcrack consists in a separation of the fibres of the hoof, owing to a want of gelatinous secretion, thus causing fissures or cracks, which sometimes are so extensive as to admit of the introduction of extraneous substances, which cause violent inflammation and sometimes even a morbid growth of the sensitive laminæ, and thus severe lameness is the result.

This disease is said to be limited to hot and dry districts entirely; but I have known as many severe cases on swamps and lowland meadows, as in upland dry pastures, and I am disposed to think that the predisposing and exciting causes are constitutional. The treatment should consist in cutting the edges of the cracks with a knife until the crust is thinned so as to be flexible, a poultice should then be applied for two days; after which the whole crust must be dressed with some stimulating application, which should be continued for some months. The best ointment consists of equal portions of grease and oil of turpentine for the first month, after which the turpentine should be considerably diminished. The horse should have his shoes removed entirely, and be put to stand on a deep bed of tan, fresh from the tanner's yard. Tan can be procured anywhere, and is the only proper material for litter when the hoof is thus diseased.

THRUSH.

Thrush proceeds from various causes, but inflammation of the frog is the immediate cause. Some horses have very soft frogs, which will become diseased by the application of cow-dung as a stopping, and contact with straw saturated with urine, which causes irritation to the sensitive frog, which contracts a diseased secretion which exudes through the cleft of the frog; which, if allowed to go on, will assume an ulcerative form, which will most probably terminate in canker. This kind of thrush is best treated by carefully avoiding the exciting cause by strict attention to providing dry litter, as well as by applying a lotion consisting of two scruples of chloride of zinc to the half-pint of water, three times daily. When thrush results from plethora, cooling diet and alteratives should be given, and the frog dressed with common tar; and if the secretion does not abate, the chloride of zinc lotion should be tried.

When either fever in the feet or navicular disease gives rise to thrush, the cleft of the frog must be left free, and the exciting causes treated as recommended hereafter. A horse with a thrush should not be ridden without knee-caps; for if he bruise the frog, he will generally fall and cut his knees severely.

CANKER.

Canker consists in ulceration of the sensitive frog, involving the sole very frequently. It is the result of severe constitutional derangement, such as a severe thrush, cracked heels, or grease, and is most common amongst cart horses, whose feet are never properly cleaned and attended to; and are generally allowed to stand for days and weeks on litter saturated with urine, which, by continuing the irritation during an attack of thrush, results in canker being established. Any inflammatory attack in the feet will produce this disease; but it must be considered as a secondary and not as a primary disease in general practice.

The discharge will be usually thin and very offensive, and the horn of the sole will break away and separate, when the extent of the mischief may be readily ascertained.

I had to treat a very severe case of canker, a few years ago, and after four months of careful treatment the horse recovered the use of his foot entirely. The case was that of a cart horse, and resulting from a neglected thrush of long standing. I first used emollient and cold poultices, which caused several fissures of the sole, and, by softening the horn, enabled it to be removed with ease. The fungoid growths were excessive, and the discharge unusually offensive. I discontinued the use of emollient poultices immediately the horn was removed, and substituted for them a strong and tough 'sock,' made of stout bag material, armed with several compresses of linen under the sole, soaked in a lotion consisting of chloride of zinc, of the strength of two scruples to the eight ounces of water for the first three weeks, and increasing the amount to four scruples during the last thirteen weeks, giving at the same time liberal but not heating diet, and being exceedingly careful that dry litter was always plentifully supplied after the first two months. I dressed the sole twice a week, and had the 'sock' well dried and warmed by the fire previously to its application; and on two or three occasions to remove excessive fungoid excrescences, it was necessary to use a strong caustic, which I deemed preferable to the use of the knife; but this should never be made use of without the supervision of a professional man. Subsequently healthy granulations, succeeded by a secretion of firm horn, took place, and a cure was effected.

The foot, however, was much altered in shape, but continued perfectly sound during four years of severe work.

QUITTOR.

This, like the former disease, is usually a secondary disease, resulting from inflammation caused by some violence or primary affection. It consists in an internal abscess of the foot, forming in sinuses.

The parts surrounding the os coronæ are generally enlarged and puffy, and hot and tender to the touch, followed, unless relieved, by a bursting of one of the abscesses at the superior border of the hoof, from which an offensive and rather thin discharge exudes.

The treatment should consist in liberal but not heating food. A free incision must be made into the abscess, for the destruction of parts by ulceration will be thus prevented; after which probes must be made use of to ascertain the extent of the injury. If synovia be apparent it will be an unfavourable sign; but in two cases under my treatment, when synovia was present, the horses became sound and resumed their work (farm work) after six months' treatment, without in any way 'favouring' the foot that had been diseased. The sinuses ascertained, either probes or bougies smeared with corrosive sublimate should be inserted, and linseed poultices applied every three hours; and if this treatment be not sufficient to bring about a sloughing of the quittor, the actual cautery must be resorted to, in which case the horse must be cast, or otherwise effectually secured.

NAVICULAR DISEASE.

Nearly every kind of foot lameness is laid to the charge of this disease. Some men adopt the only safe decision of "foot lameness," while others, less wise and prudent, presumptuously and dogmatically adopt 'navicular disease,' as if it were the only disease known to affect the foot of the horse.

It consists in :—first, inflammation of the synovial capsule of the navicular joint, resulting from inflammation of the perforans tendon, which passes under the navicular, and is attached to the pedal bone. It is met with in the very best and strongest-looking feet, and the degree of lameness occasioned by it is very variable. When ulceration occurs the synovial capsule is absorbed, and the tendon comes into contact with the bone. The horse will usually rest the affected foot when standing at his ease. He will be much more lame on leaving than on returning to the stable, the friction of the parts giving rise to a temporary secretion of synovia. When the disease is at all advanced, all treatment will be hopeless; but, in the early stages of the disease, bleeding at the toe, followed by emollient poultices, will be found beneficial, when combined with rest in a roomy and cool box, well littered with fresh tan. The insertion of setons through the elastic frog, as well as neurotomy, used to be more in vogue than at present. This disease is easily distinguished from laminitis by the horse '*walking*' perfectly sound.

A hunter or steeplechaser affected with this disease

need not be despaired of, as they will go over soft ground perfectly well and soundly. Only they should be ridden to and from cover at a pace not exceeding a walk. Indeed, on a road, no horse affected with navicular disease should be ridden at a greater speed than a walk, since more or less pain will be occasioned by the concussion.

FOUNDER, FEVER IN THE FEET, OR LAMINITIS.

This disease consists in inflammation of the laminæ and its adjacent parts of the foot. It is caused by continued exertion on hard ground, straining the crust beyond its powers; but the most frequent cause is an injury to the knee or shoulder of the horse, on account of which he is fearful of lying down, and thus the continuance of an upright position causes too severe a strain of the sensitive laminæ. In this case a lengthened rest after the cause has subsided, on puddled clay during the daytime, with a plentiful litter at night, will be absolutely necessary to effect a permanent cure. But where the horse is in training and has to continue his work, his feet should be placed into two buckets of *cool* water after coming in from exercise, and allowed to remain there so long as the horse feels disposed to maintain the same position. I have more than once seen horses neigh for the buckets and place their feet hurriedly into them of their own accord immediately they were placed before them. The softening of the hoof by water, thereby causing increased pliability of the crust, diminishes the pain occasioned by the want of room for the expansion of the blood-vessels consequent on inflammation. The symptoms will be marked by the horse standing with his hind legs in a much more forward position than usual, for the purpose of relieving his fore feet of their proper proportion of weight. If the foot be felt it will be discovered to have an unusual degree of heat, and if pressed or squeezed by a pair of pincers an unusual *flinching* will be perceptible. On running him out, the weight will be thrown principally on the heels—a marked contrast to the symptoms of navicular disease, in which the *toes* are almost the only parts of the feet placed on the ground when the horse trots. Bleeding is certainly not advisable where the inflammation is not very acute; since it weakens the foot so much that it will be unfit for hard work for many weeks afterwards.

The food should consist of bran mashes and a little hay; and, although a violent purge should be avoided when the inflammation runs very high, laxatives should be freely administered; the best dose being two drachms of emetic tartar and half an ounce of nitre, given every day for a week. In severe and long-continued cases of this disease, the coffin bone becomes separated from its attachments and is forced downwards by being unable to withstand the weight, after being deprived of its proper support, and leads to convexity of the sole, which I will consider under the head of—

PUMICED FEET.

Pumiced feet consist in a convex growth of the soles, and are sometimes attended with great 'flinching' or lameness as the horse receives any pressure on the sole. No treatment is of any avail save and except some mechanical contrivance. The object in view must be that of removing as much pressure as possible from the sole. To effect this let the shoes be wrought with 'a concave seat;' i.e. with two thirds of the inner portion of the shoe bevelled off to prevent pressure on the sole. Thus the shoes can be made thicker or deeper than usual without increasing the weight very materially, which will still more elevate the sole. Then let a strong piece of leather be placed over the sole and nailed on with the shoe very carefully; because the crust of the hoof in such cases is always very weak and brittle. This done, let the foot be stuffed with tow, smeared with tar and oil of turpentine, to stimulate the secretion of horn.

CHAPTER X.
ACCIDENTS.

WOUNDS FROM STUBS, STAKES, ETC.

In all cases of wounds from stubs, stakes, iron or wooden spikes, and other materials with blunt edges, laceration of membranes, blood-vessels, &c., must take place; and, therefore, the object must be to avoid an immediate closing or healing of the lips of the wound, or, as it is termed, 'union by first intention.'

In all cases of lacerated or torn vessels, suppuration is unavoidable; but because it is unavoidable it is not altogether desirable that it should be promoted, because it may assume dimensions at once unnecessary and dangerous.

If the wound be larger than a free egress for the hæmorrhage seems to warrant, one or two sutures or stitches should be made in the wound. The use of sutures is especially desirable where the skin is torn back in large flaps, as is often the case in wounds under the chest and abdomen; for which the interrupted suture or single stitch tied is the most convenient method; since, if the aperture of the wound be not large enough, it may be enlarged by cutting one of the stitches, without in any way disturbing the whole. Great care should be taken, however, to remove all extraneous substances previously to the insertion of sutures. Great care should be taken that the sutures be not drawn too tight—because the tighter they are drawn the sooner will they slough away; indeed, sutures rarely remain more than five or six days however artistically applied. Wounds of any extent are usually attended by constitutional disturbance—most frequently by symptomatic fever, but sometimes by lockjaw or tetanus. Wounds occurring in debilitated constitutions assume a species of mortification usually known by the name of gangrene. In all wounds by a sharp cutting instrument, such as a scythe, knife, &c., the bleeding must be first checked, and a reunion of the lips of the wound affected by sutures or compression. There is no application so good as lint soaked in tepid water, but all healing ointments and suchlike filth should be carefully avoided. The tendency of parts of the body to effect reunion are very remarkable. Indeed, parts which have been completely severed have been successfully united. I recollect a remarkable instance of this in a prize fight, where the lower half of the ear of one of the combatants was cut so severely as to retain connection with the upper portion of the ear only by a small piece of skin, which one of the seconds severed entirely, and putting the excised portion of the ear in his pocket, thought nothing of it until after the termination of the fight, when, as a joke, he attempted to reunite the severed portion of the ear merely by the aid of a little common sticking-plaster. The ear speedily reunited, and the pugilist escaped this additional disfigurement.

Great attention, in the treatment of wounds, should be paid to the state of the health at the time: if the wound does not suppurate favourably, and the discharge is profuse, a liberal diet, consisting of beans, linseed, and old oats, should be given, together with bark and aniseed powders.

In all wounds, where the small intestines protrude in consequence, they must be returned as quickly as possible into the cavity of the abdomen; for the mere displacement of the viscera is very frequently attended with fatal consequences.

If great difficulty is experienced in returning them, an attempt at the reduction of the large intestines should be made by emptying them by means of a clyster, which will usually render the operation an easy one: but in all cases where the intestines are smeared with dirt, dust, &c., they must be carefully sponged previously to being returned into the cavity; the best wash being equal parts of new milk and tepid water. For returning the intestines the use of the forefingers is most desirable—those of the one hand being used to prevent the portion returned from protruding again, while those of the other hand introduce another portion, and so on until the whole is properly returned. The intestines should be inserted in a straight direction into the abdomen, for when inserted in an oblique direction, they are liable to slip between the abdominal muscles and become strangulated. When the intestines are enormously distended with air, it will be necessary to make various small punctures with a needle to lessen their volume sufficiently to render them returnable. For this purpose round, and not flat needles should be used, since the latter would cut the fibres; but this should not be resorted to until all other means have failed, since the amount of inflammation caused by their insertion will be very great, and will be attended with extreme danger. Everything that tends to increase inflammation of the intestines should be carefully avoided; for in all wounds of the abdomen the inflammation of the peritoneum is excessive. The inflammation must be checked by bleeding, cooling applications, and laxative medicines, such as linseed oil, &c., with linseed and bran mashes as the sole food. After the return of the intestines the edges of the wound must be brought together, and as many sutures as necessary inserted, in addition to which suitable compresses and bandages will be required to retain the position of the viscera.

It is but seldom that horses can be kept in a favourable position for the successful treatment of wounds of the abdomen; and to this more than to any other cause I am inclined to attribute the few instances there are of successful treatment.

INJURIES TO THE EYE.

It very frequently happens that extraneous matter becomes lodged on the surface, or entangled in the superficial tissues, or the cellular and fatty matters surrounding the eyeball. The symptoms are marked by great impatience of light and great pain on moving the lids.

If the extraneous matter be merely dust or sand, it may be washed away by means of a syringe; but if it be of a sharp nature, such as glass, flint, or metal, it must be instantly removed. If the lids be fully opened in a good light the existence of foreign matter can be readily seen and removed. A lead pencil or the corner of a silk handkerchief should be used for removing the foreign matter. This should be done without delay, in order to avert the inflammatory action and ulceration, always consequent on injuries to the cornea.

In all wounds of the conjunctiva and surface of the eye, where no extraneous matter has become retained, lowering treatment, abstraction of blood from the facial vein, with continual application of cold spring water to ward off vascular excitement, are to be recommended. Wounds, however, of the centre of the cornea of considerable size, involving the internal structure of the organ, are necessarily fatal to the vision.

POLL EVIL.

Poll evil consists in an abscess on or behind the prominent ridge between the ears, and is caused by knocking the head violently against a low beam, or by lifting the head suddenly when eating up grains that have dropped from the manger, and striking it against the iron border. It sometimes is even produced by violent blows from the butt-end of a heavy hunting-whip, which some inhuman brutes are fond of using.

A painful swelling will be the result of the inflammation, which should be rubbed with biniodide of mercury, to bring about development of the abscess, which may be ascertained by the softness of the swelling, as well as by its fluctuation. For fear of the horse moving suddenly on feeling the knife, a sharp seton needle should be inserted from the centre of the abscess in an oblique direction: and if the abscess be immediately in the centre of the prominent ridge, or immediately over the spinal chord, insert two setons, one from the centre of the abscess to the left, and the other from the centre of the abscess to the right side. If this disease is neglected it will make terrible ravages in all directions along the cervical vertebræ, &c.; and, indeed, in some instances the spinal chord and brain have been seriously affected.

FISTULOUS WITHERS.

A fistula of the withers is generally the consequence of a common saddle gall which has been neglected. It sometimes burrows down among the muscles between the shoulder blade and the ribs, and has been known to penetrate to the sternum.

Sometimes the bones or the spines of the dorsal

vertebræ become diseased; in which cases a long and narrow knife must be passed up the sinus or pipe leading to the diseased bone, and outwards through the skin along its whole length, when the use of some escharotic lotion will be necessary. If the sinuses are of great length, long seton needles should be passed through them, and depending orifices should be made in the most convenient spot. The strength of the lotion of chloride of zinc should vary in proportion to the exigencies of the case—from one to four scruples to the pint of water.

BROKEN KNEES.

This is an accident pretty sure to fall to the lot of every owner of horses at some time or other, and it is therefore necessary that every horseman and groom should be equal to its treatment in every stage. In slight cases of broken knees when the cut is not deep the treatment should consist in well washing the wound, so as to remove all irritating and extraneous substances, and then getting the horse into a stable, and bathing the knees in warm water for an hour, after which apply a lint compress soaked in a solution of arnica and warm water—of the strength of one part of tincture of arnica to thirty parts of water—and over this tie some oiled silk. Let this be repeated for the three or four following days, and the horse's health carefully attended to, when all will be well. If, however, any proud flesh show itself, it should be burnt down by the application of bluestone. When the interior of the knee joint is penetrated, the synovia will escape, and may readily be seen on the surface of the wound. The wound should be well sponged, and immediately closed, and unition brought about if possible, and the most active measures taken to allay all inflammatory symptoms—by bran mashes, physicking, &c. Great care should also be taken that he be racked up, or he will endeavour to lie down, and not only reopen the wound, but perhaps admit extraneous substances. The most severe case that came under my notice was that of a rather undersized carthorse, which fell on coming down a hill, with thirty cwt. of bricks behind her, in a high two-wheeled cart; there was a leading horse attached to the shafts, which jumped forward immediately it heard the scuffle, and dragged the poor beast on its knees until the flesh and ligaments were completely torn away from the joints. She was brought to me about two hours after the occurrence, having walked seven miles from the place where the accident occurred. I had her racked up, sponged her knees softly, closed up the joint, and applied a lotion of chloride of zinc (of the strength of one drachm to the pint of water) with a feather. I continued this application for six weeks, about three times a day, after which the wounds healed satisfactorily; and although the scars are large, she has had the full use of her joints, and has been in hard work for three years since the occurrence. I may here say, that, owing to the amount of fatigue the mare had gone through, I did not deem it prudent to have recourse to physic and lowering treatment, but, on the contrary, I ordered liberal diet and occasional alteratives. It will never tend to any desirable results to reduce the system overmuch in severe cases of penetrated joints, since a certain amount of inflammation is necessary to the healing of the wound. The use of slings in such cases, where practicable, is much to be recommended; since the pain incurred by standing for days in the same position must, when the animal is worn out with fatigue, be inexpressibly irksome. The use of slings tends to lessen the high degree of fever which usually attacks horses which are kept on their legs too long. On this too much importance cannot be placed, for a favourable termination of a penetrated joint mainly depends on the *prevention* of a high state of inflammation. As I have said before, a moderate vascularity and redness in the integuments is to be desired; but inflammation of the capsular ligament usually leads to the formation of abscesses, and finally anchylosis, or stiffness of the joint. There is always a great derangement of the digestive organs in such cases, which is best encountered by administering mild purgative balls every other day, such as two drachms of aloes, ginger, and resin, made into one ball until the bowels act moderately.

FRACTURES AND DISLOCATIONS.

It is but very seldom that any effort is made to unite a fracture of the bones of the horse, for, being essentially an animal of labour, he ceases to be useful when any important joint or limb becomes disabled, and, therefore, owners of horses, as a rule, object to being put to the expense consequent on the proper treatment of fractures, with the prospect of having an almost useless animal at the termination of it. In all cases, therefore, of fractures of the skull, arm-bone, thigh, shoulder blade, elbow, canon bone, pastern and coffin bones, patella, and navicular bones, the horse, unless very valuable as a stallion or brood mare, should be destroyed. But cases of fractured ribs, jawbones, and face, all admit of a perfect cure if treated properly.

When the face is fractured, each piece of fractured bone should be removed by making an incision in, and laying back, the skin. This being done, the skin should be once more brought together, and, if necessary, supported by plugging the nostrils. When the jawbone is fractured, which frequently happens where cart-horses are turned out at grass with their shoes on, the bone must be set, and the jawbones kept in this position by means of straps and bandages. The horse must be fed on linseed and oatmeal gruel for some time.

In fractures of the ribs, where the bone presses on the lungs or other internal organs of importance, little or nothing can be done ; but, in cases of simple fracture, the edges of the bones should be united by applying a bandage of sufficient tightness round the trunk; which should be suffered to remain on for some time, and a cure will be effected. Fractures of the prominent head of the haunch bone, which are occasioned by horses being allowed to rush out of a narrow stable door, crashing the bone against the posts, usually unite without the aid of surgical treatment. Nevertheless, it is a great eyesore as the head of the bone becomes retracted, and the horse's frame will present an unevenness termed by horsemen *hipped*. I have seen one first-class hipped hunter, but usually there is an evident weakness in the action. Dislocation of the patella sometimes occurs, and is marked by the horse throwing upwards and outwards the hind leg with a sort of sweep when turning over in the stable, as if the limb did not belong to him and was not under his control. No treatment is of any use, since it recurs so frequently after being properly replaced.

WOUNDS OF THE FOOT.

These are generally brought about by pricks in shoeing, through the nails being improperly directed; or by treading, when the sole has been recently thinned down, on some sharp substance, as a sharp oak-stub, an iron spike, nail, glass bottles, &c. If the frog be punctured, it will not be of so much importance, and must be treated by the foreign substance being removed carefully, and a pledget of tow smeared in tar inserted. Also if the laminæ or sides of the foot are wounded, either by prick in shoeing, or in any other manner, a reduction of inflammation, and removal of the cause, will soon bring about a cure.

Where, however, the centre of the sole is cut through, and the capsular ligament or coffin bone injured, the case must be considered as a very serious one, and active measures resorted to for prevention of inflammation, suppuration, &c. First cut away the sole and enlarge the orifice of the wound as much as is necessary, then bleed freely at the toe, and insert some lint soaked in chloride of zinc, of the strength of one scruple to the pint of water, into the wound. A strong leathern shoe with two soles should be then buckled round the hoof, and the horse kept perfectly still. Cold swabs should be applied above the leathern shoe and around the pasterns, and a lowering diet, with a mild purge, administered.

OVERREACH.

This is occasioned by the horse bringing the hind foot too quickly on the fore. Sometimes the surface is merely cut, but at others it is severely bruised as well.

A due regard must be had to the nature of the injury, before commencing any treatment.

If the integuments be merely cut, the wound should be washed carefully, and then touched with Friar's balsam; after which, the lips of the wound should be immediately closed, and adhesive plaster applied to keep them in their position. If the wound, however, gives evidence of a severe bruise, inflammation and suppuration must inevitably occur.

In this case, apply, after having well cleansed the

wound, some lint compresses soaked in a solution of chloride of zinc, of the strength of one scruple to the pint of water, and continue this treatment until a cure is effected.

SPEEDY CUT.

If the skin be not broken, and the parts merely bruised, apply some lint compresses, soaked in a solution of one part of tincture of arnica to six parts of cold water, and over this tie some oiled silk. Never again, unless there was sufficient cause for the horse hitting his leg, allow him to go out without a regular speedy-cutting boot, padded with india rubber.

STRAINS.

Notwithstanding all that has been asserted to the contrary, there can be no doubt that when a muscle, tendon, or ligament is said to be strained, it has really been stretched beyond its proper limits. The fibres of the muscles, tendons, &c., are undoubtedly ruptured in addition, and an extravasation of blood and serum brought about during the violence. And this is what gives rise to the tumefaction and tenderness consequent on a strain.

STRAIN OF THE SHOULDER.

It is but very seldom that horses are strained in the shoulder; but when it does occur, it is easily detected by any careful observer, by the intense pain it gives the horse when extending the limb of his own accord, or on its being extended by manual force; and when the strain is very severe, the toe will be dragged along the ground, and the horse will hop on the other leg. No treatment is of any avail, but entire rest followed by gentle exercise.

The injury may exist in either the muscles or ligamentous attachments; but in which of the two, it will be impossible to ascertain.

Where, however, the injury lies in the triceps extensor brachii—the large bulging muscle above the arm—the heat and swelling will be very evident, and its treatment will be similar to that of any other strain: viz. a reduction of the inflammation, followed by rest and counter-irritation. Horses are very liable to this injury when galloping at great speed down hill; and on some training grounds it is of frequent occurrence.

STRAIN OF THE BACK AND LOINS.

Strained, or, as it is termed by horsemen, 'ricked back,' is marked by a stiffness and soreness of the muscles along the back and loins. It occurs usually by the horse dropping his hind legs into a ditch or drain, having at the same time a heavy weight on him. The treatment must consist of entire rest, physicking, and lowering diet. The back and loins should be well fomented by dipping flannel cloths in hot water and arnica, of the strength of one part of arnica to six parts of hot water, and applying them all along the back and loins. This treatment must be persevered in for two or three days; after which, mustard poultices should be applied every two days for a fortnight, and the rest of the treatment should be left to time alone. Such horses should be put to harness work, at which they may be useful for very many years; but, if used for saddle work, a recurrence of the injury is sure to take place. If it is ascertained by the existence of paralysis of the hind limbs that the spinal chord is injured, the animal should be destroyed.

STRAIN OF THE BACK-SINEWS, AND RUPTURE OF THE SHEATH OF THE TENDONS.

This injury is the bugbear of all trainers and hard riders, and is perfectly certain to happen to all horses which are used for racing purposes, sooner or later. When the accident occurs, the sheath of tendons is much tumefied and exquisitely tender, and great lameness is caused: indeed, I have seen a horse take half an hour to walk three hundred yards immediately after its occurrence.

In slight cases, heat, tenderness, and other evidences of inflammation resulting from strain may be readily discovered, together with a tenderness or slight lameness when in motion, and it is at this stage that treatment will be of avail in preventing the greater injury of actual rupture of the ligamentous attachments to the tendons. The treatment in either case should consist of removing all corn, and giving a mild purging ball, and applying lint compresses soaked in arnica and water—one part of arnica to twelve of water—and enveloped with oiled silk. A high-heeled shoe should be fitted on the foot to prevent extension of the sheath of the tendons. In about one month or six weeks, when the inflammation has subsided, repeated blisterings with biniodide of mercury, or firing, must be resorted to. The sheath of the tendons, however, will always present an enlarged or bowed appearance.

BREAKING DOWN, OR RUPTURE OF THE SUSPENSORY LIGAMENTS.

Rupture of the suspensory ligament rarely happens to any but the racehorse or steeple-chaser; and when it does occur, the racing career of its victim is at an end.

It consists in a rupture of the suspensory ligament, usually immediately above the fetlock joint, which generally gives way so much as to reach the ground, and causes such severe pain that the horse will hop back to the stable on three legs as best he can. The lotion recommended for the preceding injury should be used until all inflammation has abated, when the leg should be blistered with biniodide of mercury, and fired in one month's time from the period of the action of the blister.

For all fast work the horse will be utterly useless; but for farm work, and breeding purposes, his services may be of as much value as before the occurrence of the accident. Some poor wretches that have broken down, are sold by their hard-hearted masters to be butchered in hansom cabs over hard pavement, from morning till night, so long as their vital powers are in existence, who, but for this accident, might still be enjoying all the comforts and attention of the racing stables.

CURB.

It is commonly asserted that horses with 'sickle hocks' are more liable to this strain than others differently formed. And so no doubt they are; but not to the extent generally supposed.

A curb consists in a strain or extension of the ligaments at the head of the splint bone of the shank, or about six inches below the point of the hock. It results from jumping into a bog or ditch, rearing or galloping up a steep hill, &c., and usually occurs between the second and fifth year, and most frequently while the process of breaking is going on. If the strain be severe, the horse will limp soon after the extension of the ligaments has taken place, and on the next morning considerable swelling and tumefaction will take place with or without much lameness.

A high-heeled shoe should be immediately fitted on the foot of the injured limb, and cold lotions applied until the swelling subsides; a dose of physic should be administered with proper preparation, and immediately after its action, the blister composed of biniodide of mercury should be rubbed in: or what is still better—if applied by a competent person—corrosive sublimate dissolved in spirits of wine, applied with a sponge, after having wetted the adjacent parts with pure water to prevent an extended action of the blister. This admirable remedy must, however, be most cautiously used, or a blemish will be the result.

As soon as the action of the blister has subsided, gentle work should be given on level ground, which will materially promote absorption, and strengthen the ligaments.

EPIDEMIC FEVER.

In the present year (1865), in the month of January, the large towns have been peculiarly afflicted with this disease amongst horses of all denominations, whether in high or low condition.

The stages of the disease were very rapid and the symptoms very marked.

The first symptoms are general dulness, entire loss of appetite, great prostration of strength, rapid respiration, and very short and evidently painful cough about three or four times in the twenty-four hours, a greatly accelerated pulse of about 100, with entire absence of running at the nose, and cold and chilly ears and limbs, which are the usual accompaniments of all fevers.

It seems to be a severe form of low fever, in which the lungs are chiefly involved. I had three very severe cases to deal with, in which the pulse continued at 100 for no less than four days, with great prostration of strength and confined bowels. I administered two ounces of nitrous ether, with two drachms of camphor, in a pint of warm water or ale every four hours—putting two drachms of emetic tartar and an ounce of peruvian bark in a small feed of steamed bran and oats every evening —allowing as much hay as they would eat. There was no change up to the fifth day, after which the horses began to throw off the fever, recovered their appetites in some degree, and no further treatment was necessary.

The languor lasted about a week afterwards, during which an ounce of bark and aniseed was mixed with the feed every night,—the emetic tartar discontinued, and in four weeks from the disease showing itself the horses were at work again.

The course of the disease, however, was extremely rapid in many cases, and several healthy horses in fine condition fell victims to its ravages in three or four days; and in all the cases with which I was acquainted unless resolution occurred within five or six days the case proved fatal.

Bleeding did not answer in one single case that came to my knowledge; and in two cases where it was resorted to, dropsy of the chest intervened in a few days. Blistering, also, seemed to set up undue inflammation, and to be productive of more harm than good, in accelerating both the pulse and the breathing in an inordinate degree; and moreover, it prevented the horses from lying down as much as they otherwise would have done, and consequently their strength failed them more rapidly.

It matters little where the horse be placed—whether in a stall or loose box, so long as the air be pure and dry; since he evinces no desire to take any kind of exercise when labouring under this disease.

CHAPTER XI.

ADVICE TO GROOMS.

The great failing of all grooms borders on something nearly akin to extravagance, and extreme carelessness as to the limits of their masters' pockets.

I am well aware that in nine cases out of ten, the urgent touting for orders by saddlers, and dealers in oats, beans, hay, straw, &c., are too much for the nerves of most grooms to withstand, if they have not their masters' interests at heart.

If any advice, any argument of mine can succeed in partially putting an end to this wanton combination of servants and tradesmen against their employers, it is my duty as an honest man to urge upon grooms in general the necessity of forsaking the continuance of a system of dishonest pilfering, that is more heartless and unjustifiable than robbery on the highway.

I am well aware—and I have repeatedly heard stud grooms boast—that their masters' consent to orders for fodder, saddlery, &c., never once entered their heads; and that they were not going to admit of being interfered with in the requirements of the stable; or in other words, that they could not submit to the indignity of their masters' controlling their own affairs.

Really, such foolish conduct is little short of a standing danger to grooms as a class.

As surely as fox-hunters and fools were once synonymous terms, so surely will grooms and cheats defy a separate distinction in the opinion of the bulk of society.

Do not think, grooms—and I address you with deep interest—that when your masters or mistresses complain of what their carriage and horses cost them—of the amount of the saddlers' and cornfactors' accounts, that those listeners are all unlearned and fools in stable management. There may chance to be some one or more amongst them who knows better than yourselves, not only what your real expenditure ought to have been, but probably *what it has been.*

For it is no secret how much oats cost, and how much horses are able to consume; nor is it any secret how many brushes, combs, wrappers, and other stable utensils, can be honestly worn out in the course of the year.

Therefore, as often as the subject is mentioned before that person, so often do you run the risk of losing the confidence of your employer, and your own character.

The loss of character is the most serious blow that can be inflicted on a man in any situation of life; but when that man is a servant in a place of trust, it becomes a still more serious calamity.

Enough on the subject of honesty.

I will now say a few words on the subject of duty.

When your employers know nothing of the management of their stables, it is all the more your duty to see that their interests are more sedulously cared for than if they were in full possession of this knowledge, for on this depends your merit as trustworthy servants.

Carelessness, too, is a great fault in such cases.

It is absurd to offer as an excuse for careless habits that your employers do not know whether their equipages are badly turned out or not, and therefore that you feel no concern at their shabby appearance.

Is it reasonable to suppose that your employers would put themselves to enormous stable expenses, if they did not care for the manner in which their equipages were turned out?

In addition to which, your characters are invariably lost—not only amongst gentlemen who know how they ought to be turned out; but also amongst those of your own class, who are always very free in expressing their opinions respecting the character of your turn-out!

You will be sure to earn for yourself the appellation of *gardener,* whenever your name is mentioned.

Next to a badly cleaned horse, nothing looks so abominable as shabby and badly cleaned harness. It gives that sort of *jobbing* appearance to the turn-out that ought to be a cause of shame to any private servant; who, for the most part, takes a just pride in having no more duties imposed upon him than he can faithfully and properly perform.

I am well aware that some grooms have more to do than they can possibly get through properly. And when that is the case, undoubtedly the groom has a very difficult part to play. But here, too, he should be strictly honest.

If he have entered a situation not knowing the extent of the duties he would have to perform, he should at once, after having tried to do as much as he can, proceed to have an interview with either his master or mistress, as the case may be, and respectfully represent that the extent of his work is more than he can possibly get through with due regard to the proper condition of the horses, and their appurtenances, committed to his charge.

And if the employer, from ignorance of stable management, or any other cause, refuse to entertain the justice of the complaint, let him then ask to be permitted to have an interview on the subject with some friend of his employers, who is intimately acquainted with stable duties in all their intricacies. This cannot well be refused. And if it is refused, an appeal to a disinterested third party, for the adjudication of the complaint, cannot be deemed unreasonable nor unbecoming in the servant, and it may lead to a proper adjustment of the labours of the stable; after which, all should go on smoothly.

Next to this, will be the difficulty of putting forward when your horses are overworked, without giving offence. The best mode of proceeding will be to represent that the horses are falling off in their condition, and that you are of opinion that it is on account of working them too hard: and if this explanation is not admitted, a plea respectfully put forward for the opinion of a veterinary surgeon cannot but be entertained.

There is a custom which has now deep root amongst grooms and coachmen at large. I allude to the purchase of horses when the dealer and groom *stand in* as it is termed, about the two most barefaced examples of which came to my knowledge the other day, when the following conversations took place:—

Dealer.—I think that is a pretty good match for your other horse.

Coachman.—Yes. I think he will do; but how about the *sweetener?*

D.—I don't know what you mean. The price of the horse is sixty-five pounds, and I cannot take a farthing less.

C.—Then if you won't allow me anything, I'll not advise my master to buy him; and he won't buy him, unless I recommend him.

D.—Very well. I can't help that. If I give you five pounds, it must come out of your master's pocket—not mine; for I can't afford to lose it. Therefore, if I give you five pounds, I must get seventy pounds for the horse.

C.—Very well. My master shall buy him, and you shall give me five pounds out of the purchase money.

D.—Agreed. (*Aside.*) You damned scoundrel!

In a few days the coachman brought a cheque for seventy pounds; and, on presenting it, received five pounds out of it. The horse turned out no match at all for the other, and the coachman called on the dealer and requested him to take the horse back.

' No,' said the dealer, ' unless you return me the five

sovereigns, I can't give your master the seventy pounds back for the horse!'

This the coachman was unwilling or unable to do; so his master had to put up with a horse utterly unsuited to him, because the coachman and dealer had entered into a conspiracy to defraud him.

I informed the dealer of my opinion of the iniquity of thus entering into a conspiracy with a servant to defraud his master; and his answer was:—

'All the trade do it; and if I do not I cannot sell them a horse. I heartily wish half of us were sent to gaol for it for about six months, and then the custom would soon die out.'

Exactly! here it is:—'All the trade do it!' And not the horse trade only; for in proportion to the amount of the bills at butchers', bakers', grocers', chemists', &c., so are the Christmas presents to the housekeeper large or small; and in precisely the same ratio as that between cornfactors, hay and straw dealers, saddlers and coachmen. But depend on it, ye grooms, who scorn to do in secret what ye would not do openly, however much others may laugh at ye for your sensitive uprightness, ye will be rewarded by the possession of a clear conscience, and your master's benediction:—
'Well done, good and faithful servant!'

In the other case, the groom caught a Tartar with a vengeance.

His master, a wealthy gentleman in London, had, on a previous occasion in the company of a friend, looked over the stables of a noted horse-dealer in the midland counties in search of a first-class hunter, and taken a fancy to a clever weight-carrying horse, for which the sum of one hundred and sixty-five guineas was asked; whereupon he requested time for consideration, which was readily granted by the dealer; and for some few days nothing more was heard of the matter, until about eleven o'clock one morning, a person (who subsequently turned out to be the gentleman's groom) presented himself to the dealer and requested to be allowed to examine the horse—stating at the same time, that the purchase of the horse depended solely on his approval. The request was instantly complied with, and the groom—affecting the air of a professional man—went through a lengthened examination; during which, the dealer retired to his office, where he remained cogitating on the probable chances of selling his horse, until his reverie was broken into by the groom's demand of twenty-five pounds if he effected the sale of the horse; at which, the dealer expressed his most unmeasured indignation, refusing to entertain such a proposal for an instant. Whereupon, the groom once more retired, and commenced a further examination of the horse.

At about six o'clock on the same evening, he once more presented himself to the dealer, and requested the delivery of the horse; at the same time, pulling from his pocket a cheque for the amount from his master, who desired him to deliver it, and bring back the horse with a warranty as to soundness. This the dealer indignantly refused to comply with; stating as his reason, the overweening dishonesty the groom had exhibited, which he had no doubt would be repeated whenever the opportunity presented itself. And as the stables were then shut up, he further refused to deliver the horse until six o'clock on the following morning.

At this the groom exhibited great trepidation—urging, as a reason why the horse should be delivered to him, that his master would expect his arrival with the horse that evening, and that he would most likely lose his situation if he were not to arrive until the following day.

To all of which the dealer turned a deaf ear, and told him that to-morrow morning he might take the horse out of his stables, on presenting a cheque for one hundred and sixty-five pounds; but that he would not so much as warrant the horse alive to such a scoundrel. And accordingly, at six A.M., the cheque was presented and the horse delivered to the groom, who no doubt accounted for the absence of the warranty, and his non-arrival on the previous evening, by falsehood.

However this may be, the dealer heard no more of either master, servant, horse, or warranty, and so ended one of the worst of the many bad instances of dishonesty in grooms.

ON DRIVING.

The first thing required in a good coachman is to sit well up and quite square to his horses; with his chest well forward, and his elbows close to his sides, holding the reins in his left hand in a direct line with his breast-bone, by which means the whole weight and force of his body can at any moment be applied by kicking the foot board, and throwing the shoulders well back, simultaneously.

He should always keep his horses well in hand; so that he may have thorough command of them at whatever pace they are going, which should never—except under extraordinary circumstances—exceed ten miles within the hour. But many carriage horses cannot do so much; and therefore the coachman must be guided by his horses' powers entirely; always keeping them well within their pace, and making them go collectedly, easily, and well; for if they be out-paced they will lose their action, roll about, and present but a slovenly appearance, however neat their appurtenances may be.

A good coachman will never go fast round a corner; for if he does so, the horses will have to scramble, and may cross their legs and come over. A slow and well collected jog-trot is the only pace at which it is safe to turn a sharp corner with a pair of horses. On meeting any carriage or vehicle, it is always desirable to allow as much room as possible; for though a good coachman may be able to guide his own horses to great nicety, this art will avail him nothing, if the driver of the opposing vehicle come dashing along, and allow his horses—either through carelessness or bad driving—to swerve right on to him.

The safest way is to keep in the centre of the road, so as to force the driver meeting you to pull out; and immediately he does so to pull out yourself, so that by both diverging to contrary sides of the road, all will be well; whereas, by maintaining your proper—the left—side throughout, the driver of a vehicle coming along in the centre of the road, seeing what he considers plenty of room, preserves the 'even tenour of his way,' and, drawing it too fine, comes into collision.

The reckless driving of flash cab-drivers and fast young officers, with whom 'going the pace' is everything, should be strictly avoided by the coachman.

There are certain faults and vices which horses contract, such as hugging and lying off from the pole, &c.; which, for the most part, arise from overwork, and are rarely ever met with in private carriage horses, so nothing need be said on this subject.

But there is one vice very common, which may be justly laid to the charge of the coachman, i.e., 'gibbing,' or refusing to start the carriage; which is contracted through the stupidity of the coachman, in either allowing his horses to spring at the collar, or forcing them to do so by the use of his whip. In either case the effect is the same, viz., inability to start the load. For a weight can only be moved by a steady and firm pressure, or what is termed, 'a horse going into his collar quietly.'

I have cured very bad gibbers by sitting on the box perfectly still, without a whip, and allowing the horses to start the load at their pleasure—which they will do rather than stand still for any length of time, unless they have sore shoulders—and then pulling them up again and allowing them to start at their will. If this method be persevered in for a few days, the vice may be conquered effectually; but great care must be taken ever after that the horses are in no way hurried, and also that they do not see or hear the whip, or it will immediately recur again.

Carriage horses should never be reined up too tightly—even when doing short journeys; but when they are kept out for some hours, this practice becomes positively cruel; since the muscles and tendons are kept in the same restrained position, which gives rise to excessive pain and weariness, and very frequently even to paralysis of the laryngeal nerve, and consequently roaring.

The coachman should, in driving either a pair or four-in-hand, give great attention to his horses' mouths, and have his horses properly bitted; for unless they be judiciously bitted the driver can have no control over them, and every yard he drives them must be more or less of grief and pain both to him and them.

It is of almost as much importance to have horses of the same kind of mouths and temperament, as of the same colour, quality, and action, if they are to run together comfortably either in a pair or four-in-hand.

GROOMING.

The first thing to be done, on returning from work, is to take the horse into the stable, and remove all the harness: then tie him up and throw a rug loosely over him. After which take the picker and remove all the dirt, &c., from the inside and outside of the feet into the dung basket. Then take a straw wisp and rub the legs and belly till as much as possible of the filth is removed; and having done this, get two buckets of water and thoroughly cleanse the belly, legs, and feet with the water brush; and if the legs or heels be white, soft soap and washing blue must be used. Next take the sponge and use the other bucket of clean water for sponging down the legs and belly until thoroughly cleansed. The scraper must then be applied to these parts, and as much of the moisture as possible absorbed with the dry sponge; after which both legs and belly must be well rubbed with dry wrappers, and dry flannel bandages applied to all four legs from the coronets to the knees and hocks.

The rug should then be removed, the horse turned round in the stall or box, and well wisped from head to tail until quite dry.

The brush must then be passed briskly over him until the greasy scurf, dirt, &c., be entirely removed; when a damp hay wisp should be used to lay the hair, and give a healthy gloss to the coat, which will be vastly increased by a finishing touch given with the chamois-leather wrapper.

The rugs should now be adjusted, and the horse's eyes, mouth, and nose well sponged and wiped, and his mane and tail properly brushed and combed. He will then be ready for his corn, during the consumption of which he should be left perfectly quiet; after which he will require a bucket of water and a rack full of hay; when the sooner he is bedded up and allowed to rest himself the better. This dressing will take at least one hour and a half for each horse.

No one man can properly clean and take care of a carriage, harness, and pair of horses single-handed—without neglecting either the horses, carriage, or harness—the damage done to which, by neglect, would be far more than the wages of a good strong strapper or helper.

For if the dirt is allowed to dry on the carriage, and the damp to rust the harness, while the groom is cleaning his horses, considerable damage must necessarily be sustained.

I consider that a pair of horses, harness, carriage, &c., will be full work for two men if they do full justice to their master's property.

The morning's grooming, stable cleaning, &c., will take fully three hours, and exercising one hour more. And say that the carriage is absent from the yard about three hours, that the cleaning of the horses will take three hours, the harness two hours, and the carriage two hours and a half, and we shall have a day's labour of fourteen hours and a half—exclusive of time for meals and other numerous additional calls on the coachman's time, such as care of clothing, &c.

It will, therefore, be evident that the care of a carriage and pair of horses is fully as much as two men can accomplish, and that no one man should be required to attempt it.

In the case of saddle horses and hunters, I consider that one man can take care of two horses and their appurtenances, and give them the usual amount of exercise; viz., two hours.

In both cases I think it necessary to add, that grooms should always be careful never to remove the collar or saddle until the shoulders or hocks are nearly dry, or troublesome irritation and soreness will be almost sure to ensue.

CARE OF CLOTHING AND SADDLERY.

On the care of clothing and saddlery, next to the care of the horses, depends the real economy of the stable management.

In the first place, every horse should have two suits of clothing, and an exercising rug, &c.

The day suit should consist of a full suit of clothing and a large sheet; the night suit of a large sheet and common rug cut out and buckled at the chest; the exercising suit of a similar rug and roller, and knee caps.

The night suit should be removed immediately the groom enters the stable in the morning, and the horse racked up and fed. He should then be sponged over with a damp sponge to remove all stains from dung, &c., and the exercising rug thrown over him and the knee caps adjusted.

The night suit should then be well shaken, all marks of dirt removed, and then folded up and put away.

The groom should now give his horse a feed of corn, go to his own breakfast, and then take the horse to exercise; on returning to the stable he should remove the exercising rug and hang it up to dry, if wet and dirty. He should then commence cleaning the horse as above directed, and, having finished, should put on the day suit and rack the horse up; taking care to remove this suit just before bedding the horse up, which causes a good deal of unnecessary dust, chaff, &c., to adhere to this suit; which should be well shaken, brushed, folded up, and replaced by the night suit.

In this way really good clothing will last many years. But if clothing be used at all times and for all sorts of work—for night, day, and exercising—the horse will, during nine-tenths of his time, have to wear dirty and wet clothing, which must be most injurious to the skin and general health, in addition to the dirty and slovenly appearance such clothing presents, not only to the horses but to the whole stable.

Every groom should be able to stitch sufficiently well to mend the night suit when it becomes torn; which will frequently be the case from the great strain they are usually put to, when the horse lies down, rolls, and gets up again; but if either the day or exercising suits are torn, it is due to the carelessness of the groom; for if properly put on they need be subject to no strain whatever. 'A stitch in time truly saves nine' with regard to clothing, and a small tear will soon become a hopeless rent if neglected for any time.

If saddles and bridles are dry when they come into

the saddle-room they will require very little attention; but if wet and dirty they must be sponged with yellow soap and water, and then wiped as dry as possible; after which the leather will be much benefited by the application of a little of the best neatsfoot oil, or white of egg; which should be well rubbed off in the course of a few hours, with a leather kept for this especial purpose. This should be done immediately the bits, stirrups, and girths are removed. The girths should be well scraped and then scoured with soap and water—followed by pipeclay if white—when they may be hung up to dry.

The stirrups, bits, &c., should be washed with water immediately they are taken off, to remove all dirt, &c., after which they should be rubbed dry with a cloth, and then scoured with the hand and some fine silver sand slightly wetted; which should be removed by a good rubbing with a dry cloth kept for the purpose; but on no account must the sand be washed off with water, or rubbed off with oil, as the polish is soon lost thereby; but they may be polished with the burnishers to give them a still brighter appearance.

Both reins and saddles should be well rubbed with a chamois-leather wrapper previous to being used; since nothing is more nasty and disagreeable than a greasy or sticky feel on them, even if not liable to soil. If they are well rubbed until they fail to soil a clean chamois-leather wrapper, all will be well.

It will now be necessary for me to say a few words in conclusion on certain duties that every groom will be required to fulfil, and, therefore, which he ought entirely to understand; viz., drenching and physicking horses. It may seem strange that I should advert to such simple operations, but it is so seldom that the former operation is ever performed in a reasonable and proper manner by grooms, and is so often attended with fatal results, that the proper method of performing it had better be fully described.

In the first place turn the horse round in his stall or box, and make an attendant stand at the near side of the horse, and putting his hand at the bottom of the horse's jaws, elevate the nose just so much as to render the top of the gullet and lower jaw straight; but on no account must the head be raised higher than this, since swallowing then becomes more difficult; then let the person about to perform the operation, after having filled a soda-water bottle with the drench, stand on a reversed stable bucket conveniently placed, and putting his left hand under the jaws proceed to open the mouth with the neck of the bottle, and raising the bottom of it pour about a tablespoonful on the tongue, immediately withdrawing the bottle until the horse has swallowed; when the same operation will have to be repeated until the whole drench has been given.

Most horses become very tractable, and will rarely ever object to the operation, if performed in this way.

But when the drenching horn is used and the contents (fully a pint) forcibly emptied into his mouth, an unsuccessful effort to swallow is succeeded by a choking sensation; the result being that the horse endeavours to free himself from the manipulation of his unscientific tormentors, by suddenly withdrawing his head, and either ejects the whole of the contents of the horn, or a portion of it having passed into the windpipe he falls a victim to the ignorance and clumsiness of the operators.

In giving a ball, as little notice as possible should be given the horse of the intention of doing so; for if he discovers what is about to be performed, he will be sure to endeavour to defeat it, and cause a deal of trouble.

Therefore, all twitching, gagging, and the use of the balling iron should be dispensed with, unless the horse is known to be addicted to biting, when these will become absolutely necessary to protect the operator from the danger of losing one or more of his fingers.

Having racked up the horse for a few minutes prior to performing the operation, so that he may have cleansed his mouth by swallowing all food, &c., let him be turned round in the stall or box.

The operator holding the ball between his teeth, must twist the halter once round his left hand, and then pulling out the tongue with his right, should deliver it to the left, in which he should hold it gently, and then raising the head slightly, and taking hold of the ball between the ends of the three first fingers of his right hand, should pass it quickly into the pharynx, and then rapidly withdraw his hand and remove his hold of the tongue. The head should now be kept elevated, and the mouth closed until the ball has been swallowed.

THE PURCHASE OF HORSES.

If you wish to offend nine-tenths of the persons who can ride, drive, or manage a horse moderately well, tell them that they are not sufficiently good judges of horses to purchase them in the open mart. Still, if one is determined strictly to adhere to the truth, one cannot fall short of this.

The question next comes, whom can a man trust to buy for him? And here, no doubt, there arises some difficulty. There are, however, dealers of high standing and great respectability, both in London and the provinces, who, if treated in the right way, i.e., in a liberal and honest manner, can be trusted to fulfil the duties of respectable and honest tradesmen.

Many there are, doubtless, who fully merit the character usually accorded to horse-dealers in years gone by, but these soon become rightly estimated by the public in these days of competition.

Of all men in the world from whom to purchase a horse, common sense must necessarily point to the respectable dealer, for the following reasons:—In the first place, the superior judgment of the dealer selects certain horses, out of the numbers brought within his reach, as being peculiarly adapted from action, formation, performances, &c., for certain defined purposes. Therefore, in the first place, the purchaser has the advantage of the judgment of the dealer as to the horse's fitness for a certain purpose; and in the second place, he has the advantage of a horse not only purchased with a warranty (for be it known that respectable dealers do not buy above ten per cent. of their horses without a written warranty), but also considered free from unsoundness by an experienced judge.

The chief but very shallow objection usually raised is the enormous price asked by dealers of this description for their horses. But this exists merely in fancy, and not at all in reality; for sure I am that for the same class of animal the farmer or gentleman would ask an equal sum; and in the latter case you would not have the advantage of the dealer's judgment on any of the points. Some may take exception to my statement, that the farmer or gentleman will ask the same sum; but in stating this, I am merely stating the result of my experience; and the reason is easily accounted for. The farmer or gentleman who has some dozen horses to dispose of, naturally prefers to give the refusal of them to the man who will take as many off his hands in one transaction as happen to suit him; and this man, being in nine cases out of ten a dealer, becomes possessed of animals not within the reach of private individuals, and on much easier terms; for it requires no philosopher to understand that a man can afford to make a more considerable abatement in the price of each horse if he sells twelve, than if he were only to sell one, merely in a monetary point of view; to say nothing of the saving of time, trouble, and vexation.

In addition to which, some gentlemen consider it

very bad taste to offer another gentleman a less price for his horse than that demanded; and, indeed, I don't understand on what grounds this could reasonably be done, for as a general rule one private gentleman is very loth to accept the superior judgment of another, on the matter of the worth of his own horses, and will be sure to refuse to entertain such a proposal. But when a dealer respectfully puts forward that he purchases horses merely with a view of selling them at a profit, and therefore that he must clearly purchase at a price considerably below their market value, or become a loser by the transaction, any reasonable gentleman will at once see the justice of the remark, and submit to meeting the dealer's view of the worth of his horses, if he considers the offer sufficiently liberal; and it is for this reason that I assert that the dealer can afford to sell horses at fully as cheap a rate as the private individual.

A gentleman requiring a hunter frequently visits the large horse fairs in search of one, and chooses from among some hundreds of animals, unless he be a good judge, one which he thinks—and the seller says—is a hunter; but which will frequently prove an animal of no pretensions—either from his action, formation, or blood—to the appellation of a hunter; but either a harness horse, charger, or hack.

He will be pretty sure to be asked, and to give the price of a hunter for such an animal; and perhaps he will not find out his mistake until the horse has cost him some twenty pounds in keep and travelling expenses, and then in disgust he sends him to be sold by auction for what the public choose to give for him, and consequently he becomes a heavy loser.

When this happens, the blame is usually laid on bad luck instead of bad judgment; from which cause it invariably may be traced.

Such a state of things could not possibly happen in buying a horse described as a hunter from a dealer of respectability; for he would never have purchased a horse so unfitted in every way from defective form, &c., for the purpose.

And even in going into the dealer's yard, great caution must be exercised not to take a fancy to a horse in the stable because he is enamoured of his appearance, &c., for he may then purchase a charger, carriage horse, or hack, instead of a hunter: but let him distinctly give the dealer to understand exactly what he wants; viz., the nature of the country over which he hunts, whether he rides hard, and whether he requires a horse very quiet and handy, or whether he can put up with certain peculiarities; and to save giving the dealer unnecessary trouble, let him state the price he can afford to give; there need then be no misunderstanding, and there will be every chance of a horse being found in every essential particular suited to his purpose. It is a ridiculous mistake to suppose that a high class of dealer never has a low-priced horse in his stable; for it necessarily happens that out of a number of horses there must be some that he will be willing, from a variety of causes, to sell at a sacrifice;

but of course a dealer does not show such animals to his customers, unless especially asked for.

Concerning the purchase of horses of other qualifications, I need say but little, since such egregious blunders cannot be made if a gentleman knows the outline, general character, and size of horse he requires.

For it can matter little if the carriage horse or charger be a hunter in make, blood, and action; but it is of considerable importance if the hunter should prove a carriage horse or charger. I will, therefore, merely add that the better plan is to purchase each description of horse from those who deal specially in that class of animal, and not to attempt to buy a hunter from a dealer in hacks and harness horses, nor vice versâ.

Many gentlemen make a practice of purchasing at auctions, and frequently succeed in becoming possessed of a good animal at a low figure, but still more frequently in becoming possessed of ill-tempered and unsound horses.

As a general rule, it is never safe to purchase a horse at the hammer, unless he comes up in a bonâ fide stud, or unless you know something about him; and even then it is a dangerous experiment unless you are a good judge. For there are very few horses indeed that cannot make a fair show, both as to action and soundness, after having had the usual amount of preparation for sale, in the very limited trial to which they can be subjected in so small a space of ground.

There is another method of purchasing horses, which

some men of experience are very fond of resorting to. They watch the young horses that are brought into the hunting field by dealers, farmers, and colt-breakers, and purchase them merely on the strength of their performances; and in this way no doubt some good purchases are made; though very frequently such horses turn out to be no hunters at all, but merely able to jump a big fence with a clear approach to it; and the first blind or double fence they come to, down they go, as mere colts that they usually are; but from these description of fences the wary horseman, who is riding to sell, invariably keeps at a respectful distance.

Moreover, it is utterly impossible to detect the state of a horse's legs when warm and covered with mud and water, as they are sure to be on arriving at the cover side. And, in addition, many horses perform well over a country that are such execrable hacks on the road as to be positively unsafe to ride.

As a rule, if this is done, it will be the best way to visit countries precisely the opposite of the one in which you usually hunt, for by this means you will find less difficulty in obtaining the animals you require, and at a much less cost; for horses of cobby, short, and very compact build are held in no esteem in the flying countries; in the same way that the lengthy, bloodlike, raking Leicestershire hunter is considered valueless in the banking and hilly countries of Essex, Dorsetshire, Devon, Cornwall, and Wales, and its borders; and, therefore, will not be so difficult to procure at a moderate price in these districts.

But it is never advisable to purchase horses out of the hunting field, without a warranty as to soundness and freedom from vice, nor indeed without riding them a short distance on the road.

No rules can be laid down here for the use of purchasers of horses for different countries, with the exception of those that are for heavy, deep-ploughed countries; a sharp, quick, light-actioned horse, must be chosen in opposition to the heavy, clumping goers, which beat their feet into the ground, and are utterly unable to withdraw them again without soon exhausting their powers, however game they may be. And also that thorough-bred horses are necessary for these countries, owing to the amount of staying powers necessary to go through a run; which are rarely ever met with except in the pure bred animal with light and almost dainty action.

In countries where much timber is used for fencing, I am convinced a stain in the pedigree is no disadvantage; but where brooks and dykes abound it is a great disadvantage.

The best rule for a purchaser to go by, is to reckon up the horses in his own and adjoining hunts which are held in most esteem and ridden by men of similar weight, and consider the points and peculiarities—both as to size and blood—of these horses, and carry these in his mind's eye when in search of a horse to carry him.

Some men go on, year after year, purchasing horses utterly unsuited to their country, from some innate fancy for a certain class of horse, which they are utterly unable to shake off even after a life's experience. And therefore I consider it necessary, before taking leave of this subject, to warn each of my readers, to consider, if he is in the habit of getting more than his proper share of falls in the hunting field, whether he rides the proper description of horse for his country.

VETERINARY EXAMINATIONS.

In the purchase of horses a veterinary examination is the greatest possible boon both to the buyer and seller, when conducted on fair and honourable principles; but most commonly it is conducted on no principle whatever, and becomes a source of litigation, dispute, and loss to both parties, by upsetting a warranty of soundness given by the seller.

Horses are very frequently purchased warranted sound, and prove sound, so far as all absence from lameness, diseases, &c., is concerned; but the purchaser of the horse, feeling anxious from some cause about his purchase, forthwith sends for his veterinary surgeon —without having previously informed the seller of his doubts and intentions—has the horse examined, and the result is that the professional man, being overanxious to detect malformation, or a morbid tendency somewhere, succeeds in his opinion in doing so, and gives a certificate of the horse's unsoundness; which the purchaser immediately forwards to the seller, and, on the strength of the veterinary surgeon's opinion alone, requests him to take back the horse, and remit him the whole of the purchase-money.

Now, in my opinion, no man of honour or principle would be guilty of such a manifest breach of faith as this.

He purchases the horse warranted sound, by the seller who gives the warranty bonâ fide, because he has proved him to be sound from repeated trials while in his possession. And, therefore, until the horse becomes unsound, either from lameness, roaring, whistling, ophthalmia, or any other cause, which palpably must have existed at the time of sale, it is a manifest breach of faith to impugn the correctness of the warranty, by calling in the veterinary surgeon to examine him; for the horse being sold under a warranty cannot mean being sold under, or subject to the opinion of the veterinary surgeon by any trifling with words.

If a warranty means anything at all it means that the horse is to be considered sound without the opinion of the veterinary surgeon until he prove otherwise.

No man is likely to be so foolish as to sell a horse to such a man on the same terms again. Or, if he does, he will most probably run a risk, and sell him a horse he knows to be unsound, which he hopes may pass the ordeal of a veterinary examination. And it frequently happens that the horse, though notably unsound from some hidden ailment, does pass this examination; and thereby he is tempted to do the same thing again.

I have frequently known this done by sellers of horses as a set-off for previous breaches of faith.

The whole system is wrong. The only time when the opinion of the veterinary surgeon should be taken as conclusive, is when the sale of the horse is being effected; or, in other words, when the horse is purchased subject to the opinion of the veterinary surgeon; for then the seller can please himself as to whether he will run the risk of the examination. And by the risk I mean the manifest damage done to the horse's character, if he be rejected as unsound.

For it places a person in a very equivocal position in the eyes of a great portion of the public, if he subsequently sell the horse warranted sound after he has been professionally condemned. And even if he succeeds in selling him by incurring this responsibility, he most frequently has to submit to a reduction in price, and becomes a heavy sufferer through the incompetence of the veterinary surgeon.

Incompetence in the veterinary surgeon, or unfitness for giving an honest and true opinion as to the soundness of a horse, is sometimes brought about by ignorance, but far more frequently by nervousness, or constitutional inability to incur the responsibility of passing a horse sound, fearing that something may possibly cause lameness, and that he might thereby lose his character for overlooking some lurking ailment, which could not possibly be detected at the time.

Thus, if a man passes an unsound horse as sound, he gets heartily laughed at by the seller and execrated by the purchaser; by the one, because he has been the means of relieving him of an unsound and worthless animal; and by the other, because he has been the means of saddling him with a heavy loss.

Is it any wonder, then, that veterinary surgeons become so nervous and over-fearful of stating that a horse is sound, that they will scarcely ever allow a horse to pass through their hands without some imputation as to the probable chances of unsoundness?

They are forced to protect their own characters, and the only means they have of doing so is to reject seventy-five per cent. of all the horses that are brought to them for examination.

Moreover, there is an additional reason, for their credit's sake, why they should be so sparing of a certificate of soundness.

If a veterinary surgeon reject a horse because he apprehends the existence of some specified disease in futurity, and that disease happen to show itself in the course of two or three years, he will forthwith be lauded to the skies for his supernatural powers of perception, and will assuredly become a *prophetic professional* ever after; not only in his own imagination, but in that of a circle of friends and employers.

On the value of such a reputation, I have known very many set great store; but it invariably renders them ridiculous amongst the only persons capable of judging, viz., horse-dealers, trainers, and those of their own profession, who are in the habit of rightly imputing their successes to a low sort of *cunning*, and not to real ability.

For it is little short of cunning of the lowest order to

assert that a horse is likely to become lame in his feet, when it is understood that he will have to be ridden or driven at a severe pace over hard roads four or five days during every week of his existence; or that a horse, which has to carry a crushing weight to hounds over a deep or hilly country, will be likely to contract curbs and other hock lameness; or that a horse which is going to be put to severe work in an aldermanic stable will be liable to contract inflammation of the organs of respiration, and become a roarer; which prophetic wisdom the veriest tyro in horse flesh could propound, if possessed of a similar amount of impertinence and cunning.

In a great measure, the public have brought this state of things on themselves, by requiring the veterinary surgeon to dive into futurity, and give an infallible opinion as to soundness when neither lameness nor any other disease is in existence at the time of examination; so that the honest, high-minded, and highly gifted professional man is occasionally tempted to reject horses of certain formation, merely because he has known many horses similarly formed prove unsound, and not at all because the horse exhibited symptoms of unsoundness at the time of examination.

Now, it appears to me that the only correct principle of examining horses as to soundness, is to leave the consideration of peculiar formation—like colour, size, and sex—entirely to the judgment of the purchaser.

If he likes a horse with curby hocks, when no lameness exists, it is surely no affair of the advising counsel.

The same thing applies to thorough pins, contracted feet, &c., neither of which can be causes of unsoundness, when free from inflammation and disease.

For I apprehend that *general usefulness* is the great desideratum to the purchaser.

And here the real talent of the highly gifted practitioner stands forth as a beacon of safety. Repeatedly have I heard some talented professional men, when called upon to give an opinion on the soundness or general usefulness of horses with suspensory ligaments sprung and as large as walnuts, as well as horses with large unsightly curbs, but nevertheless sound and callous, pronounce them sound, giving as their reason the entire absence of inflammation, on which lameness depends, and urge their employers to become possessed of them.

This is the kind of advice which is truly valuable when it can be procured, and it proved almost a mine of silver to a gentleman of my acquaintance in one instance.

This is what horsemen especially desire to be informed of; viz., under what circumstances they may reasonably hope to make use of their horse's services without a great risk of his becoming lame and incapacitated for work. And the professional man who is competent to give this advice is the man whom the sporting public should cordially patronise; for they will rarely find that, through taking the advice of such a man, they have purchased an animal incapacitated for work; and, what is of still more importance, because it

INSTANCES OF INCOMPETENCE. 245

entails such endless vexation, they will rarely find that they have missed being possessed of a really good horse through the ignorance, pusillanimity, or caprice of their professional advisers, as is too often the case in the present day.

I was accosted by an old friend the other day with —' I wish all the vets. in England were sent over the water; for that horse (naming the animal) has won the big stake at ——, and has, in addition, stood being regularly hunted with fourteen stones on his back for two seasons, and that fool of a fellow at —— told me he had a spavin and a curb on the off hock, and would be of no use to me, since he would never stand training.'

This, no doubt, is very often the case, but it is a great pity, and still greater injustice that, because an incompetent member of the veterinary profession stultifies himself, the whole body of professional men should suffer.

I was also informed the other day by a military man of a case not a whit less absurd.

This gentleman purchased a mare of a dealer and veterinary surgeon, subject to the opinion of a professional man of large practice, to whom the mare was accordingly sent, and was, after an examination, rejected as unsound from a bone spavin.

The dealer, being much dissatisfied, named another professional man, of whom the gentleman cordially approved as being a man of still greater experience, who pronounced her unsound from defective respiration, but perfectly free from ossification of the hock. Now these two men are noted specialists, the first consulted enjoying a great reputation for keen perception of defective respiration, the second an equal reputation for fathoming both clear and occult diseases of the hock to a certainty; yet both stultified themselves, and each in a way that one would have least anticipated; for the gentleman, being unable to suit himself elsewhere, purchased the mare subsequently, and has worked her regularly for four years, during which period she has proved a thoroughly sound animal.

Another remarkable, but still more unaccountable, case occurred to the veterinary surgeon who was first consulted in the previous instance.

A noted dealer, being about to sell a high-priced brougham horse, sent for him, and desired him to examine the horse, which he did, and gave a certificate of soundness.

The horse was therefore sold, warranted sound, to a gentleman who also employed the same person as his veterinary surgeon, and on the horse reaching his stables sent for him to examine the same horse, which he did—ignorant of the fact, one would suppose, that it was the same horse—and gave a certificate of the unsoundness of the very horse he had passed sound a few days previously.

Whereupon the dealer forwarded to him the previous certificate, together with that which he had received from the purchaser, at the same time reminding him that the two certificates were for the same horse, and requesting an explanation; at which news the vet.

seemed sorely perplexed, pleaded some *mistake*, and requested another examination, which was granted, and finally, a second time, rejected the horse as unsound; so that within a week three certificates were given by the same man on the same horse, and, according to the usual order of things, the ratio was two to one in favour of unsoundness.

Surely no one will charge this very successful practitioner with neglecting his recognised duties, and say that he was willing to overlook a morbid tendency in the dealer's horse, which became a matter of paramount importance in the gentleman's.

If one ventured to allege that the horse was sound after all, the answer would assuredly be a list of his miraculous discoveries in occult cases, and his numerous triumphs over rival practitioners.

For what matters it to the monopoliser of a liberal art that a few men should exist who are sceptical of his claim to infallibility?

It is a matter of perfect indifference to him, so long as they do not succeed in robbing him of either his character or practice.

Now, we know that there are a set of men, even in these enlightened days, who—claiming to be descendants of the apostles—desire one to be satisfied with their authority, and walk with one's eyes shut in order that one may be able to see the better; and many there are who are content submissively thus to eke out their existence. But since the veterinary art in this country dates neither from the prophets nor the apostles, but chiefly from an individual hailing from Alfort, in France—one Charles Vial de St. Bel, who brought along with him a very limited stock of knowledge, not more than three-fourths of a century ago—is it asking too much to urge his pupils to invest themselves with a little less infallibility, and to descend from an imaginary pinnacle of wisdom and take up their positions, amongst men as scientific benefactors, and not as uncompromising dictators?

It really makes one smile when one considers that after eight months' successful study at the Royal Veterinary College, that smooth-faced simple-looking lad, of whom one had hoped little, gets his diploma as a qualified practitioner of the veterinary art, and from that very day he becomes infallible.

It reminds me of an absolute verdict that was passed on an old friend of mine, who went to be examined previous to insuring his life in the largest office in the kingdom, by the consulting physician; who, after going through the necessary examination, pronounced his constitution broken, and his lungs and heart diseased beyond hope of recovery; and on being twitted rather sharply with the absurdity of his opinion added, 'And if you go on as you are now, you will not be alive in twelve months.' Whereupon my friend, being of a very sportive turn of mind, and determined to bring his dogmatical friend to book for thus rashly 'numbering his days,' replied, 'I'll lay you sixty pounds to ten I shall be alive and as well as I am now, and will promise you that I will go on in precisely the same manner, except that I mean to drink port instead of sherry.' And he has been as good as his word, having seen twelve years roll by in perfect enjoyment of health and strength, which appears to have increased with the more generous diet.

After this lengthened but necessary explanation of the ridiculous position taken up by some veterinary and medical empirics, and specialists or quacks—who should give their advice gratis for all it is worth—I must hasten to resume the consideration of the fair duties of the veterinary surgeon with regard to the examination of the horse as to soundness.

In the first place, let the person conducting the examination, on approaching the horse carefully, look at the expression of the eyes and carriage of the head; for if he should notice anything peculiar, he will have time to consider and note the existence of megrims during the remainder of the examination.

Next let him examine the veins on either side of the neck, and ascertain whether the horse have been bled lately, also the larynx for any ossification or enlargement. Then let him turn his attention to the fore limbs, and examine the knees carefully for exostosis, &c. (which far more frequently exists than is generally supposed), and inside the knees for marks of speedy cutting.

He will then examine each fore leg carefully, both above and below, both inside and outside each fetlock joint, for the purpose of ascertaining whether neurotomy have been performed; during which research he will also be able to discover the formation of splints, as will as whether any injury have been done to the sheath of the tendons, ligaments, &c.

The pasterns and feet must next go through a careful examination, noting the state of the coronets, the colour and angles of the hoof, as well as its size and general formation; and if any difference in the angle or size should seem to exist between the two feet, it must be ascertained by a still more careful study and comparison that it does not arise from rasping, cutting, &c., in shoeing.

The action of the heart and respiration must then be attentively examined by putting the ear to the chest; which examination will greatly facilitate the detection of disease in the subsequent trial of these organs by rapid motion.

The spine will now require the strictest scrutiny; since the existence of a 'ricked back' is very difficult to ascertain by superficial investigation.

This done, the hind limbs will require a very rigid examination. The thighs must not only be cautiously examined as to the existence of strains, &c., but the inside of the thighs must be thoroughly observed as to the existence of pimples or farcy buds, which, even if scarcely perceptible, may be ascertained by unnatural tenderness and slight tumefaction.

The patella and stifle joints, with their muscular and ligamentous attachments, must next be examined; for this is the seat of a very troublesome lameness, especially amongst steeplechase horses, from extension of the muscles and tendons, and rupture of the fibres, through catching the hind leg on timber when going at full speed.

The hocks will give more trouble than all the rest of the parts prone to disease in the animal horse, and greater difficulty will be experienced in deciding on the existence of a spavin unless the exostosis be considerable, than a person not conversant with the different formation of the bones of the hocks would be able to credit. So much depends upon the position of the leg at the time of examination, and on the difficulty there is in making a horse adopt the position required. In addition to which, many horses have largely developed protuberant heads of the internal bones of the hock, which are very frequently mistaken for exostosis; though it is a perfectly natural though larger formation than that ordinarly met with.

When exostosis, or a real spavin, exists, it may be discovered without any difficulty by standing behind the horse's hocks, and passing the hand down the lateral edges of the internal bones, which will feel abrupt, irregular, and rarely ever of the same size on both hocks. The sheaths of the tendons of the hind legs must then be cautiously examined, more especially as they approach the fetlock joint, for they very frequently become ruptured in hilly countries.

The horse must now be walked quietly in a direct line from the person conducting the examination, and trotted quietly back again.

About fifty yards is the most convenient distance for

the purpose; as the distance may have to be gone over repeatedly, and a longer distance would distress the runner and render him unfit to keep pace with the horse without pulling his head round; which will always defeat the object of the examiner, inasmuch as it will make the horse appear lame without being so.

The saddle must next be put on his back, and after the groom has mounted him, and suitable ground for a trial have been selected—such as tan or straw ride, turf or ploughed ground—he should be put from a trot to a canter, increasing his pace as he goes on, and ridden in a circle for about two minutes; and if he has not been broken he must be longed in a cavesson for a similar length of time, in order that his organs of respiration may be tested thoroughly. Immediately after the horse has been pulled up, it will be necessary to examine once more the action of the heart and lungs previous to his being led back to the stable, where his eyes must be examined in the dark with a candle, as well as the top of his head for injuries likely to bring about poll evil. He should then be tied up and allowed to rest an hour, so that he may get perfectly cool; during which time it will be well to watch him closely, so that if he have contracted habits of crib-biting, wind sucking, pointing his toe, &c., they may be detected.

After the expiration of an hour he should again be led out, and put through a walk and trot as before; when lameness—if any exist at the time of examination —may easily be detected.

LIMITS OF PROFESSIONAL DUTIES.

Having now made a thorough examination of the horse, it will be the duty of the person conducting the examination to state in plain and decided language whether he considers the horse sound or the reverse; and if not sound what constitutes his unsoundness. If it be lameness, it should be distinctly stated, not only where it exists, but what in his opinion is the cause of it, in order that the purchaser may judge of whether he considers the lameness to arise from trivial causes; for I once recollect a horse being rejected as unsound from lameness produced from soreness of the pasterns from cracked heels.

Many veterinary surgeons object to incurring the responsibility of passing a horse sound if sent to examine him when labouring under an attack of simple catarrh, however slight, and when the feet are rather warm, and so on *ad nauseam*.

The best and most straightforward plan to adopt under these circumstances, is undoubtedly to pass the horse sound—save and except temporary unfitness for examination—and to leave the consideration of the matter in the hands of the purchaser. And if he elect to run the risk of catarrh or warm feet, he has only himself to blame or thank as the case may prove.

But, of all things, the person conducting the examination merely as to soundness, should be careful never to say anything detrimental of the horse's action, power, temper, or general suitability to the purchaser.

The matter in hand is *soundness*; and as far as the professional man departs from the matter in hand, so far does he exceed his manifest duties, and abuse his position as an impartial adviser.

I have known many dealers so grievously offended by injudicious remarks of veterinary surgeons on the action, power, quality, &c., of the horses they had come to examine—merely as to soundness—that they have refused ever again to admit of an examination by the same person on their premises. Though I think this going a little too far, I nevertheless consider that any one offering a horse for sale has just ground for complaint, if a professional man so far forgets himself, and the limits of his professional duties, as to be guilty of the bad taste of making injurious remarks on points of which he may be a far inferior judge to both seller and purchaser; for a veterinary surgeon is no more justified in arrogating to himself superior judgment of a horse's capabilities than Sir Astley Cooper would have been had he laid claim to superior judgment to the rest of the world of a pugilist, pedestrian, or wrestler, on the strength of being the best anatomist and most learned in the structure and action of the muscles. It is an authority to which neither dealers nor sportsmen, having neither asked nor accepted it, will ever subject themselves to with impunity.

YOUATT ON THE HORSE, EDITED BY GABRIEL.

Revised Edition, in 1 vol. 8vo. price 10s. 6d. cloth,

THE HORSE,

INCLUDING A TREATISE ON DRAUGHT.

By WILLIAM YOUATT.

With numerous Woodcut Illustrations chiefly from Designs by W. Harvey.

REVISED AND ENLARGED BY E. N. GABRIEL, M.R.C.S. C.V.S.
SECRETARY TO ROYAL COLLEGE OF VETERINARY SURGEONS.

YOUATT'S work, admitted to be the best and most complete practical treatise on the Horse, was originally produced under the superintendence of the Society for the Diffusion of Useful Knowledge, and subsequently published by Messrs. LONGMANS and Co. by assignment of C. KNIGHT. The edition now advertised was carefully and thoroughly revised by Mr. GABRIEL, and brought up to a level with the state of the veterinary art. Amongst numerous other additions, an account is given of Mr. RAREY'S method of horse-breaking; also a new set of illustrations of the age of the horse as indicated by his teeth. Purchasers should order Messrs. LONGMAN'S and Co.'s edition of *Youatt on the Horse,* which, besides the above-mentioned improvements, includes also the Author's latest corrections, &c. added to the second edition.

'THERE is a freshness and vigour in Mr. GABRIEL'S style which we feel certain will prove acceptable to those who read works on this subject: it is so different from the dry, technical contents of most veterinary works, that the reader is not only instructed and amused, but is impressed as he proceeds with sentiments of admiration for one of the most useful of God's creatures. YOUATT'S work on the horse is one of those few books which can be read over and over again with delight and interest. To many persons who are owners of horses, it will prove an especial boon: for in its pages will be found much that is instructive and profitable. The treatise on draught will be especially interesting to farmers and contractors; who, by adopting the Author's advice, may effect a considerable saving in horse power. The illustrations rank among the best we have ever seen. There are comparatively few artists who can draw a life-like portrait of the horse—indeed we think it all but impossible for an artist to excel in this particular branch unless he has himself well studied the anatomy and natural history of this noble animal; but here we have the various breeds, as well as the portraits of very many of our most celebrated thorough-breds, rendered with a fidelity as striking as it is instructive and beautiful. The work we unhesitatingly pronounce one of the best and most comprehensive we have ever read on the subject of the horse.'
SPORTING LIFE.

YOUATT on the DOG, 8vo. Woodcuts, 6s. may also be had.

London: LONGMANS, GREEN, and CO. Paternoster Row.

WORKS ON THE HORSE AND OX.

Lately published, in crown 8vo. price 2s. 6d.

A Plain Treatise on Horse-shoeing.

By WILLIAM MILES. Fifth Edition; with several Illustrative Figures in Lithography and on Wood.

By the same Author, New Editions.

Stables and Stable-Fittings, 15s.

Remarks on Horses' Teeth, 1s. 6d.

The Horse's Foot, and How to Keep it Sound, 12s. 6d.

Lately published, in crown 8vo. price 7s. 6d.

A New Work on the Ox,

His Diseases and their Treatment; with an Essay on Parturition in the Cow. By J. R. DOBSON, Member of the Royal College of Veterinary Surgeons. With 2 Plates (1 coloured) and 52 Woodcuts.

'THE present volume contains the most modern and approved methods of cure, expressed in simple language, unfettered as much as possible with technical terms, which renders it the more acceptable to the general reader.'
MARK LANE EXPRESS.

'A very explicit and well illustrated book of veterinary treatment—particularly explicit and well illustrated in its dicussion of the ordinary and extraordinary difficulties of parturition, but trustworthy and elaborate everywhere.'
GARDENERS' CHRONICLE.

'THE Author has furnished a work instructive to his professional brethren, full of practical advice to farmers, graziers, and dairymen, and not deficient in entertaining information to gratify the curiosity of the reading public. The numerous and well executed engravings illustrate his subjects more clearly, and will enable the uninitiated to comprehend distinctly points of which their notions would otherwise have been obscure. . . . The volume concludes with a useful APPENDIX, being a pharmacopœia of the medicines required for veterinary purposes, and the modes of preparing and using them.'
MORNING POST.

'THIS work, although copious in its explanations of the diseases treated on, and their mode of cure, is by no means abstruse or technical. The Author's explanations are, so far as compatible with a technical subject, plain and popular. The farmer and stock-keeper, for whom the work is especially intended and adapted, will have no trouble in following Mr. DOBSON through his descriptive matter, as well as his directions, diagnoses, and prescriptions. . . . The veterinary practitioner, or the cow-leech who has not read Mr. DOBSON'S book, has much to learn in his profession.' MORNING ADVERTISER.

London: LONGMANS, GREEN, and CO. Paternoster Row.

[MARCH 1863.]

GENERAL LIST OF WORKS

PUBLISHED BY

MESSRS. LONGMANS, GREEN, AND CO.

PATERNOSTER ROW, LONDON.

Historical Works.

LORD MACAULAY'S WORKS. Complete and Uniform Library Edition. Edited by his Sister, Lady TREVELYAN. 8 vols. 8vo. with Portrait, price £5 5s. cloth, or £8 8s. bound in tree-calf by Rivière.

The **HISTORY of ENGLAND** from the Fall of Wolsey to the Death of Elizabeth. By JAMES ANTHONY FROUDE, M.A. late Fellow of Exeter College, Oxford.
> VOLS. I. to IV. the Reign of Henry VIII. Third Edition, 54s.
> VOLS. V. and VI. the Reigns of Edward VI. and Mary. Second Edition, 28s.
> VOLS. VII. and VIII. the Reign of Elizabeth, VOLS. I. and II. Third Edition, 28s.

The **HISTORY of ENGLAND** from the Accession of James II. By Lord MACAULAY.
> LIBRARY EDITION, 5 vols. 8vo. £4.
> CABINET EDITION, 8 vols. post 8vo. 48s.
> PEOPLE'S EDITION, 4 vols. crown 8vo. 16s.

REVOLUTIONS in ENGLISH HISTORY. By ROBERT VAUGHAN, D.D. 3 vols. 8vo. 45s.
> VOL. I. Revolutions of Race, Second Edition, revised, 15s.
> VOL. II. Revolutions in Religion, 15s.
> VOL. III. Revolutions in Government, 15s.

An **ESSAY** on the **HISTORY of the ENGLISH GOVERNMENT** and Constitution, from the Reign of Henry VII. to the Present Time. By JOHN EARL RUSSELL. Third Edition, revised. Crown 8vo. 6s.

The **HISTORY of ENGLAND** during the Reign of George the Third. By the Right Hon. W. N. MASSEY. Cabinet Edition. 4 vols. post 8vo. 24s.

The **CONSTITUTIONAL HISTORY of ENGLAND**, since the Accession of George III. 1760—1860. By THOMAS ERSKINE MAY, C.B. Second Edition. 2 vols. 8vo. 33s.

A

CONSTITUTIONAL HISTORY of the BRITISH EMPIRE from the Accession of Charles I. to the Restoration. By G. BRODIE, Esq. Historiographer-Royal of Scotland. Second Edition. 3 vols. 8vo. 36s.

HISTORICAL STUDIES. I. On Some of the Precursors of the French Revolution; II. Studies from the History of the Seventeenth Century; III. Leisure Hours of a Tourist. By HERMAN MERIVALE, M.A. 8vo. price 12s. 6d.

LECTURES on the HISTORY of ENGLAND. By WILLIAM LONGMAN. VOL. I. from the earliest times to the Death of King Edward II. with 6 Maps, a coloured Plate, and 53 Woodcuts. 8vo. 15s.

HISTORY of CIVILISATION. By HENRY THOMAS BUCKLE. 2 vols. 8vo. £1 17s.
VOL. I. *England and France*, Fourth Edition, 21s.
VOL. II. *Spain and Scotland*, Second Edition, 16s.

DEMOCRACY in AMERICA. By ALEXIS DE TOCQUEVILLE. Translated by HENRY REEVE, with an Introductory Notice by the Translator. 2 vols. 8vo. 21s.

The SPANISH CONQUEST in AMERICA, and its Relation to the History of Slavery and to the Government of Colonies. By ARTHUR HELPS. 4 vols. 8vo. £3. VOLS. I. and II. 28s. VOLS. III. and IV. 16s. each.

HISTORY of the REFORMATION in EUROPE in the Time of Calvin. By J. H. MERLE D'AUBIGNÉ, D.D. VOLS. I. and II. 8vo. 28s. and VOL. III. 12s. VOL. IV. nearly ready.

LIBRARY HISTORY of FRANCE, in 5 vols. 8vo. By EYRE EVANS CROWE. VOL. I. 14s. VOL. II. 15s. VOL. III. 18s. VOL. IV. nearly ready.

LECTURES on the HISTORY of FRANCE. By the late Sir JAMES STEPHEN, LL.D. 2 vols. 8vo. 24s.

The HISTORY of GREECE. By C. THIRLWALL, D.D. Lord Bishop of St. David's. 8 vols. 8vo. £3; or in 8 vols. fcp. 28s.

The TALE of the GREAT PERSIAN WAR, from the Histories of Herodotus. By GEORGE W. COX, M.A. late Scholar of Trin. Coll. Oxon. Fcp. 7s. 6d.

GREEK HISTORY from Themistocles to Alexander, in a Series of Lives from Plutarch. Revised and arranged by A. H. CLOUGH. Fcp. with 44 Woodcuts, 6s.

CRITICAL HISTORY of the LANGUAGE and LITERATURE of Ancient Greece. By WILLIAM MURE, of Caldwell. 5 vols. 8vo. £3 9s.

HISTORY of the LITERATURE of ANCIENT GREECE. By Professor K. O. MÜLLER. Translated by the Right Hon. Sir GEORGE CORNEWALL LEWIS, Bart. and by J. W. DONALDSON, D.D. 3 vols. 8vo. 36s.

HISTORY of the CITY of ROME from its Foundation to the Sixteenth Century of the Christian Era. By THOMAS H. DYER, LL.D. 8vo. with 2 Maps, 15s.

HISTORY of the ROMANS under the EMPIRE. By CHARLES MERIVALE, B.D. Chaplain to the Speaker. Cabinet Edition, with Maps, complete in 8 vols. post 8vo. 48s.

The **FALL of the ROMAN REPUBLIC**: a Short History of the Last Century of the Commonwealth. By CHARLES MERIVALE, B.D. Chaplain to the Speaker. Fourth Edition. 12mo. 7s. 6d.

The **CONVERSION of the ROMAN EMPIRE**: the Boyle Lectures for the year 1864, delivered at the Chapel Royal, Whitehall. By CHARLES MERIVALE, B.D. Chaplain to the Speaker. Second Edition, 8vo. 8s. 6d.

The **CONVERSION of the NORTHERN NATIONS**; the Boyle Lectures for 1865. By the same Author. 8vo. 8s. 6d.

CRITICAL and **HISTORICAL ESSAYS** contributed to the *Edinburgh Review*. By the Right Hon. LORD MACAULAY.
    LIBRARY EDITION, 3 vols. 8vo. 36s.
    TRAVELLER'S EDITION, in 1 vol. 21s.
    CABINET EDITION, 3 vols. fcp. 21s.
    PEOPLE'S EDITION, 2 vols. crown 8vo. 8s.

HISTORICAL and **PHILOSOPHICAL ESSAYS**. By NASSAU W. SENIOR. 2 vols. post 8vo. 16s.

HISTORY of the RISE and INFLUENCE of the SPIRIT of RATIONALISM in EUROPE. By W. E. H. LECKY, M.A. Second Edition, revised. 2 vols. 8vo. 25s.

The **HISTORY of PHILOSOPHY**, from Thales to the Present Day. By GEORGE HENRY LEWES. Third Edition, partly rewritten and greatly enlarged. In 2 vols. VOL. I. *Ancient Philosophy*; VOL. II. *Modern Philosophy*. [*Nearly ready.*

HISTORY of the INDUCTIVE SCIENCES. By WILLIAM WHEWELL, D.D. F.R.S. late Master of Trin. Coll. Cantab. Third Edition. 3 vols. crown 8vo. 24s.

HISTORY of SCIENTIFIC IDEAS; being the First Part of the Philosophy of the Inductive Sciences. By the same Author. 2 vols. cr. 8vo. 14s.

EGYPT'S PLACE in UNIVERSAL HISTORY; an Historical Investigation. By C. C. J. BUNSEN, D.D. Translated by C. H. COTTRELL, M.A. With many Illustrations. 4 vols. 8vo. £5 8s. VOL. V. is nearly ready.

MAUNDER'S HISTORICAL TREASURY; comprising a General Introductory Outline of Universal History, and a series of Separate Histories. Fcp. 10s.

HISTORICAL and CHRONOLOGICAL ENCYCLOPÆDIA, presenting in a brief and convenient form Chronological Notices of all the Great Events of Universal History. By B. B. WOODWARD, F.S.A. Librarian to the Queen. [*In the press.*

HISTORY of the CHRISTIAN CHURCH, from the Ascension of Christ to the Conversion of Constantine. By E. BURTON, D.D. late Prof. of Divinity in the Univ. of Oxford. Eighth Edition. Fcp. 3s. 6d.

SKETCH of the HISTORY of the CHURCH of ENGLAND to the Revolution of 1688. By the Right Rev. T. V. SHORT, D.D. Lord Bishop of St. Asaph. Seventh Edition. Crown 8vo. 10s. 6d.

HISTORY of the EARLY CHURCH, from the First Preaching of the Gospel to the Council of Nicæa, A.D. 325. By the Author of 'Amy Herbert.' Fcp. 4s. 6d.

The **ENGLISH REFORMATION.** By F. C. MASSINGBERD, M.A. Chancellor of Lincoln and Rector of South Ormsby. Fourth Edition, revised. Fcp. 8vo. [*Nearly ready.*

HISTORY of WESLEYAN METHODISM. By GEORGE SMITH, F.A.S. Fourth Edition, with numerous Portraits. 3 vols. cr. 8vo. 7s. each.

LECTURES on the HISTORY of MODERN MUSIC, delivered at the Royal Institution. By JOHN HULLAH. FIRST COURSE, with Chronological Tables, post 8vo. 6s. 6d. SECOND COURSE, on the Transition Period, with 40 Specimens, 8vo. 16s.

Biography and *Memoirs.*

EXTRACTS of the JOURNALS and CORRESPONDENCE of MISS BERRY, from the Year 1783 to 1852. Edited by Lady THERESA LEWIS. Second Edition, with 3 Portraits. 3 vols. 8vo. 42s.

The DIARY of the Right Hon. WILLIAM WINDHAM, M.P. From 1783 to 1809. Edited by Mrs. HENRY BARING. 8vo. 18s.

LIFE of the DUKE of WELLINGTON. By the Rev. G. R. GLEIG, M.A. Popular Edition, carefully revised; with copious Additions. Crown 8vo. with Portrait, 5s.

Brialmont and Gleig's Life of the Duke of Wellington. (The Parent Work.) 4 vols. 8vo. with Illustrations, £2 14s.

Life of the Duke of Wellington, Intermediate Edition, partly from the French of M. BRIALMONT, partly from Original Documents. By the Rev. G. R. GLEIG, M.A. 8vo. with Portrait, 15s.

HISTORY of MY RELIGIOUS OPINIONS. By J. H. NEWMAN, D.D. Being the Substance of Apologia pro Vitâ Suâ. Post 8vo. 6s.

FATHER MATHEW: a Biography. By JOHN FRANCIS MAGUIRE, M.P. Popular Edition, with Portrait. Crown 8vo. 3s. 6d.

Rome; its Rulers and its Institutions. By the same Author. New Edition in preparation.

LIFE of AMELIA WILHELMINA SIEVEKING, from the German. Edited, with the Author's sanction, by CATHERINE WINKWORTH. Post 8vo. with Portrait, 12s.

MOZART'S LETTERS (1769–1791), translated from the Collection of Dr. LUDWIG NOHL by Lady WALLACE. 2 vols. post 8vo. with Portrait and Facsimile, 18s.

BEETHOVEN'S LETTERS (1790–1826), from the Two Collections of Drs. NOHL and discovered Letters to the Archduke Rudolph, Cardinal-Archbishop of Olmütz, VON KÖCHEL. Translated by Lady WALLACE. 2 vols. post 8vo. with Portrait.

FELIX MENDELSSOHN'S LETTERS from *Italy and Switzerland,* and *Letters from* 1833 *to* 1847, translated by Lady WALLACE. New Edition, with Portrait. 2 vols. crown 8vo. 5s. each.

NEW WORKS PUBLISHED BY LONGMANS AND CO.   5

RECOLLECTIONS of the late WILLIAM WILBERFORCE, M.P. for the County of York during nearly 30 Years. By J. S. HARFORD, F.R.S. Second Edition. Post 8vo. 7s.

MEMOIRS of SIR HENRY HAVELOCK, K.C.B. By JOHN CLARK MARSHMAN. Second Edition. 8vo. with Portrait, 12s. 6d.

THOMAS MOORE'S MEMOIRS, JOURNAL, and CORRESPONDENCE. Edited and abridged from the First Edition by Earl RUSSELL. Square crown 8vo. with 8 Portraits, 12s. 6d.

MEMOIR of the Rev. SYDNEY SMITH. By his Daughter, Lady HOLLAND. With a Selection from his Letters, edited by Mrs. AUSTIN. 2 vols. 8vo. 28s.

VICISSITUDES of FAMILIES. By Sir BERNARD BURKE, Ulster King of Arms. FIRST, SECOND, and THIRD SERIES. 3 vols. crown 8vo. 12s. 6d. each.

ESSAYS in ECCLESIASTICAL BIOGRAPHY. By the Right Hon. Sir J. STEPHEN, LL.D. Fourth Edition. 8vo. 14s.

BIOGRAPHIES of DISTINGUISHED SCIENTIFIC MEN. By FRANÇOIS ARAGO. Translated by Admiral W. H. SMYTH, F.R.S. the Rev. B. POWELL, M.A. and R. GRANT, M.A. 8vo. 18s.

MAUNDER'S BIOGRAPHICAL TREASURY: Memoirs, Sketches, and Brief Notices of above 12,000 Eminent Persons of All Ages and Nations. Fcp. 10s.

LETTERS and LIFE of FRANCIS BACON, including all his Occasional Works. Collected and edited, with a Commentary, by J. SPEDDING, Trin. Coll. Cantab. VOLS. I. and II. 8vo. 24s.

Criticism, Philosophy, Polity, &c.

The INSTITUTES of JUSTINIAN; with English Introduction, Translation, and Notes. By T. C. SANDARS, M.A. Barrister, late Fellow of Oriel Coll. Oxon. Third Edition. 8vo. 15s.

The ETHICS of ARISTOTLE. Illustrated with Essays and Notes. By Sir A. GRANT, Bart. M.A. LL.D. Director of Public Instruction in the Bombay Presidency. Second Edition, revised and completed. 2 vols. 8vo.

ELEMENTS of LOGIC. By R. WHATELY, D.D. late Archbishop of Dublin. Ninth Edition. 8vo. 10s. 6d. crown 8vo. 4s. 6d.

Elements of Rhetoric. By the same Author. Seventh Edition. 8vo. 10s. 6d. crown 8vo. 4s. 6d.

English Synonymes. Edited by Archbishop WHATELY. 5th Edition. Fcp. 3s.

BACON'S ESSAYS with ANNOTATIONS. By R. WHATELY, D.D. late Archbishop of Dublin. Sixth Edition. 8vo. 10s. 6d.

LORD BACON'S WORKS, collected and edited by R. L. ELLIS, M.A. J. SPEDDING, M.A. and D. D. HEATH. Vols. I. to V. *Philosophical Works,* 5 vols. 8vo. £4 6s. VOLS. VI. and VII. *Literary and Professional Works,* 2 vols. £1 16s.

On **REPRESENTATIVE GOVERNMENT.** By JOHN STUART MILL, M.P. for Westminster. Third Edition, 8vo. 9s. crown 8vo. 2s.

On Liberty. By the same Author. Third Edition. Post 8vo. 7s. 6d. crown 8vo. 1s. 4d.

Principles of Political Economy. By the same. Sixth Edition. 2 vols. 8vo. 30s. or in 1 vol. crown 8vo. 5s.

A System of Logic, Ratiocinative and Inductive. By the same. Sixth Edition. Two vols. 8vo. 25s.

Utilitarianism. By the same. Second Edition. 8vo. 5s.

Dissertations and Discussions. By the same Author. 2 vols. 8vo. price 24s.

Examination of Sir W. Hamilton's Philosophy, and of the Principal Philosophical Question discussed in his Writings. By the same Author. Second Edition. 8vo. 14s.

MISCELLANEOUS REMAINS from the Common-place Book of RICHARD WHATELY, D.D. late Archbishop of Dublin. Edited by Miss E. J. WHATELY. Crown 8vo. 7s. 6d.

ESSAYS on the ADMINISTRATIONS of GREAT BRITAIN from 1783 to 1830. By the Right Hon. Sir G. C. LEWIS, Bart. Edited by the Right Hon. Sir E. HEAD, Bart. 8vo. with Portrait, 15s.

By the same Author.

Inquiry into the Credibility of the Early Roman History, 2 vols. price 30s.

On the Methods of Observation and Reasoning in Politics, 2 vols. price 28s.

Irish Disturbances and Irish Church Question, 12s.

Remarks on the Use and Abuse of some Political Terms, 9s.

The Fables of Babrius, Greek Text with Latin Notes, PART I. 5s. 6d. PART II. 3s. 6d.

An OUTLINE of the NECESSARY LAWS of THOUGHT: a Treatise on Pure and Applied Logic. By the Most Rev. W. THOMSON, D.D. Archbishop of York. Crown 8vo. 5s. 6d.

The ELEMENTS of LOGIC. By THOMAS SHEDDEN, M.A. of St. Peter's Coll. Cantab. 12mo. 4s. 6d.

ANALYSIS of Mr. MILL'S SYSTEM of LOGIC. By W. STEBBING, M.A. Fellow of Worcester College, Oxford. Second Edition. 12mo. 3s. 6d.

The ELECTION of REPRESENTATIVES, Parliamentary and Municipal; a Treatise. By THOMAS HARE, Barrister-at-Law. Third Edition, with Additions. Crown 8vo. 6s.

SPEECHES of the RIGHT HON. LORD MACAULAY, corrected by
Himself. Library Edition, 8vo. 12s. People's Edition, crown 8vo. 3s. 6d.

LORD MACAULAY'S SPEECHES on PARLIAMENTARY REFORM
in 1831 and 1832. 16mo. 1s.

A DICTIONARY of the ENGLISH LANGUAGE. By R. G. LATHAM,
M.A. M.D. F.R.S. Founded on the Dictionary of Dr. S. JOHNSON, as edited
by the Rev. H. J. TODD, with numerous Emendations and Additions.
Publishing in 36 Parts, price 3s. 6d. each, to form 2 vols. 4to.

THESAURUS of ENGLISH WORDS and PHRASES, classified and
arranged so as to facilitate the Expression of Ideas, and assist in Literary
Composition. By P. M. ROGET, M.D. 18th Edition. Crown 8vo. 10s. 6d.

LECTURES on the SCIENCE of LANGUAGE, delivered at the Royal
Institution. By MAX MÜLLER, M.A. Taylorian Professor in the University
of Oxford. FIRST SERIES, Fourth Edition, 12s. SECOND SERIES, 18s.

CHAPTERS on LANGUAGE. By FREDERIC W. FARRAR, M.A. late
Fellow of Trin. Coll. Cambridge, Author of 'The Origin of Language,' &c.
Crown 8vo. 8s. 6d.

The **DEBATER**; a Series of Complete Debates, Outlines of Debates,
and Questions for Discussion. By F. ROWTON. Fcp. 6s.

A COURSE of ENGLISH READING, adapted to every taste and
capacity; or, How and What to Read. By the Rev. J. PYCROFT, B.A.
Fourth Edition. Fcp. 5s.

MANUAL of ENGLISH LITERATURE, Historical and Critical: with
a Chapter on English Metres. By THOMAS ARNOLD, B.A. Post 8vo. 10s. 6d.

SOUTHEY'S DOCTOR, complete in One Volume. Edited by the Rev.
J. W. WARTER, B.D. Square crown 8vo. 12s. 6d.

HISTORICAL and CRITICAL COMMENTARY on the OLD TESTA-
MENT; with a New Translation. By M. M. KALISCH, Ph.D. VOL. I.
Genesis, 8vo. 18s. or adapted for the General Reader, 12s. VOL. II. *Exodus,*
15s. or adapted for the General Reader, 12s.

A Hebrew Grammar, with Exercises. By the same. PART I. *Outlines with Exercises,* 8vo. 12s. 6d. KEY, 5s. PART II. *Exceptional Forms
and Constructions,* 12s. 6d.

A LATIN-ENGLISH DICTIONARY. By J. T. WHITE, M.A. of
Corpus Christi College, and J. E. RIDDLE, M.A. of St. Edmund Hall, Oxford.
Imperial 8vo. pp. 2,128, price 42s. cloth.

A New Latin-English Dictionary, abridged from the larger work
of *White* and *Riddle* (as above), by J. T. WHITE, M.A. Joint-Author.
Medium 8vo. pp. 1,048, price 18s. cloth.

The Junior Scholar's Latin-English Dictionary, abridged from the
larger works of *White* and *Riddle* (as above), by J. T. White, M.A. surviving
Joint-Author. Square 12mo. pp. 662, price 7s. 6d. cloth.

An **ENGLISH-GREEK LEXICON**, containing all the Greek Words used by Writers of good authority. By C. D. YONGE, B.A. Fifth Edition. 4to. 21s.

Mr. **YONGE'S NEW LEXICON**, English and Greek, abridged from his larger work (as above). Revised Edition. Square 12mo. 8s. 6d.

A **GREEK-ENGLISH LEXICON.** Compiled by H. G. LIDDELL, D.D. Dean of Christ Church, and R. SCOTT, D.D. Master of Balliol. Fifth Edition. Crown 4to. 31s. 6d.

A **Lexicon, Greek and English**, abridged from LIDDELL and SCOTT's *Greek-English Lexicon.* Eleventh Edition. Square 12mo. 7s. 6d.

A **SANSKRIT-ENGLISH DICTIONARY**, the Sanskrit words printed both in the original Devanagari and in Roman letters; with References to the Best Editions of Sanskrit Authors, and with Etymologies and Comparisons of Cognate Words chiefly in Greek, Latin. Gothic, and Anglo-Saxon. Compiled by T. BENFEY, Prof. in the Univ. of Göttingen. 8vo. 52s. 6d.

A **PRACTICAL DICTIONARY of the FRENCH and ENGLISH LANGUAGES.** By L. CONTANSEAU. Tenth Edition. Post 8vo. 10s. 6d.

Contanseau's Pocket Dictionary, French and English, abridged from the above by the Author. Third Edition, 18mo. 5s.

NEW PRACTICAL DICTIONARY of the GERMAN LANGUAGE; German-English and English-German. By the Rev. W. L. BLACKLEY, M.A. and Dr. CARL MARTIN FRIEDLANDER. Post 8vo. [*Nearly ready.*

Miscellaneous Works and *Popular Metaphysics.*

RECREATIONS of a COUNTRY PARSON. By A. K. H. B. FIRST SERIES, with 41 Woodcut Illustrations from Designs by R. T. Pritchett. Crown 8vo. 12s. 6d.

Recreations of a Country Parson. SECOND SERIES. Cr. 8vo. 3s. 6d.

The Common-place Philosopher in Town and Country. By the same Author. Crown 8vo. 3s. 6d.

Leisure Hours in Town; Essays Consolatory, Æsthetical, Moral, Social, and Domestic. By the same Author. Crown 8vo. 3s. 6d.

The Autumn Holidays of a Country Parson; Essays contributed to *Fraser's Magazine* and to *Good Words.* By the same. Crown 8vo. 3s. 6d.

The Graver Thoughts of a Country Parson. SECOND SERIES. By the same Author. Crown 8vo. 3s. 6d.

Critical Essays of a Country Parson. Selected from Essays contributed to *Fraser's Magazine.* By the same Author. Post 8vo. 9s.

A **CAMPAIGNER AT HOME.** By SHIRLEY, Author of 'Thalatta' and 'Nugæ Criticæ.' Post 8vo. with Vignette, 7s. 6d.

STUDIES in PARLIAMENT. A Series of Sketches of Leading Politicians. By R. H. HUTTON. [Reprinted from the 'Pall Mall Gazette.'] Crown 8vo. 4s. 6d.

LORD MACAULAY'S MISCELLANEOUS WRITINGS.
LIBRARY EDITION. 2 vols. 8vo. Portrait, 21s.
PEOPLE'S EDITION. 1 vol. crown 8vo. 4s. 6d.

The REV. SYDNEY SMITH'S MISCELLANEOUS WORKS; including his Contributions to the *Edinburgh Review*.
LIBRARY EDITION, 3 vols. 8vo. 36s.
TRAVELLER'S EDITION, in 1 vol. 21s.
CABINET EDITION, 3 vols. fcp. 21s.
PEOPLE'S EDITION, 2 vols. crown 8vo. 8s.

Elementary Sketches of Moral Philosophy, delivered at the Royal Institution. By the same Author. Fcp. 7s.

The Wit and Wisdom of the Rev. Sydney Smith: a Selection of the most memorable Passages in his Writings and Conversation. 16mo. 5s.

EPIGRAMS, Ancient and Modern; Humorous, Witty, Satirical, Moral, and Panegyrical. Edited by Rev. JOHN BOOTH, B.A. Cambridge. Second Edition, revised and enlarged. Fcp. 7s. 6d.

From MATTER to SPIRIT: the Result of Ten Years' Experience in Spirit Manifestations. By SOPHIA E. DE MORGAN. With a PREFACE by Professor DE MORGAN. Post 8vo. 8s. 6d.

ESSAYS selected from CONTRIBUTIONS to the *Edinburgh Review.* By HENRY ROGERS. Second Edition. 3 vols. fcp. 21s.

The Eclipse of Faith; or, a Visit to a Religious Sceptic. By the same Author. Eleventh Edition. Fcp. 5s.

Defence of the Eclipse of Faith, by its Author; a rejoinder to Dr. Newman's *Reply.* Third Edition. Fcp. 3s. 6d.

Selections from the Correspondence of R. E. H. Greyson. By the same Author. Third Edition. Crown 8vo. 7s. 6d.

Fulleriana, or the Wisdom and Wit of THOMAS FULLER, with Essay on his Life and Genius. By the same Author. 16mo. 2s. 6d.

An ESSAY on HUMAN NATURE; showing the Necessity of a Divine Revelation for the Perfect Development of Man's Capacities. By HENRY S. BOASE, M.D. F.R.S. and G.S.

The PHILOSOPHY of NATURE; a Systematic Treatise on the Causes and Laws of Natural Phænomena. By the same Author. 8vo. 12s.

An INTRODUCTION to MENTAL PHILOSOPHY, on the Inductive Method. By J. D. MORELL, M.A. LL.D. 8vo. 12s.

Elements of Psychology, containing the Analysis of the Intellectual Powers. By the same Author. Post 8vo. 7s. 6d.

B

The **SECRET of HEGEL**: being the Hegelian System in Origin, Principle, Form, and Matter. By JAMES HUTCHISON STIRLING. 2 vols. 8vo. 28s.

SIGHT and TOUCH: an Attempt to Disprove the Received (or Berkeleian) Theory of Vision. By THOMAS K. ABBOTT, M.A. Fellow and Tutor of Trin. Coll. Dublin. 8vo. with 21 Woodcuts, 5s. 6d.

The **SENSES and the INTELLECT**. By ALEXANDER BAIN, M.A. Professor of Logic in the University of Aberdeen. Second Edition. 8vo. price 15s.

The **Emotions and the Will**, by the same Author; completing a Systematic Exposition of the Human Mind. 8vo. 15s.

On the Study of Character, including an Estimate of Phrenology. By the same Author. 8vo. 9s.

TIME and SPACE: a Metaphysical Essay. By SHADWORTH H. HODGSON. 8vo. pp. 588, price 16s.

The **WAY to REST**: Results from a Life-search after Religious Truth. By R. VAUGHAN, D.D.

HOURS WITH THE MYSTICS: a Contribution to the History of Religious Opinion. By ROBERT ALFRED VAUGHAN, B.A. Second Edition. 2 vols. crown 8vo. 12s.

The **PHILOSOPHY of NECESSITY**; or Natural Law as applicable to Mental, Moral, and Social Science. By CHARLES BRAY. Second Edition. 8vo. 9s.

The **Education of the Feelings and Affections**. By the same Author. Third Edition. 8vo. 3s. 6d.

CHRISTIANITY and COMMON SENSE. By Sir WILLOUGHBY JONES, Bart. M.A. Trin. Coll. Cantab. 8vo. 6s.

Astronomy, Meteorology, Popular Geography, &c.

OUTLINES of ASTRONOMY. By Sir J. F. W. HERSCHEL, Bart. M.A. Eighth Edition, revised; with Plates and Woodcuts. 8vo. 18s.

ARAGO'S POPULAR ASTRONOMY. Translated by Admiral W. H. SMYTH, F.R.S. and R. GRANT, M.A. With 25 Plates and 358 Woodcuts. 2 vols. 8vo. £2 5s.

SATURN and its SYSTEM. By RICHARD A. PROCTOR, B.A. late Scholar of St John's Coll. Camb. and King's Coll. London. 8vo. with 14 Plates, 14s.

CELESTIAL OBJECTS for COMMON TELESCOPES. By the Rev. T. W. WEBB, M.A. F.R.A.S. With Map of the Moon, and Woodcuts. 16mo. 7s.

PHYSICAL GEOGRAPHY for SCHOOLS and GENERAL READERS. By M. F. MAURY, LL.D. Fcp. with 2 Charts, 2s. 6d.

M'CULLOCH'S DICTIONARY, Geographical, Statistical, and Historical, of the various Countries, Places, and Principal Natural Objects in the World. Revised Edit. printed in a larger type, with Maps, and with the Statistical Information throughout brought up to the latest returns by F. MARTIN. 4 vols. 8vo. 21s. each. VOL. I. now ready.

A GENERAL DICTIONARY of GEOGRAPHY, Descriptive, Physical, Statistical, and Historical: forming a complete Gazetteer of the World. By A. KEITH JOHNSTON, F.R.S.E. 8vo. 31s. 6d.

A MANUAL of GEOGRAPHY, Physical, Industrial, and Political. By W. HUGHES, F.R.G.S. Professor of Geography in King's College, and in Queen's College, London. With 6 Maps. Fcp. 7s. 6d.

The Geography of British History; a Geographical Description of the British Islands at Successive Periods. By the same. With 6 Maps. Fcp. 8s. 6d.

Abridged Text-Book of British Geography. By the same. Fcp. 1s. 6d.

MAUNDER'S TREASURY of GEOGRAPHY, Physical, Historical, Descriptive, and Political. Edited by W. HUGHES, F.R.G.S. With 7 Maps and 16 Plates. Fcp. 10s. 6d.

Natural History and *Popular Science.*

The ELEMENTS of PHYSICS or NATURAL PHILOSOPHY. By NEIL ARNOTT, M.D. F.R.S. Physician Extraordinary to the Queen. Sixth Edition, rewritten and completed. 2 Parts, 8vo. 21s.

HEAT CONSIDERED as a MODE of MOTION. By Professor JOHN TYNDALL, LL.D. F.R.S. Second Edition. Crown 8vo. with Woodcuts, 12s. 6d.

VOLCANOS, the Character of their Phenomena, their Share in the Structure and Composition of the Surface of the Globe, &c. By G. POULETT SCROPE, M.P. F.R.S. Second Edition. 8vo. with Illustrations, 15s.

A TREATISE on ELECTRICITY, in Theory and Practice. By A. DE LA RIVE, Prof. in the Academy of Geneva. Translated by C. V. WALKER, F.R.S. 3 vols. 8vo. with Woodcuts, £3 13s.

The CORRELATION of PHYSICAL FORCES. By W. R. GROVE, Q.C. V.P.R.S. Fourth Edition. 8vo. 7s. 6d.

MANUAL of GEOLOGY. By S. HAUGHTON, M.D. F.R.S. Fellow of Trin. Coll. and Prof. of Geol. in the Univ. of Dublin. Revised Edition, with 66 Woodcuts. Fcp. 6s.

A GUIDE to GEOLOGY. By J. PHILLIPS, M.A. Professor of Geology in the University of Oxford. Fifth Edition, with Plates. Fcp. 4s.

A GLOSSARY of MINERALOGY. By H. W. BRISTOW, F.G.S. of the Geological Survey of Great Britain. With 486 Figures. Crown 8vo. 12s.

PHILLIPS'S ELEMENTARY INTRODUCTION to MINERALOGY, with extensive Alterations and Additions, by H. J. BROOKE, F.R.S. and W. H. MILLER, F.G.S. Post 8vo. with Woodcuts, 18s.

VAN DER HOEVEN'S HANDBOOK of ZOOLOGY. Translated from the Second Dutch Edition by the Rev. W. CLARK, M.D. F.R.S. 2 vols. 8vo. with 24 Plates of Figures, 60s.

The COMPARATIVE ANATOMY and PHYSIOLOGY of the VERTEbrate Animals. By RICHARD OWEN, F.R.S. D.C.L. 3 vols. 8vo. with upwards of 1,200 Woodcuts. VOLS. I. and II. price 21s. each, now ready.

HOMES WITHOUT HANDS: a Description of the Habitations of Animals, classed according to their Principle of Construction. By Rev. J. G. WOOD, M.A. F.L.S. With about 140 Vignettes on Wood (20 full size of page). Second Edition. 8vo. 21s.

MANUAL of CORALS and SEA JELLIES. By J. R. GREENE, B.A. Edited by the Rev. J. A. GALBRAITH, M.A. and the Rev. S. HAUGHTON, M.D. Fcp. with 39 Woodcuts, 5s.

Manual of Sponges and Animalculæ; with a General Introduction on the Principles of Zoology. By the same Author and Editors. Fcp. with 16 Woodcuts, 2s.

Manual of the Metalloids. By J. APJOHN, M.D. F.R.S. and the same Editors. Revised Edition. Fcp. with 38 Woodcuts, 7s. 6d.

The HARMONIES of NATURE and UNITY of CREATION. By Dr. GEORGE HARTWIG. 8vo. with numerous Illustrations.

The Sea and its Living Wonders. By the same Author. Second (English) Edition. 8vo. with many Illustrations. 18s.

The Tropical World. By the same Author. With 8 Chromoxylographs and 172 Woodcuts. 8vo. 21s.

SKETCHES of the NATURAL HISTORY of CEYLON. By Sir J. EMERSON TENNENT, K.C.S. LL.D. With 82 Wood Engravings. Post 8vo. price 12s. 6d.

Ceylon. By the same Author. Fifth Edition; with Maps, &c. and 90 Wood Engravings. 2 vols. 8vo. £2 10s

A FAMILIAR HISTORY of BIRDS. By E. STANLEY, D.D. F.R.S. late Lord Bishop of Norwich. Seventh Edition, with Woodcuts. Fcp. 3s. 6d.

MARVELS and MYSTERIES of INSTINCT; or, Curiosities of Animal Life. By G. GARRATT. Third Edition. Fcp. 7s.

HOME WALKS and HOLIDAY RAMBLES. By the Rev. C. A. JOHNS, B.A. F.L.S. Fcp. 8vo. with 10 Illustrations, 6s.

KIRBY and SPENCE'S INTRODUCTION to ENTOMOLOGY, or Elements of the Natural History of Insects. Seventh Edition. Crown 8vo. price 5s.

MAUNDER'S TREASURY of NATURAL HISTORY, or Popular Dictionary of Zoology. Revised and corrected by T. S. COBBOLD, M.D. Fcp. with 900 Woodcuts, 10s.

The TREASURY of BOTANY, or Popular Dictionary of the Vegetable Kingdom; with which is incorporated a Glossary of Botanical Terms. Edited by J. LINDLEY, F.R.S. and T. MOORE, F.L.S. assisted by eminent Contributors. Pp. 1,274, with 274 Woodcuts and 20 Steel Plates. 2 Parts, fcp. 20s.

The **ELEMENTS of BOTANY** for **FAMILIES** and **SCHOOLS**.
Tenth Edition, revised by THOMAS MOORE, F.L.S. Fcp. with 154 Woodcuts, 2s. 6d.

The **ROSE AMATEUR'S GUIDE**. By THOMAS RIVERS. New Edition.
Fcp. 4s.

The **BRITISH FLORA**; comprising the Phænogamous or Flowering Plants and the Ferns. By Sir W. J. HOOKER, K.H. and G. A. WALKER-ARNOTT, LL.D. 12mo. with 12 Plates, 14s. or coloured, 21s.

BRYOLOGIA BRITANNICA; containing the Mosses of Great Britain and Ireland, arranged and described. By W. WILSON. 8vo. with 61 Plates 42s. or coloured, £4 4s.

The **INDOOR GARDENER**. By Miss MALING. Fcp. with Frontispiece, printed in Colours. 5s.

LOUDON'S ENCYCLOPÆDIA of PLANTS; comprising the Specific Character, Description, Culture, History, &c. of all the Plants found in Great Britain. With upwards of 12,000 Woodcuts. 8vo. £3 13s. 6d.

Loudon's Encyclopædia of Trees and Shrubs; containing the Hardy Trees and Shrubs of Great Britain scientifically and popularly described. With 2,000 Woodcuts. 8vo. 50s.

MAUNDER'S SCIENTIFIC and LITERARY TREASURY; a Popular Encyclopædia of Science, Literature, and Art. Fcp. 10s.

A DICTIONARY of SCIENCE, LITERATURE, and ART. Fourth Edition, re-edited by W. T. BRANDE (the Author), and GEORGE W. COX. M.A. assisted by gentlemen of eminent Scientific and Literary Acquirements. 3 vols. medium 8vo. price 63s. cloth.

ESSAYS on SCIENTIFIC and other SUBJECTS, contributed to Reviews. By Sir H. HOLLAND, Bart. M.D. Second Edition. 8vo. 14s.

ESSAYS from the EDINBURGH and QUARTERLY REVIEWS; with Addresses and other Pieces. By Sir J. F. W. HERSCHEL, Bart. M.A. 8vo. 18s.

Chemistry, Medicine, Surgery, and the *Allied Sciences*.

A DICTIONARY of CHEMISTRY and the Allied Branches of other Sciences; founded on that of the late Dr. Ure. By HENRY WATTS, F.C.S. assisted by eminent Contributors. 5 vols. medium 8vo. in course of publication in Parts. VOL. I. 31s. 6d. VOL. II. 26s. VOL. III. 31s. 6d. are now ready.

HANDBOOK of CHEMICAL ANALYSIS. Adapted to the Unitary System of Notation. By F. T. CONINGTON, M.A. F.C.S. Post 8vo. 7s. 6d.—TABLES of QUALITATIVE ANALYSIS adapted to the same, 2s. 6d.

A HANDBOOK of VOLUMETRICAL ANALYSIS. By ROBERT H. SCOTT, M.A. T.C.D. Post 8vo. 4s. 6d.

ELEMENTS of CHEMISTRY, Theoretical and Practical. By WILLIAM
A. MILLER, M.D. LL.D. F.R.S. F.G.S. Professor of Chemistry, King's
College, London. 3 vols. 8vo. £2 13s. PART I. CHEMICAL PHYSICS.
Third Edition, 12s. PART II. INORGANIC CHEMISTRY, 21s. PART III.
ORGANIC CHEMISTRY, Second Edition, 20s.

A MANUAL of CHEMISTRY, Descriptive and Theoretical. By
WILLIAM ODLING, M.B. F.R.S. PART I. 8vo. 9s.

A Course of Practical Chemistry, for the use of Medical Students.
By the same Author. Second Edition, with 70 new Woodcuts. Crown 8vo.
price 7s. 6d.

Lectures on Animal Chemistry, delivered at the Royal College of Physicians in 1865. By the same Author. Crown 8vo. 4s. 6d.

The DIAGNOSIS and TREATMENT of the DISEASES of WOMEN;
including the Diagnosis of Pregnancy. By GRAILY HEWITT, M.D. 8vo. 16s.

LECTURES on the DISEASES of INFANCY and CHILDHOOD. By
CHARLES WEST, M.D. &c. Fifth Edition, revised and enlarged. 8vo. 16s.

EXPOSITION of the SIGNS and SYMPTOMS of PREGNANCY:
with other Papers on subjects connected with Midwifery. By W. F.
MONTGOMERY, M.A. M.D. M.R.I.A. 8vo. with Illustrations, 25s.

A SYSTEM of SURGERY, Theoretical and Practical. In Treatises
by Various Authors. Edited by T. HOLMES, M.A. Cantab. Assistant-Surgeon
to St. George's Hospital. 4 vols. 8vo. £4 13s.

Vol. I. **General Pathology.** 21s.

Vol. II. **Local Injuries:** Gunshot Wounds, Injuries of the Head,
Back, Face, Neck, Chest, Abdomen, Pelvis, of the Upper and Lower Extremities, and Diseases of the Eye. 21s.

Vol. III. **Operative Surgery** Diseases of the Organs of Circulation, Locomotion, &c. 21s.

Vol. IV. **Diseases of the Organs of Digestion, of the Genito-Urinary System,** and of the Breast, Thyroid Gland, and Skin; with
APPENDIX and GENERAL INDEX. 30s.

LECTURES on the PRINCIPLES and PRACTICE of PHYSIC. By
THOMAS WATSON, M.D. Physician-Extraordinary to the Queen. Fourth
Edition. 2 vols. 8vo. 34s.

LECTURES on SURGICAL PATHOLOGY. By J. PAGET, F.R.S. Surgeon-Extraordinary to the Queen. Edited by W. TURNER, M.B. 8vo. with
117 Woodcuts, 21s.

A TREATISE on the CONTINUED FEVERS of GREAT BRITAIN.
By C. MURCHISON, M.D. Senior Physician to the London Fever Hospital.
8vo. with coloured Plates, 18s.

ANATOMY, DESCRIPTIVE and SURGICAL. By HENRY GRAY,
F.R.S. With 410 Wood Engravings from Dissections. Third Edition, by
T. HOLMES, M.A. Cantab. Royal 8vo. 28s.

The CYCLOPÆDIA of ANATOMY and PHYSIOLOGY. Edited by
the late R. B. TODD, M.D. F.R.S. Assisted by nearly all the most eminent
cultivators of Physiological Science of the present age. 5 vols. 8vo. with
2,853 Woodcuts, £6 6s.

PHYSIOLOGICAL ANATOMY and PHYSIOLOGY of MAN. By the late R. B. TODD, M.D. F.R.S. and W. BOWMAN, F.R.S. of King's College. With numerous Illustrations. VOL. II. 8vo. 25s.

A DICTIONARY of PRACTICAL MEDICINE. By J. COPLAND, M.D. F.R.S. Abridged from the larger work by the Author, assisted by J. C. COPLAND, M.R.C.S. and throughout brought down to the present State of Medical Science. Pp. 1,560 in 8vo. price 36s.

Dr. Copland's Dictionary of Practical Medicine (the larger work). 3 vols. 8vo. £5 11s.

The WORKS of SIR B. C. BRODIE, Bart. collected and arranged by CHARLES HAWKINS, F.R.C.S.E. 3 vols. 8vo. with Medallion and Facsimile, 48s.

Autobiography of Sir B. C. Brodie, Bart. Printed from the Author's materials left in MS. Second Edition. Fcp. 4s. 6d.

The TOXICOLOGIST'S GUIDE: a New Manual on Poisons, giving the Best Methods to be pursued for the Detection of Poisons (post-mortem or otherwise). By JOHN HORSLEY, F.C.S. Analytical Chemist.

A MANUAL of MATERIA MEDICA and THERAPEUTICS, abridged from Dr. PEREIRA'S *Elements* by F. J. FARRE, M.D. assisted by R. BENTLEY, M.R.C.S. and by R. WARINGTON, F.R.S. 8vo. with 90 Woodcuts, 21s.

Dr. Pereira's Elements of Materia Medica and Therapeutics. Third Edition. By A. S. TAYLOR, M.D. and G. O. REES, M.D. 3 vols. 8vo. with Woodcuts, £3 15s.

THOMSON'S CONSPECTUS of the BRITISH PHARMACOPŒIA. Twenty-fourth Edition, corrected and made conformable throughout to the New Pharmacopœia of the General Council of Medical Education. By E. LLOYD BIRKETT, M.D. 18mo. 5s. 6d.

MANUAL of the DOMESTIC PRACTICE of MEDICINE. By W. B. KESTEVEN, F.R.C.S.E. Second Edition, revised, with Additions. Fcp. 5s.

The RESTORATION of HEALTH; or, the Application of the Laws of Hygiene to the Recovery of Health: a Manual for the Invalid, and a Guide in the Sick Room. By W. STRANGE, M.D. Fcp. 6s.

SEA-AIR and SEA-BATHING for CHILDREN and INVALIDS By the same Author. Fcp. boards, 3s.

MANUAL for the CLASSIFICATION, TRAINING, and EDUCATION of the Feeble-Minded, Imbecile, and Idiotic. By P. MARTIN DUNCAN, M.B. and WILLIAM MILLARD. Crown 8vo. 5s.

The Fine Arts, and *Illustrated Editions*.

The NEW TESTAMENT, illustrated with Wood Engravings after the Early Masters, chiefly of the Italian School. Crown 4to. 63s. cloth, gilt top or £5 5s. elegantly bound in morocco.

LYRA GERMANICA; Hymns for the Sundays and Chief Festivals of the Christian Year. Translated by CATHERINE WINKWORTH; 125 Illustrations on Wood drawn by J. LEIGHTON, F.S.A. Fcp. 4to. 21s.

The **LIFE of MAN SYMBOLISED** by the **MONTHS** of the **YEAR** in their Seasons and Phases; with Passages selected from Ancient and Modern Authors. By RICHARD PIGOT. Accompanied by a Series of 25 full-page Illustrations and numerous Marginal Devices, Decorative Initial Letters, and Tailpieces, engraved on Wood from Original Designs by JOHN LEIGHTON, F.S.A. 4to. 42s.

CATS' and FARLIE'S MORAL EMBLEMS; with Aphorisms, Adages, and Proverbs of all Nations: comprising 121 Illustrations on Wood by J. LEIGHTON, F.S.A. with an appropriate Text by R. PIGOT. Imperial 8vo. 31s. 6d.

SHAKSPEARE'S SENTIMENTS and SIMILES, printed in Black and Gold, and Illuminated in the Missal Style by HENRY NOEL HUMPHREYS. In massive covers, containing the Medallion and Cypher of Shakspeare. Square post 8vo. 21s.

The **HISTORY of OUR LORD**, as exemplified in Works of Art. Being the fourth and concluding series of 'Sacred and Legendary Art.' By Mrs. JAMESON and Lady EASTLAKE. Second Edition, with 13 Etchings and 281 Woodcuts. 2 vols. square crown 8vo. 42s.

In the same Series, by Mrs. JAMESON.

Legends of the Saints and Martyrs. Fourth Edition, with 19 Etchings and 187 Woodcuts. 2 vols. 31s. 6d.

Legends of the Monastic Orders. Third Edition, with 11 Etchings and 88 Woodcuts. 1 vol. 21s.

Legends of the Madonna. Third Edition, with 27 Etchings and 165 Woodcuts. 1 vol. 21s.

Arts, Manufactures, &c.

DRAWING from NATURE; a Series of Progressive Instructions in Sketching, from Elementary Studies to Finished Views, with Examples from Switzerland and the Pyrenees. By GEORGE BARNARD, Professor of Drawing at Rugby School. With 18 Lithographic Plates, and 108 Wood Engravings. Imp. 8vo. 25s.

ENCYCLOPÆDIA of ARCHITECTURE, Historical, Theoretical, and Practical. By JOSEPH GWILT. With more than 1,000 Woodcuts. 8vo. 42s.

TUSCAN SCULPTORS, their Lives, Works, and Times. With 45 Etchings and 28 Woodcuts from Original Drawings and Photographs. By CHARLES C. PERKINS. 2 vols. imperial 8vo. 63s.

The **GRAMMAR of HERALDRY**: containing a Description of all the Principal Charges used in Armory, the Signification of Heraldic Terms, and the Rules to be observed in Blazoning and Marshalling. By JOHN E. CUSSANS. Fcp. with 196 Woodcuts, 4s. 6d.

The **ENGINEER'S HANDBOOK**; explaining the Principles which should guide the young Engineer in the Construction of Machinery. By C. S. LOWNDES. Post 8vo. 5s.

NEW WORKS PUBLISHED BY LONGMANS AND CO. 17

The ELEMENTS of MECHANISM. By T. M. GOODEVE, M.A.
Professor of Mechanics at the R. M. Acad. Woolwich. Second Edition,
with 217 Woodcuts. Post 8vo. 6s. 6d.

URE'S DICTIONARY of ARTS, MANUFACTURES, and MINES.
Re-written and enlarged by ROBERT HUNT, F.R.S. assisted by numerous
gentlemen eminent in Science and the Arts. With 2,000 Woodcuts. 3 vols.
8vo. £4.

ENCYCLOPÆDIA of CIVIL ENGINEERING, Historical, Theoretical,
and Practical. By E. CRESY, C.E. With above 3,000 Woodcuts. 8vo. 42s.

TREATISE on MILLS and MILLWORK. By W. FAIRBAIRN, C.E.
Second Edition, with 18 Plates and 322 Woodcuts. 2 vols. 8vo. 32s.

Useful Information for Engineers. By the same Author. FIRST
and SECOND SERIES, with many Plates and Woodcuts. 2 vols. crown 8vo.
10s. 6d. each.

The Application of Cast and Wrought Iron to Building Purposes.
By the same Author. Third Edition, with 6 Plates and 118 Woodcuts. 8vo. 16s.

IRON SHIP BUILDING, its History and Progress, as comprised in a
Series of Experimental Researches on the Laws of Strain; the Strengths,
Forms, and other conditions of the Material; and an Inquiry into the Present
and Prospective State of the Navy, including the Experimental Results on
the Resisting Powers of Armour Plates and Shot at High Velocities. By the
same Author. With 4 Plates and 130 Woodcuts. 8vo. 18s.

The PRACTICAL MECHANIC'S JOURNAL: an Illustrated Record
of Mechanical and Engineering Science, and Epitome of Patent Inventions.
4to. price 1s. monthly.

The PRACTICAL DRAUGHTSMAN'S BOOK of INDUSTRIAL DE-
SIGN. By W. JOHNSON, Assoc. Inst. C.E. With many hundred Illustrations.
4to. 28s. 6d.

The PATENTEE'S MANUAL. a Treatise on the Law and Practice of
Letters Patent for the use of Patentees and Inventors. By J. and J. H.
JOHNSON. Post 8vo. 7s. 6d.

The ARTISAN CLUB'S TREATISE on the STEAM ENGINE, in its
various Applications to Mines, Mills, Steam Navigation, Railways and Agriculture. By J. BOURNE, C.E. Seventh Edition; with 37 Plates and 546
Woodcuts. 4to. 42s.

Catechism of the Steam Engine, in its various Applications to
Mines, Mills, Steam Navigation, Railways, and Agriculture. By the same
Author. With 199 Woodcuts. Fcp. 9s. The INTRODUCTION of 'Recent
Improvements' may be had separately, with 110 Woodcuts, price 3s. 6d.

Handbook of the Steam Engine. By the same Author, forming a
KEY to the Catechism of the Steam Engine, with 67 Woodcuts. Fcp. 9s.

A TREATISE on the SCREW PROPELLER, SCREW VESSELS, and
Screw Engines, as adapted for purposes of Peace and War; illustrated by
many Plates and Woodcuts. By the same Author. New and enlarged
Edition, in course of publication in 24 Parts. Royal 4to. 2s. 6d. each.

The THEORY of WAR Illustrated by numerous Examples from
History. By Lieut.-Col. P. L. MACDOUGALL. Third Edition, with 10 Plans.
Post 8vo. 10s. 6d.

C

The **ART of PERFUMERY**; the History and Theory of Odours, and the Methods of Extracting the Aromas of Plants. By Dr. PIESSE, F.C.S. Third Edition, with 53 Woodcuts. Crown 8vo. 10s. 6d.

Chemical, Natural, and Physical Magic, for Juveniles during the Holidays. By the same Author. Third Edition, enlarged, with 38 Woodcuts. Fcp. 6s.

TALPA; or the Chronicles of a Clay Farm. By C. W. HOSKYNS, Esq. Sixth Edition, with 24 Woodcuts by G. CRUIKSHANK. 16mo. 5s. 6d.

LOUDON'S ENCYCLOPÆDIA of AGRICULTURE: comprising the Laying-out, Improvement, and Management of Landed Property, and the Cultivation and Economy of the Productions of Agriculture. With 1,100 Woodcuts. 8vo. 31s. 6d.

Loudon's Encylopædia of Gardening: comprising the Theory and Practice of Horticulture, Floriculture, Arboriculture, and Landscape Gardening. With 1,000 Woodcuts. 8vo. 31s. 6d.

Loudon's Encyclopædia of Cottage, Farm, and Villa Architecture and Furniture. With more than 2,000 Woodcuts. 8vo. 42s.

HISTORY of WINDSOR GREAT PARK and WINDSOR FOREST. By WILLIAM MENZIES, Resident Deputy Surveyor. With 2 Maps and 20 Photographs. Imp. folio, £8 8s.

BAYLDON'S ART of VALUING RENTS and TILLAGES, and Claims of Tenants upon Quitting Farms, both at Michaelmas and Lady-Day. Eighth Edition, revised by J. C. MORTON. 8vo. 10s. 6d.

Religious and *Moral Works.*

An **EXPOSITION of the 39 ARTICLES**, Historical and Doctrinal. By E. HAROLD BROWNE, D.D. Lord Bishop of Ely. Seventh Edit. 8vo. 16s.

The Pentateuch and the Elohistic Psalms, in Reply to Bishop Colenso. By the same. Second Edition. 8vo. 2s.

Examination Questions on Bishop Browne's Exposition of the Articles. By the Rev. J. GORLE, M.A. Fcp. 3s. 6d.

FIVE LECTURES on the CHARACTER of ST. PAUL; being the Hulsean Lectures for 1862. By the Rev. J. S. HOWSON, D.D. Second Edition. 8vo. 9s.

The LIFE and EPISTLES of ST. PAUL. By W. J. CONYBEARE, M.A. late Fellow of Trin. Coll. Cantab. and J. S. HOWSON, D.D. late Principal of Liverpool College.

LIBRARY EDITION, with all the Original Illustrations, Maps, Landscapes on Steel, Woodcuts, &c. 2 vols. 4to. 48s.

INTERMEDIATE EDITION, with a Selection of Maps, Plates, and Woodcuts. 2 vols. square crown 8vo. 31s. 6d.

PEOPLE'S EDITION, revised and condensed, with 46 Illustrations and Maps. 2 vols. crown 8vo. 12s.

The VOYAGE and SHIPWRECK of ST. PAUL; with Dissertations on the Ships and Navigation of the Ancients. By JAMES SMITH, F.R.S. Crown 8vo. Charts, 8s. 6d.

FASTI SACRI, or a Key to the Chronology of the New Testament; comprising an Historical Harmony of the Four Gospels, and Chronological Tables generally from B.C. 70 to A.D. 70 : with a Preliminary Dissertation on the Chronology of the New Testament, and other Aids to the elucidation of the subject. By THOMAS LEWIN, M.A. F.S.A. Imperial 8vo. 42s.

A CRITICAL and GRAMMATICAL COMMENTARY on ST. PAUL'S Epistles. By C. J. ELLICOTT, D.D. Lord Bishop of Gloucester and Bristol. 8vo.

Galatians, Third Edition, 8s. 6d.

Ephesians, Third Edition, 8s. 6d.

Pastoral Epistles, Third Edition, 10s. 6d.

Philippians, Colossians, and Philemon, Third Edition, 10s. 6d.

Thessalonians, Second Edition, 7s. 6d.

Historical Lectures on the Life of our Lord Jesus Christ: being the Hulsean Lectures for 1859. By the same Author. Fourth Edition. 8vo. price 10s. 6d.

The Destiny of the Creature; and other Sermons preached before the University of Cambridge. By the same. Fourth Edition. Post 8vo. 5s.

The Broad and the Narrow Way; Two Sermons preached before the University of Cambridge. By the same. Crown 8vo. 2s.

Rev. T. H. HORNE'S INTRODUCTION to the CRITICAL STUDY and Knowledge of the Holy Scriptures. Eleventh Edition, corrected and extended under careful Editorial revision. With 4 Maps and 22 Woodcuts and Facsimiles. 4 vols. 8vo. £3 13s. 6d.

Rev. T. H. Horne's Compendious Introduction to the Study of the Bible, being an Analysis of the larger work by the same Author. Re-edited by the Rev. JOHN AYRE, M.A. With Maps. &c. Post 8vo. 9s.

The TREASURY of BIBLE KNOWLEDGE; being a Dictionary of the Books, Persons, Places, Events, and other matters of which mention is made in Holy Scripture: intended to establish its Authority and illustrate its Contents. By Rev. J. AYRE, M.A. With Maps, 16 Plates, and numerous Woodcuts. Fcp. 10s. 6d.

The GREEK TESTAMENT; with Notes, Grammatical and Exegetical. By the Rev. W. WEBSTER, M.A. and the Rev. W. F. WILKINSON, M.A. 2 vols. 8vo. £2 4s.

VOL. I. the Gospels and Acts, 20s.

VOL. II. the Epistles and Apocalypse, 24s.

EVERY-DAY SCRIPTURE DIFFICULTIES explained and illustrated. By J. E. PRESCOTT, M.A. VOL. I. *Matthew* and *Mark*; VOL. II. *Luke* and *John*. 2 vols. 8vo. 9s. each.

The PENTATEUCH and BOOK of JOSHUA CRITICALLY EXAMINED. By the Right Rev. J. W. COLENSO, D.D. Lord Bishop of Natal. People's Edition, in 1 vol. crown 8vo. 6s. or in 5 Parts, 1s. each.

The PENTATEUCH and BOOK of JOSHUA CRITICALLY EXAMINED. By Prof. A. KUENEN, of Leyden. Translated from the Dutch, and edited with Notes, by J. W. COLENSO, D.D. Bishop of Natal. 8vo. 8s. 6d.

The CHURCH and the WORLD: Essays on Questions of the Day. By Various Writers. Edited by the Rev. ORBY SHIPLEY, M.A. 8vo.

The **FORMATION of CHRISTENDOM.** Part I. By T. W. Allies, 8vo. 12s.

CHRISTENDOM'S DIVISIONS: a Philosophical Sketch of the Divisions of the Christian Family in East and West. By Edmund S. Ffoulkes, formerly Fellow and Tutor of Jesus Coll. Oxford. Post 8vo. 7s. 6d.

Christendom's Divisions, Part II. Greeks and Latins, being a History of their Dissensions and Overtures for Peace down to the Reformation. By the same Author. [*Nearly ready*.

The **LIFE of CHRIST**: an Eclectic Gospel, from the Old and New Testaments, arranged on a New Principle, with Analytical Tables, &c. By Charles De la Pryme, M.A. Trin. Coll. Camb. Revised Edition. 8vo. 5s.

The **HIDDEN WISDOM of CHRIST** and the **KEY of KNOWLEDGE**; or, History of the Apocrypha. By Ernest de Bunsen. 2 vols. 8vo. 28s.

ESSAYS on RELIGION and LITERATURE. Edited by the Most Rev. Archbishop Manning. 8vo. 10s. 6d.

The **TEMPORAL MISSION of the HOLY GHOST**; or, Reason and Revelation. By the Most Rev. Archbishop Manning. Second Edition. Crown 8vo. 8s. 6d.

ESSAYS and REVIEWS. By the Rev. W. Temple, D.D. the Rev. R. Williams, B.D. the Rev. B. Powell, M.A. the Rev. H. B. Wilson, B.D. C. W. Goodwin, M.A. the Rev. M. Pattison, B.D. and the Rev. B. Jowett, M.A. Twelfth Edition. Fcp. 8vo. 5s.

MOSHEIM'S ECCLESIASTICAL HISTORY. Murdock and Soames's Translation and Notes, re-edited by the Rev. W. Stubbs, M.A. 3 vols. 8vo. 45s.

BISHOP JEREMY TAYLOR'S ENTIRE WORKS: With Life by Bishop Heber. Revised and corrected by the Rev. C. P. Eden, 10 vols. price £5 5s.

PASSING THOUGHTS on RELIGION. By the Author of 'Amy Herbert.' New Edition. Fcp. 8vo. 5s.

Thoughts for the Holy Week, for Young Persons. By the same Author. Third Edition. Fcp. 8vo. 2s.

Night Lessons from Scripture. By the same Author. Second Edition. 32mo. 3s.

Self-Examination before Confirmation. By the same Author. 32mo. price 1s. 6d.

Readings for a Month Preparatory to Confirmation, from Writers of the Early and English Church. By the same. Fcp. 4s.

Readings for Every Day in Lent, compiled from the Writings of Bishop Jeremy Taylor. By the same. Fcp. 5s.

Preparation for the Holy Communion; the Devotions chiefly from the works of Jeremy Taylor. By the same. 32mo. 3s.

MORNING CLOUDS. Second Edition. Fcp. 5s.

PRINCIPLES of EDUCATION Drawn from Nature and Revelation, and applied to Female Education in the Upper Classes. By the same. 2 vols. fcp. 12s. 6d.

The **WIFE'S MANUAL**; or, Prayers, Thoughts, and Songs on Several Occasions of a Matron's Life. By the Rev. W. CALVERT, M.A. Crown 8vo. price 10s. 6d.

SPIRITUAL SONGS for the **SUNDAYS** and **HOLIDAYS** throughout the Year. By J. S. B. MONSELL, LL.D. Vicar of Egham. Fourth Edition. Fcp. 4s. 6d.

The Beatitudes: Abasement before God; Sorrow for Sin; Meekness of Spirit; Desire for Holiness; Gentleness; Purity of Heart; the Peacemakers; Sufferings for Christ. By the same. Second Edition, fcp. 3s. 6d.

LYRA DOMESTICA; Christian Songs for Domestic Edification. Translated from the *Psaltery and Harp* of C. J. P. SPITTA, and from other sources, by RICHARD MASSIE. FIRST and SECOND SERIES, fcp. 4s. 6d. each.

LYRA SACRA; Hymns, Ancient and Modern, Odes and Fragments of Sacred Poetry. Edited by the Rev. B. W. SAVILE, M.A. Third Edition, enlarged and improved. Fcp. 5s.

LYRA GERMANICA, translated from the German by Miss C. WINKWORTH. FIRST SERIES, Hymns for the Sundays and Chief Festivals; SECOND SERIES, the Christian Life. Fcp. 5s. each SERIES.

Hymns from Lyra Germanica, 18mo. 1s.

LYRA EUCHARISTICA; Hymns and Verses on the Holy Communion, Ancient and Modern: with other Poems. Edited by the Rev. ORBY SHIPLEY, M.A. Second Edition. Fcp. 7s. 6d.

Lyra Messianica; Hymns and Verses on the Life of Christ, Ancient and Modern; with other Poems. By the same Editor. Second Edition, altered and enlarged. Fcp. 7s. 6d.

Lyra Mystica; Hymns and Verses on Sacred Subjects, Ancient and Modern. By the same Editor. Fcp. 7s. 6d.

The CHORALE BOOK for ENGLAND; a complete Hymn-Book in accordance with the Services and Festivals of the Church of England: the Hymns translated by Miss C. WINKWORTH; the tunes arranged by Prof. W. S. BENNETT and OTTO GOLDSCHMIDT. Fcp. 4to. 12s. 6d.

Congregational Edition. Fcp. 2s.

The CATHOLIC DOCTRINE of the ATONEMENT: an Historical Inquiry into its Development in the Church; with an Introduction on the Principle of Theological Developments. By H. N. OXENHAM, M.A. formerly Scholar of Balliol College, Oxford. 8vo. 8s. 6d.

FROM SUNDAY TO SUNDAY: an attempt to consider familiarly the Weekday Life and Labours of a Country Clergyman. By R. GEE, M.A Vicar of Abbott's Langley and Rural Dean. Fcp. 5s.

FIRST SUNDAYS at CHURCH; or, Familiar Conversations on the Morning and Evening Services of the Church of England. By J. E. RIDDLE, M.A. Fcp. 2s. 6d.

The JUDGMENT of CONSCIENCE, and other Sermons. By RICHARD WHATELY, D.D. late Archbishop of Dublin. Crown 8vo. 4s. 6d.

PALEY'S MORAL PHILOSOPHY, with Annotations. By RICHARD WHATELY, D.D. late Archbishop of Dublin. 8vo. 7s.

Travels, Voyages, &c.

OUTLINE SKETCHES of the HIGH ALPS of DAUPHINÉ. By T. G. BONNEY, M.A. F.G.S. M.A.C. Fellow of St. John's Coll. Camb. With 13 Plates and a Coloured Map. Post 4to. 16s.

ICE-CAVES of FRANCE and SWITZERLAND; a Narrative of Subterranean Exploration. By the Rev. G. F. BROWNE, M.A. Fellow and Assistant-Tutor of St. Catherine's Coll. Cambridge, M.A.C. With 11 Illustrations on Wood. Square crown 8vo. 12s. 6d.

VILLAGE LIFE in SWITZERLAND. By SOPHIA D. DELMARD. Post 8vo. 9s. 6d.

HOW WE SPENT the SUMMER; or, a Voyage en Zigzag in Switzerland and Tyrol with some Members of the ALPINE CLUB. From the Sketch-Book of one of the Party. Third Edition, re-drawn. In oblong 4to. with about 300 Illustrations, 15s.

BEATEN TRACKS; or, Pen and Pencil Sketches in Italy. By the Authoress of 'A Voyage en Zigzag.' With 42 Plates, containing about 200 Sketches from Drawings made on the Spot. 8vo. 16s.

MAP of the CHAIN of MONT BLANC, from an actual Survey in 1863—1864. By A. ADAMS-REILLY, F.R.G.S. M.A.C. Published under the Authority of the Alpine Club. In Chromolithography on extra stout drawing-paper 28in. × 17in. price 10s. or mounted on canvas in a folding case, 12s. 6d.

TRANSYLVANIA, its PRODUCTS and its PEOPLE. By CHARLES BONER. With 5 Maps and 43 Illustrations on Wood and in Chromolithography. 8vo. 21s.

EXPLORATIONS in SOUTH WEST AFRICA, from Walvisch Bay to Lake Ngami and the Victoria Falls. By THOMAS BAINES, F.R.G.S. 8vo. with Map and Illustrations, 21s.

VANCOUVER ISLAND and BRITISH COLUMBIA; their History, Resources, and Prospects. By MATTHEW MACFIE, F.R.G.S. With Maps and Illustrations. 8vo. 18s.

HISTORY of DISCOVERY in our AUSTRALASIAN COLONIES, Australia, Tasmania, and New Zealand, from the Earliest Date to the Present Day. By WILLIAM HOWITT. With 3 Maps of the Recent Explorations from Official Sources. 2 vols. 8vo. 28s.

The CAPITAL of the TYCOON; a Narrative of a Three Years' Residence in Japan. By Sir RUTHERFORD ALCOCK, K.C.B. 2 vols. 8vo. with numerous Illustrations, 42s.

LAST WINTER in ROME. By C. R. WELD. With Portrait and Engravings on Wood. Post 8vo. 14s.

AUTUMN RAMBLES in NORTH AFRICA. By JOHN ORMSBY, of the Middle Temple. With 16 Illustrations. Post 8vo. 8s. 6d.

The DOLOMITE MOUNTAINS. Excursions through Tyrol, Carinthia, Carniola, and Friuli in 1861, 1862, and 1863. By J. GILBERT and G. C. CHURCHILL, F.R.G.S. With numerous Illustrations. Square crown 8vo. 21s.

A SUMMER TOUR in the GRISONS and ITALIAN VALLEYS of the Bernina. By Mrs. HENRY FRESHFIELD. With 2 Coloured Maps and 4 Views. Post 8vo. 10s. 6d.

Alpine Byeways; or, Light Leaves gathered in 1859 and 1860. By the same Authoress. Post 8vo. with Illustrations, 10s. 6d.

A LADY'S TOUR ROUND MONTE ROSA; including Visits to the Italian Valleys. With Map and Illustrations. Post 8vo. 14s.

GUIDE to the PYRENEES, for the use of Mountaineers. By CHARLES PACKE. With Maps, &c. and Appendix. Fcp. 6s.

The ALPINE GUIDE. By JOHN BALL, M.R.I.A. late President of the Alpine Club. Post 8vo. with Maps and other Illustrations.

Guide to the Eastern Alps, *nearly ready.*

Guide to the Western Alps, including Mont Blanc, Monte Rosa, Zermatt, &c. 7s. 6d.

Guide to the Oberland and all Switzerland, excepting the Neighbourhood of Monte Rosa and the Great St. Bernard; with Lombardy and the adjoining portion of Tyrol. 7s. 6d.

A GUIDE to SPAIN. By H. O'SHEA. Post 8vo. with Travelling Map, 15s.

CHRISTOPHER COLUMBUS; his Life, Voyages, and Discoveries. Revised Edition, with 4 Woodcuts. 18mo. 2s. 6d.

CAPTAIN JAMES COOK; his Life, Voyages, and Discoveries. Revised Edition, with numerous Woodcuts. 18mo. 2s. 6d.

HUMBOLDT'S TRAVELS and DISCOVERIES in SOUTH AMERICA. Third Edition, with numerous Woodcuts. 18mo. 2s. 6d.

MUNGO PARK'S LIFE and TRAVELS in AFRICA, with an Account of his Death and the Substance of Later Discoveries. Sixth Edition, with Woodcuts. 18mo. 2s. 6d.

NARRATIVES of SHIPWRECKS of the ROYAL NAVY between 1793 and 1857, compiled from Official Documents in the Admiralty by W. O. S. GILLY; with a Preface by W. S. GILLY, D.D. Third Edition, fcp. 5s.

A WEEK at the LAND'S END. By J. T. BLIGHT; assisted by E. H. RODD, R. Q. COUCH, and J. RALFS. With Map and 96 Woodcuts. Fcp. price 6s. 6d.

VISITS to REMARKABLE PLACES: Old Halls, Battle-Fields, and Scenes Illustrative of Striking Passages in English History and Poetry. By WILLIAM HOWITT. 2 vols. square crown 8vo. with Wood Engravings, price 25s.

The RURAL LIFE of ENGLAND. By the same Author. With Woodcuts by Bewick and Williams. Medium 8vo. 12s. 6d.

Works of *Fiction.*

ATHERSTONE PRIORY. By L. N. COMYN. 2 vols. post 8vo. 21s.

Ellice: a Tale. By the same Author. Post 8vo. 9s. 6d.

STORIES and TALES by the Author of 'Amy Herbert,' uniform Edition, each Tale or Story complete in a single Volume.

AMY HERBERT, 2s. 6d.
GERTRUDE. 2s. 6d.
EARL'S DAUGHTER, 2s. 6d.
EXPERIENCE OF LIFE, 2s. 6d.
CLEVE HALL, 3s. 6d.

IVORS, 3s. 6d.
KATHARINE ASHTON, 3s. 6d.
MARGARET PERCIVAL, 5s.
LANETON PARSONAGE, 4s. 6d.
URSULA, 4s. 6d.

A Glimpse of the World. By the Author of 'Amy Herbert.' Fcp. 7s. 6d.

THE SIX SISTERS of the VALLEYS: an Historical Romance. By W. BRAMLEY-MOORE, M.A. Incumbent of Gerrard's Cross, Bucks. Third Edition, with 14 Illustrations. Crown 8vo. 5s.

The GLADIATORS: A Tale of Rome and Judæa. By G. J. WHYTE MELVILLE. Crown 8vo. 5s.

Digby Grand, an Autobiography. By the same Author. 1 vol. 5s.

Kate Coventry, an Autobiography. By the same. 1 vol. 5s.

General Bounce, or the Lady and the Locusts. By the same. 1 vol. 5s.

Holmby House, a Tale of Old Northamptonshire. 1 vol. 5s.

Good for Nothing, or All Down Hill. By the same. 1 vol. 6s.

The Queen's Maries, a Romance of Holyrood. 1 vol. 6s.

The Interpreter, a Tale of the War. By the same. 1 vol. 5s.

TALES from GREEK MYTHOLOGY. By George W. Cox, M.A. late Scholar of Trin. Coll. Oxon. Second Edition. Square 16mo. 3s. 6d.

Tales of the Gods and Heroes. By the same Author. Second Edition. Fcp. 5s.

Tales of Thebes and Argos. By the same Author. Fcp. 4s. 6d.

BECKER'S GALLUS; or, Roman Scenes of the Time of Augustus: with Notes and Excursuses illustrative of the Manners and Customs of the Ancient Romans. New Edition. [Nearly ready.

BECKER'S CHARICLES; a Tale illustrative of Private Life among the Ancient Greeks: with Notes and Excursuses. New Edition. [Nearly ready.

ICELANDIC LEGENDS. Collected by JON ARNASON. Selected and Translated from the Icelandic by G. E. J. POWELL and E. MAGNUSSON. SECOND SERIES, with Notes and an Introductory Essay on the Origin and Genius of the Icelandic Folk-Lore, and 3 Illustrations on Wood. Cr. 8vo. 21s.

The WARDEN: a Novel. By ANTHONY TROLLOPE. Crown 8vo. 3s. 6d.

Barchester Towers: a Sequel to 'The Warden.' By the same Author. Crown 8vo. 5s.

Poetry and The *Drama.*

GOETHE'S SECOND FAUST. Translated by JOHN ANSTER, LL.D. M.R.I.A. Regius Professor of Civil Law in the University of Dublin. Post 8vo. 15s.

TASSO'S JERUSALEM DELIVERED. Translated into English Verse by Sir J. KINGSTON JAMES, Kt. M.A. 2 vols. fcp. with Facsimile, 14s.

POETICAL WORKS of JOHN EDMUND READE; with final Revision and Additions. 3 vols. fcp. 18s. or each vol. separately, 6s.

MOORE'S POETICAL WORKS, Cheapest Editions complete in 1 vol. including the Autobiographical Prefaces and Author's last Notes, which are still copyright. Crown 8vo. ruby type, with Portrait, 6s. or People's Edition, in larger type, 12s. 6d.

Moore's Poetical Works, as above, Library Edition, medium 8vo. with Portrait and Vignette, 14s. or in 10 vols. fcp. 3s. 6d. each.

MOORE'S IRISH MELODIES, 32mo. Portrait, 1s. 16mo. Vignette, 2s. 6d.

Maclise's Edition of Moore's Irish Melodies, with 161 Steel Plates from Original Drawings. Super-royal 8vo. 31s. 6d.

Maclise's Edition of Moore's Irish Melodies with all the Original Designs (as above) reduced by a New Process. Imp. 16mo. 10s. 6d.

MOORE'S LALLA ROOKH. 32mo. Plate, 1s. 16mo. Vignette, 2s. 6d.

Tenniel's Edition of Moore's Lalla Rookh, with 68 Wood Engravings from original Drawings and other Illustrations. Fcp. 4to. 21s.

SOUTHEY'S POETICAL WORKS, with the Author's last Corrections and copyright Additions. Library Edition, in 1 vol. medium 8vo. with Portrait and Vignette, 14s. or in 10 vols. fcp. 3s. 6d. each.

LAYS of ANCIENT ROME; with *Ivry* and the *Armada*. By the Right Hon. LORD MACAULAY. 16mo. 4s. 6d.

Lord Macaulay's Lays of Ancient Rome. With 90 Illustrations on Wood, Original and from the Antique, from Drawings by G. SCHARF. Fcp. 4to. 21s.

POEMS. By JEAN INGELOW. Tenth Edition. Fcp. 8vo. 5s.

POETICAL WORKS of LETITIA ELIZABETH LANDON (L.E.L.) 2 vols. 16mo 10s.

PLAYTIME with the POETS: a Selection of the best English Poetry for the use of Children. By a LADY. Revised Edition. Crown 8vo. 5s.

BOWDLER'S FAMILY SHAKSPEARE, cheaper Genuine Edition, complete in 1 vol. large type, with 36 Woodcut Illustrations, price 14s. or with the same ILLUSTRATIONS, in 6 pocket vols. 3s. 6d. each.

ARUNDINES CAMI, sive Musarum Cantabrigiensium Lusus canori. Collegit atque edidit H. DRURY, M.A. Editio Sexta, curavit H. J. HODGSON, M.A. Crown 8vo. 7s. 6d.

The ILIAD of HOMER TRANSLATED into BLANK VERSE. By ICHABOD CHARLES WRIGHT, M.A. late Fellow of Magd. Coll. Oxon. 2 vols. crown 8vo. 21s.

The ILIAD of HOMER in ENGLISH HEXAMETER VERSE. By J. HENRY DART, M.A. of Exeter College, Oxford: Author of 'The Exile of St. Helena, Newdigate, 1838.' Square crown 8vo. 21s.

D

DANTE'S DIVINE COMEDY, translated in English Terza Rima by JOHN DAYMAN, M.A. [With the Italian Text, after *Brunetti*, interpaged.] 8vo. 21s.

Rural Sports, &c.

ENCYCLOPÆDIA of RURAL SPORTS; a complete Account, Historical, Practical, and Descriptive, of Hunting, Shooting, Fishing, Racing, &c. By D. P. BLAINE. With above 600 Woodcuts (20 from Designs by JOHN LEECH). 8vo. 42s.

NOTES on RIFLE SHOOTING. By Captain HEATON, Adjutant of the Third Manchester Rifle Volunteer Corps. Revised Edition. Fcp. 2s. 6d.

COL. HAWKER'S INSTRUCTIONS to YOUNG SPORTSMEN in all that relates to Guns and Shooting. Revised by the Author's SON. Square crown 8vo. with Illustrations, 18s.

The RIFLE, its THEORY and PRACTICE. By ARTHUR WALKER (79th Highlanders), Staff. Hythe and Fleetwood Schools of Musketry. Second Edition. Crown 8vo. with 125 Woodcuts, 5s.

The DEAD SHOT, or Sportsman's Complete Guide; a Treatise on the Use of the Gun, Dog-breaking, Pigeon-shooting, &c. By MARKSMAN. Revised Edition. Fcp. 8vo. with Plates, 5s.

HINTS on SHOOTING, FISHING, &c. both on Sea and Land and in the Fresh and Saltwater Lochs of Scotland; being the Experiences of C. IDLE. Second Edition, revised. Fcp. 6s.

The FLY-FISHER'S ENTOMOLOGY. By ALFRED RONALDS. With coloured Representations of the Natural and Artificial Insect. Sixth Edition; with 20 coloured Plates. 8vo. 14s.

HANDBOOK of ANGLING: Teaching Fly-fishing, Trolling, Bottom-fishing, Salmon-fishing; with the Natural History of River Fish, and the best modes of Catching them. By EPHEMERA. Fcp. Woodcuts, 5s.

The CRICKET FIELD; or, the History and the Science of the Game of Cricket. By JAMES PYCROFT, B.A. Fourth Edition. Fcp. 5s.

The Cricket Tutor; a Treatise exclusively Practical. By the same. 18mo. 1s.

Cricketana. By the same Author. With 7 Portraits. Fcp. 5s.

The HORSE-TRAINER'S and SPORTMAN'S GUIDE: with Considerations on the Duties of Grooms, on Purchasing Blood Stock, and on Veterinary Examination. By DIGBY COLLINS. Post 8vo. 6s.

The HORSE'S FOOT, and HOW to KEEP IT SOUND. By W. MILES, Esq. Ninth Edition, with Illustrations. Imperial 8vo. 12s. 6d.

A Plain Treatise on Horse-Shoeing. By the same Author. Post 8vo. with Illustrations, 2s. 6d.

Stables and Stable-Fittings. By the same. Imp. 8vo. with 13 Plates, 15s.

Remarks on Horses' Teeth, addressed to Purchasers. By the same. Post 8vo. 1s. 6d.

On DRILL and MANŒUVRES of CAVALRY, combined with Horse Artillery. By Major-Gen. MICHAEL W. SMITH, C.B. Commanding the Poonah Division of the Bombay Army. 8vo. 12s. 6d.

BLAINE'S VETERINARY ART; a Treatise on the Anatomy, Physiology, and Curative Treatment of the Diseases of the Horse, Neat Cattle and Sheep. Seventh Edition, revised and enlarged by C. STEEL, M.R.C.V.S.L. 8vo. with Plates and Woodcuts, 18s.

The HORSE: with a Treatise on Draught. By WILLIAM YOUATT. New Edition, revised and enlarged. 8vo. with numerous Woodcuts, 10s. 6d.

The Dog. By the same Author. 8vo. with numerous Woodcuts, 6s.

The DOG in HEALTH and DISEASE. By STONEHENGE. With 70 Wood Engravings. Square crown 8vo. 15s.

The Greyhound. By the same Author. Revised Edition, with 24 Portraits of Greyhounds. Square crown 8vo. 21s.

The OX; his Diseases and their Treatment: with an Essay on Parturition in the Cow. By J. R. DOBSON, M.R.C.V.S. Crown 8vo. with Illustrations. price 7s. 6d.

Commerce, Navigation, and *Mercantile Affairs.*

PRACTICAL GUIDE for BRITISH SHIPMASTERS to UNITED States Ports. By PIERREPONT EDWARDS, Her Britannic Majesty's Vice-Consul at New York. Post 8vo. 8s. 6d.

A NAUTICAL DICTIONARY, defining the Technical Language relative to the Building and Equipment of Sailing Vessels and Steamers, &c. By ARTHUR YOUNG. Second Edition; with Plates and 150 Woodcuts. 8vo. 18s.

A DICTIONARY, Practical, Theoretical, and Historical, of Commerce and Commercial Navigation. By J. R. M'CULLOCH, Esq. 8vo. with Maps and Plans, 50s.

A MANUAL for NAVAL CADETS. By J. M'NEIL BOYD, late Captain R.N. Third Edition; with 240 Woodcuts and 11 coloured Plates. Post 8vo. 12s. 6d.

The LAW of NATIONS Considered as Independent Political Communities. By TRAVERS TWISS, D.C.L. Regius Professor of Civil Law in the University of Oxford. 2 vols. 8vo. 30s. or separately, PART I. *Peace,* 12s. PART II. *War,* 18s.

Works of Utility and *General Information.*

MODERN COOKERY for PRIVATE FAMILIES, reduced to a System of Easy Practice in a Series of carefully-tested Receipts. By ELIZA ACTON. Newly revised and enlarged; with 8 Plates, Figures, and 150 Woodcuts. Fcp. 7s. 6d.

The HANDBOOK of DINING; or, Corpulency and Leanness scientifically considered. By BRILLAT-SAVARIN, Author of 'Physiologie du Goût.' Translated by L. F. SIMPSON. Revised Edition, with Additions. Fcp. 3s. 6d.

On FOOD and its DIGESTION; an Introduction to Dietetics. By W. BRINTON, M.D. Physician to St. Thomas's Hospital, &c. With 48 Woodcuts. Post 8vo. 12s.

WINE, the VINE, and the CELLAR. By THOMAS G. SHAW. Second Edition, revised and enlarged, with Frontispiece and 31 Illustrations on Wood. 8vo. 16s.

HOW TO BREW GOOD BEER: a complete Guide to the Art of Brewing Ale, Bitter Ale, Table Ale, Brown Stout, Porter, and Table Beer. By JOHN PITT. Revised Edition. Fcp. 4s. 6d.

A PRACTICAL TREATISE on BREWING; with Formulæ for Public Brewers, and Instructions for Private Families. By W. BLACK. 8vo. 10s. 6d.

SHORT WHIST. By MAJOR A. Sixteenth Edition, revised, with an Essay on the Theory of the Modern Scientific Game by PROF. P. Fcp. 3s. 6d.

WHIST, WHAT TO LEAD. By CAM. Third Edition. 32mo. 1s.

HINTS on ETIQUETTE and the USAGES of SOCIETY; with a Glance at Bad Habits. Revised, with Additions, by a LADY of RANK. Fcp. price 2s. 6d.

TWO HUNDRED CHESS PROBLEMS, composed by F. HEALEY, including the Problems to which the Prizes were awarded by the Committees of the Era, the Manchester, the Birmingham, and the Bristol Chess Problem Tournaments; accompanied by the SOLUTIONS. Crown 8vo. with 200 Diagrams, 5s.

The CABINET LAWYER; a Popular Digest of the Laws of England, Civil and Criminal. Twenty-first Edition, extended by the Author; including the Acts of the Sessions 1864 and 1865. Fcp. 10s. 6d.

The PHILOSOPHY of HEALTH; or, an Exposition of the Physiological and Sanitary Conditions conducive to Human Longevity and Happiness. By SOUTHWOOD SMITH, M.D. Eleventh Edition, revised and enlarged: with 113 Woodcuts, 8vo. 15s.

HINTS to MOTHERS on the MANAGEMENT of their HEALTH during the Period of Pregnancy and in the Lying-in Room. By T. BULL, M.D. Fcp. 5s.

The Maternal Management of Children in Health and Disease. By the same Author. Fcp. 5s.

The LAW RELATING to BENEFIT BUILDING SOCIETIES; with Practical Observations on the Act and all the Cases decided thereon; also a Form of Rules and Forms of Mortgages. By W. TIDD PRATT, Barrister. Second Edition. Fcp. 3s. 6d.

NOTES on HOSPITALS. By FLORENCE NIGHTINGALE. Third Edition, enlarged; with 13 Plans. Post 4to. 18s.

C. M. WILLICH'S POPULAR TABLES for ascertaining the Value of Lifehold, Leasehold, and Church Property, Renewal Fines, &c.; the Public Funds; Annual Average Price and Interest on Consols from 1731 to 1861; Chemical, Geographical, Astronomical, Trigonometrical Tables, &c. Post 8vo. 10s.

THOMSON'S TABLES of INTEREST, at Three, Four, Four and a Half, and Five per Cent. from One Pound to Ten Thousand and from 1 to 365 Days. 12mo. 3s. 6d.

MAUNDER'S TREASURY of KNOWLEDGE and LIBRARY of Reference: comprising an English Dictionary and Grammar, Universal Gazetteer, Classical Dictionary, Chronology, Law Dictionary, a Synopsis of the Peerage, useful Tables, &c. Fcp. 10s.

INDEX.

Abbott on Sight and Touch 10
Acton's Modern Cookery 27
Alcock's Residence in Japan 22
Allies on Formation of Christendom 20
Alpine Guide (The) 22
Apjohn's Manual of the Metalloids 12
Arago's Biographies of Scientific Men .. 5
—— Popular Astronomy 10
Arnold's Manual of English Literature .. 7
Arnott's Elements of Physics 11
Arundines Cami 25
Atherstone Priory 23
Autumn holidays of a Country Parson .. 8
Ayre's Treasury of Bible Knowledge 19

Bacon's Essays, by Whately 5
—— Life and Letters, by Spedding .. 5
—— Works 6
Bain on the Emotions and Will 10
—— on the Senses and Intellect 10
—— on the Study of Character 10
Baines's Explorations in S. W. Africa .. 22
Ball's Alpine Guide 23
Barnard's Drawing from Nature 16
Bayldon's Rents and Tillages 18
Beaten Tracks 22
Becker's Charicles and Gallus 24
Beethoven's Letters 4
Benfey's Sanskrit Dictionary 8
Berry's Journals and Correspondence ... 4
Black's Treatise on Brewing 28
Blackley and Friedlander's German and English Dictionary 8
Blaine's Rural Sports 26
—— Veterinary Art 27
Bright's Week at the Land's End 23
Boase's Essay on Human Nature 9
—— Philosophy of Nature 9
Booth's Epigrams 9
Boner's Transylvania 22
Bonney's Alps of Dauphiné 22
Bourne on Screw Propeller 17
Bourne's Catechism of the Steam Engine 17
—— Handbook of Steam Engine 17
—— Treatise on the Steam Engine .. 17
Bowdler's Family Shakspeare 25
Boyd's Manual for Naval Cadets 27
Bramley-Moore's Six Sisters of the Valleys 24
Brande's Dictionary of Science, Literature, and Art 13
Bray's (C.) Education of the Feelings .. 10
—— Philosophy of Necessity 10
Brinton on Food and Digestion 27
Bristow's Glossary of Mineralogy 11
Brodie's (Sir C. B.) Works 15
—— Autobiography 15
—— Constitutional History 2

Browne's Ice Caves of France and Switzerland 15
—— Exposition 39 Articles 18
—— Pentateuch 18
Buckle's History of Civilization 2
Bull's Hints to Mothers 26
—— Maternal Management of Children 26
Bunsen's Ancient Egypt 3
Bunsen on Apocrypha 20
Burke's Vicissitudes of Families 5
Burton's Christian Church 3

Cabinet Lawyer 26
Calvert's Wife's Manual 21
Campaigner at Home 8
Cats and Farlie's Moral Emblems 16
Chorale Book for England 21
Clough's Lives from Plutarch 2
Colenso (Bishop) on Pentateuch and Book of Joshua 19
Collins's Horse-Trainer's Guide 26
Columbus's Voyages 23
Commonplace Philosopher in Town and Country 8
Conington's Handbook of Chemical Analysis 13
Contanseau's Pocket French and English Dictionary 8
—— Practical ditto 8
Conybeare and Howson's Life and Epistles of St. Paul 18
Cook's Voyages 23
Copland's Dictionary of Practical Medicine 15
—— Abridgment of ditto 15
Cox's Tales of the Great Persian War .. 2
—— Tales from Greek Mythology 24
—— Tales of the Gods and Heroes .. 24
—— Tales of Thebes and Argos 24
Cresy's Encyclopædia of Civil Engineering 17
Critical Essays of a Country Parson ... 8
Crowe's History of France 2
Cussans's Grammar of Heraldry 16

Dart's Iliad of Homer 25
Dayman's Dante's Divina Commedia 26
D'Aubigné's History of the Reformation in the time of Calvin 2
Dead Shot (The), by Marksman 26
De la Rive's Treatise on Electricity .. 11
Delmard's Village Life in Switzerland . 22
De la Pryme's Life of Christ 20
De Morgan on Matter and Spirit 9
De Tocqueville's Democracy in America 2
Dobson on the Ox 27
Duncan and Millard on Classification, &c. of the Idiotic 15
Dyer's City of Rome 2

NEW WORKS PUBLISHED BY LONGMANS AND CO.

Edwards' Shipmaster's Guide 27
Elements of Botany 15
Ellice, a Tale 23
Ellicott's Broad and Narrow Way 19
———— Commentary on Ephesians 19
———— Destiny of the Creature 19
———— Lectures on Life of Christ 19
———— Commentary on Galatians 19
———————————————Pastoral Epist... 19
——————————————————Philippians, &c.. 19
——————————————————Thessalonians... 19
Essays and Reviews 20
———— on Religion and Literature, edited by Manning 20

Fairbairn on Iron Shipbuilding 17
Fairbairn's Application of Cast and Wrought Iron to Building 17
———————— Information for Engineers... 17
———————— Treatise on Mills & Millwork 17
Farrar's Chapters on Language 7
Foulkes's Christendom's Divisions 20
Freshfield's Alpine Byways 23
———————— Tour in the Grisons 23
Friends in Council 9
Froude's History of England 1

Garratt's Marvels and Mysteries of Instinct 12
Gee's Sunday to Sunday 21
Gilbert and Churchill's Dolomite Mountains 22
Gilly's Shipwrecks of the Navy 23
Goethe's Second Faust, by Anster 24
Goodeve's Elements of Mechanism 17
Gorle's Questions on Browne's Exposition of the 39 Articles 18
Grant's Ethics of Aristotle 5
Graver Thoughts of a Country Parson 8
Gray's Anatomy 14
Greene's Corals and Sea Jellies 12
———————— Sponges and Animalcule 12
Grove on Correlation of Physical Forces.. 11
Gwilt's Encyclopædia of Architecture 16

Handbook of Angling, by Ephemera 26
Hare on Election of Representatives 6
Hartwig's Sea and its Living Wonders 12
———————— Harmonies of Nature 12
———————— Tropical World 12
Haughton's Manual of Geology 11
Hawker's Instructions to Young Sportsmen 26
Healey's Chess Problems 28
Heaton's Notes on Rifle Shooting 26
Helps's Spanish Conquest in America 2
Herschel's Essays from the Edinburgh and Quarterly Reviews 13
———————— Outlines of Astronomy 10
Hewitt on the Diseases of Women 14
Hints on Etiquette 28
Hodgson's Time and Space 10
Holland's Essays on Scientific Subjects... 13
Holmes's System of Surgery 14
Hooker and Walker-Arnott's British Flora 13
Horne's Introduction to the Scriptures 19
———————— Compendium of ditto 19
Horsley's Manual of Poisons 15
Hoskyns's Talpa 18
How we Spent the Summer 22
Howitt's Australian Discovery 22
———————— Rural Life of England 22
———————— Visits to Remarkable Places...... 23
Howson's Hulsean Lectures on St. Paul.... 18

Hughes's (W.) Geography of British History 11
———————— Manual of Geography 11
Hullah's History of Modern Music 4
———————— Transition Musical Lectures 4
Humboldt's Travels in South America 23
Humphreys' Sentiments of Shakspeare 16
Hutton's Studies in Parliament 9
Hymns from Lyra Germanica 21

Icelandic Legends. Second Series 24
Idle's Hints on Shooting 26
Inglow's Poems 25

Jameson's Legends of the Saints and Martyrs 16
———————— Legends of the Madonna 16
———————— Legends of the Monastic Orders 16
Jameson and Eastlake's History of Our Lord 16
Johns's Home Walks and Holiday Rambles 12
Johnson's Patentee's Manual 17
———————— Practical Draughtsman 17
Johnston's Gazetteer, or Geographical Dictionary 11
Jones's Christianity and Common Sense.... 10

Kalisch's Commentary on the Bible 7
———————— Hebrew Grammar 7
Kesteven's Domestic Medicine 15
Kirby and Spence's Entomology 12
Koenen on Pentateuch and Joshua 19

Lady's Tour Round Monte Rosa 23
Landon's (L. E. L.) Poetical Works 25
Latham's English Dictionary 7
Lecky's History of Rationalism 3
Leisure Hours in Town 8
Lewes' History of Philosophy 3
Lewin's Fasti Sacri 19
Lewis on Early Roman History 6
———————— Essays on Administrations 6
———————— Fables of Babrius 6
———————— on Foreign Jurisdiction 6
———————— on Irish Disturbances 6
———————— on Observation and Reasoning in Politics 6
———————— on Political Terms 6
Liddell and Scott's Greek-English Lexicon 8
———————— Abridged ditto 8
Life of Man Symbolised 16
Lindley and Moore's Treasury of Botany 12
Longman's Lectures on the History of England 2
Loudon's Agriculture 18
———————— Cottage, Farm,Villa Architecture 18
———————— Gardening 18
———————— Plants 13
———————— Trees and Shrubs 13
Lowndes's Engineer's Handbook 16
Lyra Domestica 21
———— Eucharistica 21
———— Germanica 16, 21
———— Messianica 21
———— Mystica 21
———— Sacra 21

Macaulay's (Lord) Essays 3
———————— History of England 1
———————— Lays of Ancient Rome 25
———————— Miscellaneous Writings ... 8
———————— Speeches 7
———————— Works 1

NEW WORKS PUBLISHED BY LONGMANS AND CO. 31

MACDOUGALL's Theory of War.............. 17
McCULLOCH's Dictionary of Commerce..... 27
———————Geographical Dictionary...... 11
MACFIE's Vancouver Island 22
MAGUIRE's Life of Father Mathew........... 4
———— Rome and its Rulers............ 4
MALING's Indoor Gardener 13
MANNING on Holy Ghost................... 20
MARSHMAN's Life of Havelock.............. 5
MASSEY's History of England 1
MASSINGBERD's History of the Reformation.. 4
MAUNDER's Biographical Treasury 5
———— Geographical Treasury 11
———— Historical Treasury 3
———— Scientific and Literary Treasury 13
———— Treasury of Knowledge........ 28
———— Treasury of Natural History .. 12
MAURY's Physical Geography 10
MAY's Constitutional History of England.. 1
MELVILLE's Digby Grand.................... 24
———— General Bounce 24
———— Gladiators 24
———— Good for Nothing 24
———— Holmby House 24
———— Interpreter 24
———— Kate Coventry 24
———— Queen's Maries.................. 24
MENDELSSOHN's Letters..................... 4
MENZIES' Windsor Great Park............... 18
MERIVALE's (H.) Historical Studies 3
———— (C.) Fall of the Roman Republic 3
———— Boyle Lectures 3
———— Romans under the Empire 2
MILES on Horse's Foot and Horseshoeing... 26
———— on Horses' Teeth and Stables........ 26
MILL on Liberty............................ 6
———— on Representative Government...... 6
———— on Utilitarianism................. 6
MILL's Dissertations and Discussions 6
———— Political Economy 6
———— System of Logic 6
———— Hamilton's Philosophy 6
MILLER's Elements of Chemistry 14
MONSELL's Spiritual Songs 21
———— Beatitudes 21
MONTGOMERY on Pregnancy 20
MOORE's Irish Melodies..................... 25
———— Lalla Rookh 25
———— Journal and Correspondence 5
———— Poetical Works 25
MORELL's Elements of Psychology 9
———— Mental Philosophy 9
Morning Clouds 20
MOSHEIM's Ecclesiastical History 20
MOZART's Letters........................... 4
MÜLLER's (Max) Lectures on the Science of
  Language 7
———— (K. O.) Literature of Ancient
  Greece 2
MURCHISON on Continued Fevers............ 14
MURE's Language and Literature of Greece 2

New Testament, illustrated with Wood Engravings from the Old Masters............ 16
NEWMAN's History of his Religious Opinions 4
NIGHTINGALE's Notes on Hospitals 28

ODLING's Animal Chemistry 14
———— Course of Practical Chemistry 14
———— Manual of Chemistry 14
ORMSBY's Rambles in Algeria and Tunis.... 22
O'SHEA's Guide to Spain 23
OWEN's Comparative Anatomy and Physiology of Vertebrate Animals 12
OXENHAM on Atonement.................... 21

PACKE's Guide to the Pyrenees 23
PAGET's Lectures on Surgical Pathology .. 14
PARK's Life and Travels.................... 23
PEREIRA's Elements of Materia Medica..... 15
———— Manual of Materia Medica 15
PERKINS's Tuscan Sculptors 16
PHILLIPS's Guide to Geology 11
———— Introduction to Mineralogy 11
PIESSE's Art of Perfumery 18
———— Chemical, Natural, and Physical
  Magic 18
PITT on Brewing 28
Playtime with the Poets 25
Practical Mechanic's Journal............... 17
PRATT's Law of Building Societies 28
PRESCOTT's Scripture Difficulties 19
PROCTOR's Saturn 10
PYCROFT's Course of English Reading...... 7
———— Cricket Field 26
———— Cricket Tutor 26
———— Cricketana 26

READE's Poetical Works 25
Recreations of a Country Parson.......... 8
REILY's Map of Mont Blanc 22
RIDDLE's First Sundays at Church......... 21
RIVERS's Rose Amateur's Guide............ 13
ROGERS's Correspondence of Greyson 9
———— Eclipse of Faith 9
———— Defence of ditto 9
———— Essays from the Edinburgh Review 9
———— Fullerians..................... 9
ROGET's Thesaurus of English Words and
  Phrases.............................. 7
RONALDS's Fly-Fisher's Entomology 26
ROWTON's Debater......................... 7
RUSSELL on Government and Constitution.. 1

SANDARS's Justinian's Institutes............ 5
SCOTT's Handbook of Volumetrical Analysis 13
SCROPE on Volcanos 11
SENIOR's Essays 3
SEWELL's Amy Herbert 24
———— Cleve Hall..................... 24
———— Earl's Daughter................. 24
———— Examination for Confirmation ... 20
———— Experience of Life.............. 24
———— Gertrude...................... 24
———— Glimpse of the World.......... 24
———— History of the Early Church..... 3
———— Ivors.......................... 24
———— Katharine Ashton.............. 24
———— Laneton Parsonage............ 24
———— Margaret Percival............. 24
———— Night Lessons from Scripture ... 20
———— Passing Thoughts on Religion.... 20
———— Preparation for Communion 20
———— Principles of Education 20
———— Readings for Confirmation..... 20
———— Readings for Lent.............. 20
———— Stories and Tales............... 24
———— Thoughts for the Holy Week ... 20
———— Ursula......................... 24
SHAW's Work on Wine 28
SHEDDEN's Elements of Logic 6
SHIPLEY's Church and the World 19
Short Whist 28
SHORT's Church History 3
SIEVEKING's (AMELIA) Life, by WINKWORTH 4
SIMPSON's Handbook of Dining 27
SMITH's (SOUTHWOOD) Philosophy of Health 28
———— (J.) Paul's Voyage and Shipwreck.. 18
———— (G.) Wesleyan Methodism 4
———— (SYDNEY) Memoir and Letters...... 5
———— Miscellaneous Works 9
———— Moral Philosophy 9
———— Wit and Wisdom............. 9

SMITH on Cavalry Drill and Manœuvres.... 26
SOUTHEY's (Doctor)............................ 7
——— Poetical Works................. 25
STANLEY's History of British Birds 12
STEBBING's Analysis of MILL's Logic........ 6
STEPHEN's Essays in Ecclesiastical Biography................................... 5
——— Lectures on History of France.. 2
STIRLING's Secret of Hegel.................. 10
STONEHENGE on the Dog 27
——— on the Greyhound.............. 27
STRANGE on Sea Air 15
——— on Restoration of Health 15

TASSO's Jerusalem, by JAMES................ 25
TAYLOR's (Jeremy) Works, edited by EDEN 20
TENNENT's Ceylon 12
——— Natural History of Ceylon...... 12
THIRLWALL's History of Greece 2
THOMSON's (Archbishop) Laws of Thought 6
——— (J.) Tables of Interest 28
——— Conspectus, by BIRKETT........ 15
TODD's Cyclopædia of Anatomy and Physiology 14
——— and BOWMAN's Anatomy and Physiology of Man 15
TROLLOPE's Barchester Towers.............. 24
——— Warden........................... 24
TWISS's Law of Nations 27
TYNDALL's Lectures on Heat................ 11

URE's Dictionary of Arts, Manufactures, and Mines 17

VAN DER HOEVEN's Handbook of Zoology.. 12
VAUGHAN's (R.) Revolutions in English History...................................... 1
——— Way to Rest..................... 10
——— (R. A.) Hours with the Mystics 10

WALKER on the Rifle 26
WATSON's Principles and Practice of Physic 14
WATTS's Dictionary of Chemistry.......... 13
WEBB's Objects for Common Telescopes.... 10
WEBSTER & WILKINSON's Greek Testament 19
WELD's Last Winter in Rome................ 22
WELLINGTON's Life, by BRIALMONT and GLEIG 4
——— by GLEIG 4
WEST on Children's Diseases................ 14
WHATELY's English Synonymes 5
——— Logic.......................... 5
——— Remains 6
——— Rhetoric 5
——— Sermons 21
——— Paley's Moral Philosophy 21
WHEWELL's History of the Inductive Sciences 3
——— Scientific Ideas 3
Whist, what to lead, by CAM................ 28
WHITE and RIDDLE's Latin-English Dictionaries 7
WILBERFORCE (W.) Recollections of, by HARFORD..................................... 5
WILLICH's Popular Tables 28
WILSON's Bryologia Britannica 13
WINDHAM's Diary 4
WOOD's Homes without Hands............... 12
WOODWARD's Historical and Chronological Encyclopædia 3
WRIGHT's Homer's Iliad..................... 25

YONGE's English-Greek Lexicon 8
——— Abridged ditto 8
YOUNG's Nautical Dictionary 27
YOUATT on the Dog 27
——— on the Horse 27

SPOTTISWOODE AND CO., PRINTERS, NEW STREET-SQUARE, LONDON

www.ingramcontent.com/pod-product-compliance
Lightning Source LLC
Chambersburg PA
CBHW021958220426
43663CB00007B/873